T0291234

# Contours of Value Capture

Stagnation in manufacturing and the delinking of growth and employment have been a major concern in the context of industrialising India. Policy debates in the past three decades have been confined to binaries such as public versus private, manufacturing versus services, production versus finance or inward- versus outward-looking strategies. These are important choices in strategising industrialisation. *Contours of Value Capture* highlights how these immediate choices are influenced by class processes of accumulation. It foregrounds 'value capture' as the critical concept in analysing accumulation in the realm of production and finance articulated through exploitation, expropriation and exclusion.

This book discusses how India and other developing countries figure in global production networks, the asymmetric distribution of gains, how financialisation creeps into India's corporate sector, and, although not always similar to advanced countries, how these manifest a reification of 'objectivity' that helps in reproducing capital relations. It takes capital as an integral relation and aims to analyse the complex causal relationship between apparently disparate trends such as stagnation in productive investment, rising financial profits, declining share of wages, informality, self-employment and dispossession.

Contesting the ideological view that economies are neutral containers and economic transactions are powerless exchanges between equally placed agents, it sees power and hegemonic discourse as constitutive of the world of production and finance realised through hierarchies of capital and architecture of institutions. These norms and institutions normalise expropriation and legitimise exclusion. This book discusses how power and profit explain the making and unmaking of the neoliberal path of industrialisation in India.

**Satyaki Roy** is Associate Professor at the Institute for Studies in Industrial Development, New Delhi.

# Contours of Value Capture

## India's Neoliberal Path of Industrial Development

*Satyaki Roy*

CAMBRIDGE
UNIVERSITY PRESS

# CAMBRIDGE
## UNIVERSITY PRESS

University Printing House, Cambridge CB2 8BS, United Kingdom

One Liberty Plaza, 20th Floor, New York, NY 10006, USA

477 Williamstown Road, Port Melbourne, vic 3207, Australia

314 to 321, 3rd Floor, Plot No.3, Splendor Forum, Jasola District Centre, New Delhi 110025, India

79 Anson Road, #06–04/06, Singapore 079906

Cambridge University Press is part of the University of Cambridge.

It furthers the University's mission by disseminating knowledge in the pursuit of education, learning and research at the highest international levels of excellence.

www.cambridge.org
Information on this title: www.cambridge.org/9781108486910

© Satyaki Roy 2020

First published 2020

Printed in India

*A catalogue record for this publication is available from the British Library*

ISBN 978-1-108-48691-0 Hardback

*For Baba and Ma*

# Contents

# Tables and Figures

## Tables

## Figures

# Preface

Early development discourse emerged on acknowledging the fact of unevenness of capitalist growth, with underdevelopment syndromes persisting in large parts of the world simultaneously with advanced economies recording high industrial growth. The general observation was that persistent gap in development indicators between advanced and lagging economies would not mend automatically with time. In other words, although it appears that some of the social and economic symptoms of underdevelopment resemble the past of advanced economies, they may not logically transform into the present of those economies and, therefore, asymmetry, structural dependence and strategic intervention crept into economic analyses of making and unmaking of under-development. The central problem was to transform economies by moving people from low-productivity segments to high-productivity activities. Spontaneous innovation of technology, facilitated by competition that would continuously replace less productive processes, requires the creation of capital relations, and industrialisation epitomised the process of rapid diffusion of development. In developing countries, transition was subject to attaining autonomy from the imperialist powers and, in many cases, the post-colonial state became an active protagonist in mobilising capital, infrastructure and technology, initiating an independent path of industrial development. There were successes and failures which had been analysed from different perspectives including the view that failures manifest the limitations of the ruling combination who were hesitant to fully utilise the potential of redistributive justice. But more importantly, over time, the discourse of development was increasingly subsumed into the neoliberal doctrine which essentially establishes overwhelming faith in the market.

From such a perspective, societies or economies are nothing but neutral containers and the role of respective states should be restricted to facilitating free flow of inputs and outputs according to price signals. Its fascinating attraction seems to flow from the 'objectification' of social relations that are reified as an uncompromising verdict of market, as the rational choice for efficient allocation of resources and rewards to factors. Hence, solution to the problem either of inequality within countries or of divide between advanced and developing countries at the global level have relied on the cardinal faith that through free flow of factors, and because of the instinctive impulses of private gains, disparities in productivity and, therefore, of returns to factors would eventually be wiped out. Banishing power relations from economic analyses and confining it to the discourse of rational individuals, neoliberalism makes the world look flat, factories appear as laboratories with given production functions, dispossession as collateral damage of buying and selling, profit as returns for risk or entrepreneurship as pure and simple, distilled from speculative churning in financial transactions, worker as the owner of human capital who receives returns according to his skills and the question of redistribution is nothing but a moral reconciliation for rising inequality that, beyond an admissible political high point, threatens the legitimacy of the system.

This paradigmatic shift in policy discourse has considerable influence on the debate on industrial stagnation in India. There has been a rich tradition of counterpoints to the dominant discourse of market-led industrialisation, but somehow the debates were largely caught up in binaries such as state versus market or public versus private sectors, inward- versus outward-looking strategies, manufacturing versus services, productive sectors versus finance or labour-intensive versus capital-intensive industrialisation, and so on. These are undoubtedly important markers in identifying changes in policies during the neoliberal regime and its likely impact on economic outcomes, but what seems to be missing in these debates is how choices of policy sets are intrinsically linked to class processes that are more structural in nature and define proximate choices of economic policies. The trajectory of capitalist industrialisation is not only about identifying an appropriate mix of physical and human capital and of technology, but something more than that. In a deeper sense, it is about the regime of value capture, the way produced values are captured and accumulated by capital, and the question of distribution, therefore, cannot be separated from the particular mode of production.

Industrial development or technological innovation cannot be a goal in itself. Rather, it is a means to achieve human well-being. This involves productivity growth by way of which social labour time required to meet necessities for human well-being declines over time. It is about pushing the frontiers of capabilities through enhancing 'free time', such that people can actively and creatively contribute to the process of development rather than being enslaved into the compulsive act of repetitive physical labour. Human civilisation and collective wisdom have been creating immense opportunities through technological innovation towards such a goal, but values captured through exploitation and expropriation define a trajectory of industrial development both at the global and country levels that could not be inclusive in nature. This book aims to demystify the debate on industrial stagnation in India and bring value capture to the centrestage. Exploitation and expropriation in this narrative are not pushed to the margin, but considered to be constitutive of the neoliberal path of industrialisation. In various chapters, it intends to problematise the existing binaries within the discourse on industrialisation, foregrounding class process as one of the cardinal elements in the analyses of industrial growth.

This book, of course, confines itself to contemporary trends in India's industrial growth but, first, it does not see these trends as independent of the global circuit of capital. Hence, it tries to locate the problems of industrialisation in India within the larger frame of hierarchies of capital. Second, while restricting the scope of analyses to the present, the approach, however, has never been ahistoric. Instead, it aims to extend the rich tradition of class-focused analyses of post-colonial India's industrial trajectory to contemporary times.

The book is an outcome of research on various related issues carried out for more than a decade. At the outset, I would like to extend my sincere gratitude to the Institute for Studies in Industrial Development (ISID) for extending a conducive environment for independent research. I am thankful to my colleagues at ISID, faculty and non-academic staff, for always being supportive and particularly for the stimulating debates in various formal and informal discussions which helped to strengthen and affirm my views. My special thanks to Divya Sharma and Swati Verma for helping me in culling out data from various sources used in one of the chapters. I sincerely thank the Indian Council for Social Science Research, the Planning Commission of India, Department of Science and Technology, GOI, for extending support on various projects that I undertook over the years. Findings of these projects feed into some of the topics discussed in this book. I extend my sincere gratitude to the three anonymous referees who went through the initial proposal and encouraged me with their comments to take up the current work. I am immensely thankful to Anwesha Rana of Cambridge University Press who has been extremely professional and, at the same time, generously flexible in persuading me to complete the manuscript. My special thanks to Aniruddha De of Cambridge University Press for his sincere and meticulous copy editing which significantly improved the flow of the text.

I extend my sincere gratitude to Surajit Mazumdar, Chirashree Das Gupta and Anjan Chakrabarti, whose intellectual inputs through debates and discussions over a long period of association helped me attain greater clarity on various issues. My special thanks to them for taking the pain of going through drafts of some of the chapters of this work. I am immensely indebted for their continuous support and comradeship.

Many insights and arguments put forward in the current work in their formative stage were presented at various conferences and were published as papers in journals or in edited volumes. I am thankful to the referees, commentators and discussants for their inputs. I am thankful to my students at Ambedkar University, Delhi, critical engagements with whom have helped enrich my understanding.

This book is a tribute to my parents, Saroj Kumar Roy and Swapna Roy, who supported us throughout in persuading independent opinion without being driven always by immediate gains and losses. I was immensely influenced in my childhood by my grand-uncle Sachindra Nath Roy who stood for the cause of the poor and the oppressed throughout his life. My continuous and unending conversation and debates with my elder brother, Saugata Roy, have kept me alert to the different dimensions of realities that need to be addressed. These precious emotions, ideas and lived experience of my family, friends and comrades have helped shape my objectives of academic work. I am grateful to Lekha Guha, Shukla Raha, Shekharendra Nath Ghosh, Krishnakoli Ghosh and Chitra Ghosh for their continuous encouragement and support. To Ujjayini, I am in debt forever for providing continuous support and strength to stand by what I believe in. My deep gratitude to her for being with me and supporting my academic and non-academic pursuits. Our daughter, Krittika, has always been a motivation. Her observations familiarise me with young minds.

# 1

# Introduction

We often acknowledge the fascinating changes around us – changes embedded in a globalised world with increased trade and interdependence between nations, speed and depth of communication, innovation in technology, sharing of knowledge, movement of people across borders, rise of the global middle class, and homogenisation of culture and lifestyles. Glitches in the growth process, episodes of slowing down, rising inequality, delinking growth and employment, financialisation, and dwindling growth in physical investment are seen as reconcilable perturbations within the larger picture of a stable and ubiquitous capitalism. The Indian story appears to be even more exciting. It is no longer about just 'catching up' with the North. With consistent high growth, the two Asian giants, India and China, seem to have emerged as the drivers of global growth in the recent past. In the case of India, a major concern of policy-makers and experts is the industrialisation conundrum amid high growth. Though services contribute a major share, in terms of output and employment, a stagnant manufacturing sector is worrisome. In large democracies like India, the distribution of growth is directly linked to the electoral fortunes of contesting political parties as rising inequality beyond a point leads to social tensions and resentment against the ruling establishment. Though the relation between political outcome and economic performance need not be linear, pitting growth against distribution, the doctrine of gains trickling down, and the patience of the majority of people waiting for market-driven desired outcomes seem to have lost steam.

The policy discourse in this regard has been largely confined to certain broad binaries: state versus market when it comes to economic mediation; to promote public or private sectors; services or manufacturing sector to drive the desired growth path; inward- or outward-looking policies on the question of degree of openness; regulate finance to redirect capital flow towards productive sectors or enjoy the swings of speculation; relax labour laws for flexibility, or provide social security to unprotected workers; and so on. Industry requires land and minerals and the state has to be decisive in releasing the supply side constraints. Therefore, land that has so far been used for low-productivity agriculture has to be transformed – forcibly, if required – towards high-productivity industrial activities. These themes broadly constitute policy debates in the recent past. Agrarian distress, farmers' suicide and issues such as minimum support price or agricultural subsidies did hit the streets as popular unrest, but these were viewed by the ruling elite as responses of the unfortunate. Rural people may require occasional political attention either in the form of subsidies or cash transfers, not because they contribute to the growth of 'emerging' India, but because agriculture still employs the largest share of rural India.

The purpose of this book is largely to dwell on the same important issues of contemporary India, but from a different perspective. The nodal signifiers of our discussion are not growth, distribution, or inequality. Here, we talk about accumulation and value capture so as to locate the industrialisation conundrum from the perspective of class process. In the succeeding chapters, our sensory tools and instruments are not limited to seeing mismatches in demand and supply which certainly reflect policy failure, but go beyond those interpretations. We will focus on what constitute mismatches, priorities, and flows of capital and perceived failures. It is more about conflicts and contestations that are structural in nature, *longue duree* tendencies that influence immediate economic outcomes. The frame of analyses is essentially Marxian which adds an important dimension – class process – to other processes such as economic, ideological, natural, and cultural that constitutes a particular social outcome.

The book intends to go beyond the ideology of assuming exchanges between equivalents as the imagery of the real world. Instead, it sees power as constitutive of economic process. The appropriation of surplus by capital is not benign as the term 'growth' seems to suggest. It is value capture from labour and distributed as subsumed class payments to hierarchies of capital that create conditions for the production and appropriation of surplus value. The trajectory of growth and its distributional dimensions are also not independent of the class process both with reference to the domestic economy as well as for international engagements. Rising inequality in the economy, imparting global norms of production and profit across the globe, declining share of working people in output and huge gains for a few through financial returns, persistent technology gap between the North and the South and shifting manufacturing to developing countries entailing a labour regime that subverts existing protective institutions for labour are not issues independent of each other. Tools and disciplines make them appear as separate, as inconsequential to each other. And to see the interlinkages, this book uses the unifying motive of value capture that exists in different layers at home and abroad. There is no claim that this is the only way of comprehending the set of problems at hand, but the kind of solution we conceive as desirable largely depends on how we approach the problem.

## Value Capture

The society and economy we are talking about is largely based on commodity production. This implies that goods and services are produced for sale and members of the society who participate in this process of production earn income with which they buy their required commodities. The mediation between buyers and sellers takes place through a market and monetary values of commodities in terms of prices are realised through an exchange. But this benign portrayal of our economy misses out that only a handful of people in the population own the means of production while the majority sell their labour power to them because they do not possess any other asset by which they can earn a livelihood. Classical economists as well as Karl Marx and John Maynard Keynes held that addition of value is basically the act of labour with different degrees of brains and brawn. Materials and inputs are transformed into new products through human intervention and this creation is measured as a value addition. This value addition is, therefore, the difference between the price of output and the price of input at various stages of production. This is aggregated as the national product of a country and its changes are captured as growth. The addition to national product are exchanged in the form of factor incomes as profits, wages, rents, and interests as payments for the contribution to capitalists, workers, asset holders or property owners who lend their property to capitalists and financers respectively.

It is also true that what is output for a particular stage of production is the input for the next stage and if the factor payments for the preceding stage can be reduced, then input prices for the next stage also fall. Hence, even if output prices of that stage remain the same, value addition may increase. Simply put, if less profit, wage, rent, and interest can be paid, then the value of input falls for the immediate next stage and, hence, value addition increases. But for the sake of increasing value addition, the share of labour is reduced. Since the worker has no other alternative but to sell his labour power, suppressing their returns will not stop supply of labour. On the other hand, returns to the property-owning classes grow since they will not lend their property as a means of production if they do not get expected returns. And most importantly, this asymmetric distribution of ownership has to be reproduced. Otherwise, making the worker work at a declining share of value added would not be possible.

Now the question is what determines the share of workers in value added and this is not only about physical work in factories, roads, and ports, but also includes all forms of mental and physical labour offered for sale in exchange of remuneration. Adhering to the classical norm, Marx argued that assuming exchanges take place on the basis of equivalence of value, labour power should be paid in the market according to its value. And the value of labour power is determined not by what the worker produces, but what he sells, the labour power. The value of this commodity is simply the aggregate value of goods and services required to maintain the worker and the future stream of labour supply required for production. Now even if the value in the production process is created by the work of human labour, workers receive wages representing the value of the labour power and the rest of the value added is captured by the capitalist and the property-owning classes. This value capture is mediated by the market in the form of exchange through monetary transactions.

Marx's determination of the value of a commodity is distinct from the classical economists in that it is an outcome of a systemic process instead of depending on the technical conditions of production at a particular stage. The value of a commodity is not the amount of labour congealed in the commodity. Rather, it is determined by the 'socially necessary labour' or the amount of labour that is socially sanctioned to produce a particular commodity. This social determination of value is mediated through the market by acts of numerous exchanges reflected through demand and supply, contestations of forces and interests finally arriving to a price which signals socially necessary labour for that particular commodity. The values and prices mutually constitute each other and the same is true for labour power. There is no hard and fast rule or any objective criterion that determines the value of labour power or equivalently the value of goods and services that constitute the value of labour power. It is determined by class contestations given the particularity of a country, its institutions, culture, and ideology which ultimately defines the social sanction of what is considered to be necessary for the worker. Therefore, the veil of 'objectivity' which engulfs the narrative of growth and productivity is a misrepresentation of real contestations between classes. Productivity of workers do not necessarily determine their returns. Even though productivity increases how the gain will be shared with the workers in the form of rising wages depends not on the objectivity of the specific product or technology involved but by the concrete conditions of class contestations.

Value captured is, therefore, value added or produced net of the value of labour power. Thus, the value captured by property owners can be increased in two ways or by a mix of both. The first is by making workers work for more hours while maintaining the value of labour power which Marx termed as absolute surplus value. This has to be supported by a cultural and ideological promotion of work ethic or by relaxing the existing norms of employment which allow employers to extend working hours. The second option is increasing workers' productivity by introducing new technology. In this process, even if the working day remains the same, the worker would produce more per unit of time and would require less time to produce the value equivalent to labour power. This means increasing relative surplus value by cheapening labour power without making the worker work longer or not denying a payment that is considered to be socially necessary at that point in time.

Apart from these two major ways of value capture, there can be a third way which is denying the exchange on the basis of equivalence of value altogether. This can be done in many ways. One way would be to pay workers less than the value of labour power and forcing them to sacrifice rights and entitlements that define 'socially necessary labour time' or paying them below the socially sanctioned norm. In other words, extracting more value from the worker by paying him less. The other way could be alienating direct producers from the means of production, forcefully or otherwise. This is expropriation of resources or inputs at zero or very little cost and converting them into assets for capital accumulation. Appropriation of value in these cases is basically transforming the means of livelihood into investable capital without paying compensation to owners on the basis of equivalence of value.

The share of value added that is appropriated by the capitalist class is not immediately translated into capitalists' profits. The process of exploitation and expropriation involves social, cultural, political, and ideological processes that create preconditions for value capture. Hence, a part of the appropriated surplus has to be distributed to entities and institutions that provide legal, political, and cultural processes that support and constitute value capture. Also, the share of surplus appropriated as profits by individual capitalists depend on their respective contributions to the total pool of capital. This raises the question of hierarchies of capital and their respective returns. Accumulation and distribution of surplus plays out at a global scale and, therefore, the process of value capture from different parts of the world by global circuit of capital needs to be appreciated. Sharing of the surplus among various layers of capital involved in the process determines the return to domestic players once they are integrated into the global circuit of capital.

This book intends to understand the problem of industrialisation and its various facets in the light of this conflictual structure of value capture. The nature of the conflicts and momentary resolutions, at particular points in history, define the regime of accumulation and the corresponding path of growth and distribution. In a globalised regime, free flow of capital asserts uniformity in the rate of profit while differential rates of exploitation continue to exist in different countries and also within countries, giving rise to unequal exchange. Exploitation and expropriation remain hidden in the garb of market exchange. This book claims to make a limited point that the outcomes of industrial development in contemporary India can be analysed in various ways, but a narrative through the lens of value capture might add another crucial dimension in comprehending contemporary realities of industrial development.

## About the Book

Our entry point to the complex problem of premature deindustrialisation in India is the stagnating share of the manufacturing sector in terms of output and employment and the delinking of growth and employment in the recent past. The narrative is not typical of India since most developing countries barring China show a similar pattern of the rising importance of services. In a neoliberal regime, there is hardly any comprehensive industrial strategy and, therefore, the pattern of growth manifests the preferred path of accumulation by capital in a market-driven regime. The presumed advantages of manufacturing derived from the experiences of early capitalist countries often give rise to a normative discourse, that manufacturing 'ought to be' the engine of growth and services show a relatively slow productivity growth and, hence, cannot trigger a high-productivity, employment-augmenting growth path. Somewhere, this narrative of exalting manufacturing as having some intrinsic virtues diverts our attention from the actual problem of how and when higher productivity growth leads to growing employment. The changing production and consumption patterns also need to be taken into account which entails synergies between manufacturing and services that destabilise the presumed sequence of the relative importance of sectors. In this context, the next chapter locates the current industrialisation conundrum in the larger context of rising inequality and distribution.

In today's globalised world, the dominant view of industrial development suggests that developing countries can industrialise through specialised engagement with the global production networks that define the new international division of labour. It is also true that there has been a significant shift in the share of global manufacturing in favour of developing countries. Hence, as the global value of total manufacturing output increases, developing countries are supposed to gain by increasing their manufacturing output and employment by integrating with global production networks. After the financial crisis, there has been increased focus on rebalancing growth, relying more on domestic demand and contraction of global production chains as a fallout of new protectionism. But it continues to be the dominant form of industrial engagement between nations, de-centred and dispersed, but controlled by multinational companies representing far more centralised and concentrated capital than ever before. Chapter 3 identifies which countries gain out of this participation and how the relocation of industry affects global labour in general and employment in India in particular.

The current phase of capital accumulation is largely dominated by financial interests. It is really difficult to draw universal features of financialisation as the process involves specificities of institutions, history, and the culture of countries. But some general traits derived from experiences from advanced countries offer us reference points for analysing particular contexts. Financialisation generally means faster growth of profit than that of investment, a trade-off between growth and profitability that constrains a firm's decision-making process, a general suppression of long-term investment growth and increasing concern on maximising shareholder's returns. While corporates rely more on retained profits, banks shift from their conventional banking activities and target household income through non-banking services, and household savings decline while debt-financed or wealth-based consumption increases. Chapter 4 looks into the Indian case through the trope of the corporate sector primarily with the purpose of identifying trends of financialisation that are similar or may be different from the patterns discernable from advanced countries.

The Marxian theory of capital accumulation offers the concepts, categories, and language to comprehend the process of value capture in the realm of production and that of finance as an integral whole. Within the heterodox tradition, the critique of dominance of finance assumes a dichotomy between capitals operating in the realms of production and finance. It assigns an ontological privilege to productive capital as against finance. Such analyses see differentiated capital involved in productive or financial activities as self-conscious 'subjects'. Marxian notion, on the contrary, allows us to trace the metamorphosis of industrial capital as a totality passing through the integral phases of production and circulation. Production and appropriation of surplus, its realisation and distribution through the architecture of finance, is the core of the analysis of value capture. Chapter 5 intends to offer an analysis of value capture actualised through global production networks and financialisation. Surplus production and its distribution through hierarchies of capital as a systemic process, appropriation of rents through defined property rights, super-profits generated through labour arbitrage and the reification of capitalist norms through commodification and securitisation of risks through a maze of financial transactions is what characterises today's empire of capital.

This grand edifice of exploitative structure, however, demands a conducive labour regime, a supply of unprotected and devalued labour. With reference to India, we see informality as a regime of accumulation in the larger context of combined and uneven development of capitalism. The image of capitalism centred on the notion of 'wage labour', particularly 'formal' workers, needs to be historicised, because capitalism always existed with petty-producers, subcontracted devalued labour, labour by chattel, slave labour, lumpen and various other forms of proletariat and only in a particular juncture of history did some of the workers' rights attain juridical recognition. The imagery of formal workers as 'free labour' who sell their labour power on the basis of equivalence of value, where exploitation is rule-based, contracts well-defined and devoid of any coercion becomes the nodal signifier of capitalism. Chapter 6 argues that informality predicated on the notion of 'formal' is a mode of instrumentalising discipline on the vast majority of workforce in the neoliberal regime. The denial of rights is based on idealising formal and delegitimising informal workers and the informality discourse works as an instrument of power that capitalism uses, pushing the majority of the workforce at the margin of illegality.

Chapter 7 addresses the peculiar trend of persistent, high, non-wage employment in India. This is sometimes attributed to cyclical fluctuations as people resort to self-employment in periods of low growth, but in India, the share of non-wage employment remained high independent of growth fluctuations. Apparently, this creates a conceptual discomfort as capitalism is characterised by commodification of labour power. We engage with debates on the relationship between capital and non-capital in this context and intend to explain the persistence of this huge segment of non-capital and the way it interacts with the realm of capital relations. Sometimes, the expansion of self-employment is seen as the proliferation of entrepreneurship and a response to the need of flexibilisation in production. We see high self-employment in India as fragmentation rather than manifesting real autonomy and a result of the absence of standardised market rather than a response to customised demand.

Chapter 8 discusses land acquisition as a form of expropriation. Land gains importance as a financial asset independent of its productive capacity particularly in the backdrop of the financial crisis and the resultant distrust of existing financial instruments. On top of that, mending the 'yield gap' by using land for activities that give higher returns is the dominant mainstream argument for land acquisition. In the context of India, converting small peasant land holdings into large agribusiness units of industrial agriculture or real estate is the key process of securitising land and making it attractive to domestic and foreign investors. Foreign investors are pumping money into India's real estate sector due to decline in asset prices in advanced economies and because huge capital overhang leads them to search for high returns. The expropriation involves a cultural process of creating demand for lifestyles approximating global standards. India's agriculture, however, persists mostly as subsistence economy without any endogenous dynamic of capital accumulation. Hence, the agrarian question remains unresolved and development is misread as de-peasantisation. The Marxian notion of primitive accumulation of capital and all its later avatars are revisited in this context to underline the fact that devaluing human labour as well as nature is a prominent way by which capitalism aims to displace the crisis of overaccumulation.

In the next chapter, the book discusses resistance and the mediation of conflicts between labour and capital. The history of capitalism has not been the story of capital alone. Rather, the trajectory of accumulation can be better explained by looking into realities of value capture as a process of contestation between classes. Moments of crisis in capitalism, either of profitability or of legitimacy, had been preceded by high tides of labour resistance and capital responded by imparting new dimensions of reorganising the production process that ultimately empowers capital. In the current phase of globalisation, global capital gets access to global labour reserve and labour's share declines across the globe. Though inequalities manifest class oppressions, class becomes apparently invisible and the politics of resistance seems to be increasingly limited to sporadic resentments and populist manoeuvring. But the change in the production process throws a new challenge of constructing resistance which is no longer confined to the factory. Instead, society itself emerges as an arena of capital–labour conflict. Finally, the book ends with some cursory remarks on the future of industrial development, particularly in the context of new technology. The conflictual frame that runs through the book will perhaps help us identify the cardinal fissures that the trajectory of neoliberal industrialisation is bound to face.

# 2

# Manufacturing versus Services

## A Misplaced Debate

Trajectories of economic development, particularly industrialisation, have largely been conceived in terms of stylised phases marked by structural changes in output and employment. The sequential pattern of the relative importance of sectors such as agriculture, manufacturing and services in terms of output and employment in advanced countries spanning the second half of the nineteenth century to the first half of the twentieth century seems to provide the benchmarks of industrial progress for late industrialisers. Different versions of the classical theories of development[1] assume a virtuous circle of rising productivity translated into capital accumulation in a labour-surplus scenario together with declining production costs diffused across the economy by way of rising real income and, hence, higher demand. The idealised path of moving people from low-productivity agriculture to manufacturing activities with a subsistence–plus wage begins with an initial extensive phase when the industrial sector absorbs labour. This is followed by an intensive phase of employing people in higher productivity manufacturing. With rising income and consequent changes in demand due to varying income elasticities, the importance of agriculture and then manufacturing declines and that of services rises. However, barring China, the experiences of most post-colonial latecomers do not conform with the assumed sequence. The deviation from the stylised sequence for most developing countries where de-industrialisation sets in at a low level of per capita income and at a low peak has been a major concern for policy makers. Contemporary debates on development underline the fact that colonial structures and the imperatives of imperial power led to a peculiar growth trajectory for ex-colonies, making their future completely different from that of advanced countries. It became important eventually to recognise that growth and structural change engage in a double causation rather than in a linear relationship, where the pattern of growth and relative importance of sectors in terms of output and employment are mutually constitutive of each other.

---

[1] See Clark (1940), Fisher (1935), Chenery (1960), Kuznets and Murphy (1966) and Lewis (1954).

The immediate concern for policy makers in developing countries was primarily to deal with the problem of delinking of employment from growth. In most developing countries, huge supply of unskilled labour remains unutilised which makes high growth politically unsustainable. This once again highlights the importance of manufacturing which has the capacity to absorb low-skilled labour and trigger a growth path that will enhance productivity over time. Since it is assumed that services do not possess similar attributes of fast productivity growth derived from static and dynamic scale economies, services are largely non-tradeable and hardly have economy-wide spillover effects, a structural change that bypasses the manufacturing phase and moves people from agriculture to services is an unwanted derailment having grave consequences as growth becomes both economically unsustainable and politically unacceptable. Most debates in this context take a normative turn that manufacturing ought to be the 'engine of growth', but reality favours the rising importance of services in terms of both output and employment share. In the context of India, there has been a series of policy papers arguing for manufacturing-led growth and a tentative trajectory to attain faster employment generation and absorb new additions in the labour force. However, the share of manufacturing both in terms of output and employment remained more or less the same for decades.

R. Nagaraj[2] offers a detailed account of India's manufacturing performance arguing that even if the share of manufacturing in GDP did not decline, it stagnated for a quarter of a century and annual growth of merchandise exports declined. C. P. Chandrasekhar discusses various phases of industrial growth and slowdown in the post-colonial pre-liberalisation era which includes two phases of creditable growth (1951–65 and 1980–90) and stagnation (1965–80) and since 1991 even though growth was more volatile, but moderately high during the 2000s. Early emergence of monopoly in post-Independence India and dependence on a few who could invest in emerging sectors, as well as other forms of non-price competition made competition based on innovation less important. In the past few decades, industrial growth was heavily influenced by the emergence of domestic stock markets and access to private sources of international finance.[3] This chapter aims to further problematise the manufacturing-versus-services debate that assumes some features as intrinsic to sectors largely derived from the early development experiences of capitalism.

We begin with the premise that in a world of free entrepreneurs in a globalised regime of market society, the outcome of structural change in output and employment is not a result of a preconceived design orchestrated by a collective

---

[2] Nagaraj (2017).
[3] Chandrasekhar (2015).

goal. Rather, it is driven by entrepreneurs in search of higher gains. Employment in various sectors also depends on relative gains that workers may derive depending on their position in the skill scale. Increase in productivity has been the key driving force of technological development that reduces unit costs. Whether higher productivity results in higher employment depends on the distribution of gains derived out of the rise in productivity. Therefore, the virtuous circle presumed in a linear causal chain of higher productivity driven by innovation and complementary skills, lower unit costs, higher real income, greater demand and diversification of demand motivating further productivity could be truncated, if not aborted, if the distribution does not allow 'massification' of goods and services. The issue becomes further complicated when technology increasingly displaces labour both in manufacturing and services and there is no other mechanism to pass on the gains derived from improved technology, but to distribute gains as factor incomes to hired labour. Hence, unemployment disrupts the chain of causality creating a skewed distribution of productivity gains.

One can argue that in a globalised economy, demand is not restricted to geographical boundaries nor are technology choices determined by domestic configuration of factors. Hence, there is no limit to scale as such and the choice is only about where to get placed in the hierarchy of global division of labour. Hence, it is a global churning of roles as one moves up from a low to a higher order of technology, passing the job of low-end manufacturing to a relatively less developed country resembling the famous 'flying geese model'. In this apparently smooth global exchange, high technology imports demand higher export earnings through increased specialisation in the division of labour that often runs the risk of relative decline in returns due to declining terms of trade for exports of less developed countries. The more important question, however, is how such a trajectory can be linked to a process of utilising the available labour force which is mostly unskilled in developing economies. If this cannot be done, then a huge labour force may be stuck in a low productivity segment comprising agriculture, low-end manufacturing and low-end services, none of which resemble the assumed virtues of the dynamic high productivity growth path conceived in classical models of transition. It is also difficult in today's world to think of manufacturing and services as mutually exclusive. Emerging synergies between the two will define new-age technological changes. Therefore, assuming that demand for agricultural, manufacturing and services output would show up in sequential phases depending on income grades as it happened earlier would be too simplistic a proposition. Instead of sticking to sectors, it might be important to explore how trajectories of growth and distribution influence structural change in output and employment and it is not manufacturing *per se*, but the critical dynamic features of a production-distribution path incubated in an inclusive milieu that gives rise to a virtuous path of higher productivity together with gainful employment.

The next section primarily identifies the stylised facts of manufacturing both for India and the world and sees how global integration influences manufacturing and services outcomes in India. Next, we closely engage with the manufacturing versus service debate and the emerging synergies between the two and how distribution and demand structure influence growth patterns and vice versa.

## Some Stylised Facts on Manufacturing: India and the World

The origin of deindustrialisation in the South has colonial roots. Deepak Nayyar[4] used the Maddison online database to show that Asia, Africa and South America accounted for 81.8 per cent of the world population and 83.3 per cent of world output in circa 1000. In 1820, the share of these countries in world GDP continued to be 63.1 per cent while the population share was 74.4 per cent. The decline in terms of global output share became prominent between 1820 and 1950 when the share of output for the South declined sharply from 63.1 per cent to 27.1 per cent. Paul Bairoch's[5] study on international industrialisation levels suggests that Asia, Africa and Latin America together accounted for roughly three-fourths of the world industrial output in 1750 and the share declined to 6.5 per cent in 1953. In fact, in terms of world manufacturing output in 1860, China ranked second and India third, just after the United Kingdom. Over a century and a half ending at 1950, the process of deindustrialisation was meant to trigger a dependent development where economic activities of colonies were restricted to supplying primary commodities to industries in the West and as a source of imperial extraction of rents. In the post-colonial phase, the share of developing countries in world output again rose from 27.1 per cent in 1950 to 49.4 per cent in 2008.[6]

The rising share of manufacturing of individual countries of the South in world manufacturing output was paradoxically coupled with the dominant trend of declining share of manufacturing in their respective domestic output and employment. During the period 1994 to 2015, India's share in global manufacturing value added increased from 1.1 per cent to 2.8 per cent while China's share around this time span increased five-fold from less than 5 per cent to 25 per cent.[7] Interestingly, both countries and those which increased their

---

[4] D. Nayyar (2013: 13–15).
[5] Bairoch (1982).
[6] D. Nayyar (2013: 50).
[7] Hallward-Driemeier and Nayyar (2018: 45–46).

share in global manufacturing experienced a stagnation or decline of manufacturing in domestic share in value added. In the most recent period 2011–12 to 2017–18, growth of manufacturing in India was an average 7.5 per cent, slightly higher than the average growth of GDP of 6.9 per cent and the share of manufacturing value added in total output was 17.6 per cent.[8] The share of manufacturing in total employment was 12.6 per cent till the last available NSS data. The composition of manufactured exports remained more or less the same. Resource-based products continue to dominate, although the share of engineering goods and chemicals increased during the recent past together with a fall in the share of textiles. Notably since the 1980s, India experienced massive shift of employment from agriculture to non-agriculture along with a remarkable decline in the share of agriculture in GDP. However, services increased its share both in terms of output and employment as a result of this structural change. The average growth rate of services during 2011–12 to 2017–18 was 8.6 per cent and its share in GDP during this period was 51.8 per cent.[9] Therefore, the share of manufacturing in GDP and total employment suffered a relative decline although the absolute number of workers involved in manufacturing increased despite episodes of absolute decline in 2014 to 2015.

The real GDP of manufacturing has increased at the world level while its share in world GDP declined between 1997 and 2015.[10] In other words, the relatively low share of manufacturing in domestic GDP compared to services and a stable share of manufacturing in domestic output and employment and increasing services seems to be the dominant trend for the world today. In fact, three-fourths of the countries in the world including China show a declining share of manufacturing in their domestic output. The relocation of manufacturing towards developing countries is the other side of global manufacturing. In spite of a significant increase in the share of developing countries in world manufacturing output, high income countries still account for 69 per cent of world manufacturing value added and 17 per cent of manufacturing employment. China emerged as the biggest gainer in the process of relocation and is the 'factory of the world' accounting for one-fourth of world manufacturing value added and roughly 40 per cent of employment.[11] This shows that huge productivity gaps exist between advanced and developing countries with regard to manufacturing production. The relatively stable share of manufacturing in

---

[8] Author's calculation from National Accounts Statistics, available at http://www.mospi.gov.in/13-national-accounts-statistics (accessed 8 September 2019).
[9] Author's calculation from National Accounts Statistics.
[10] Hallward-Driemeier and Nayyar (2018: 45–46).
[11] Ibid., 46.

domestic output and employment is explained by faster productivity growth of manufacturing that reduces unit costs of production and price. Because of a fall in prices, there is a rise in demand directly and indirectly, leading to a rise in manufacturing output. The output growth could prevent a fall in the share of manufacturing in domestic value added even if prices fell due to rise in productivity, but the volume did not increase to an extent which could prevent fall in employment share. In other words, the relative increase in the share of services in domestic value added could largely be because of the slow growth of average productivity in services causing the relative price of services to increase. Faster innovation keeping pace with changing demand, economies of scale advantages derived from domestic and export markets, and speedy diffusion of technology drives higher productivity growth and accumulation. However, such a virtuous trajectory of manufacturing can be compromised by a change in the production structure that increasingly relies on the low-productivity informal sector engaged through subcontracting and outsourcing. On an average, productivity in the unorganised manufacturing in India is roughly one-seventh of that in organised manufacturing. Hence, reliance on informal segments reduces productivity growth of the manufacturing sector as a whole although the labour productivity of organised manufacturing might have grown by 6.4 per cent during the period 2005–06 to 2011–12.[12] William Baumol's cost disease hypothesis suggests that sectors having productivity growth below the economy's average would tend to record over-average cost increases.[13] The resulting cost increase termed as 'cost disease' of stagnant sectors becomes a permanent drag on the economy with above-average price increase, financial pressure and declining quality. It was argued that low-productivity growth of stagnant sectors might lead to a rising share of nominal output of those stagnant sectors. Most of the workers relieved from agriculture in the past four decades in India were absorbed in construction, wholesale and retail trade and unorganised manufacturing which are basically labour-intensive services and low-productivity manufacturing.

High-productivity growth led by manufacturing does not in itself ensure a virtuous growth path. In the context of developing countries, it is important how the vast mass of unskilled labour is put to a high-productivity trajectory. The advantage of manufacturing has been the possibility of easily transforming a person involved in agriculture to a low-skilled factory worker, say in garments or leather, and then move up the value ladder involving higher order of technology.

---

[12] Sundaram (2008); Roy (2016).
[13] Baumol (1967).

The 'flying geese' paradigm[14] or stages of comparative advantage[15] primarily captures this international division of labour where latecomers specialise in relatively matured products according to product cycle stages.[16] High-income countries usually initiate innovation for new products driven by demand and as this technology gets diffused and the product enters the mature phase of production, it is relocated to developing countries. In this process, latecomers are put to a high-productivity growth path through manufacturing growth. Now if the product cycle shrinks or the demand for new goods remains restricted to few people, the process of diffusion of technology and employment in manufacturing subsides at a low peak and at a low level of per capita income.

A study by Dani Rodrik using a sample of 42 countries for the period 1950 to 2012 shows that decline in the share of manufacturing sets in at a low peak and this process of decline becomes faster after the 1960s.[17] High income countries, particularly industrialised countries, recorded a peak of manufacturing share of 25 per cent to 35 per cent in their respective GDPs. It is also important to note that capital intensity in manufacturing has increased over time, particularly for relative cheapening of capital. Hence, employment elasticity of manufacturing declined sharply. In India, capital intensity increased in organised manufacturing. In the 1980s, 10 million rupees of fixed capital (in 2015 prices) supported 90 jobs while it reduced to 10 jobs in 2010.[18] In the second half of the 2000s, capital intensity in manufacturing increased faster.[19] Therefore, even if productivity in manufacturing is increasing, it seems no longer able to employ and upgrade the growing supply of unskilled labour force.

One proposition could be to promote the growth of labour-intensive sectors in manufacturing that might increase manufacturing output with growing employment. In the context of India, the top ten labour-intensive sectors account for 48 per cent of the total employment in the factory segment, but their share in gross value added has been 21 per cent and accounts for 37 per cent of the wages paid in this segment. Tobacco products, the sector which recorded the highest labour intensity within the factory segment, is also the sector that recorded the least average wage per worker during the reference period. Moreover, six of the top ten labour-intensive sectors namely tobacco products, wood and wood products, food products, leather and leather product, apparel and textiles figure

---

[14] Akamatsu (1962).
[15] Balassa (1977).
[16] Vernon (1966).
[17] Rodrik (2016).
[18] Centre for Sustainable Employment (2018: 19).
[19] Roy (2016).

in the group of ten lowest paying wage rates.[20] In other words, these are the sectors which employ relatively more, their contribution to value added is relatively less and they also pay relatively lower wages. Labour intensity coupled with low productivity and low profitability is the 'low road' of survival strategy that hardly contributes to mending the gap between production and consumption.

The question of generating employment in the manufacturing sector, therefore, relates to the challenge of creating gainful employment. Assuming a neoclassical production function producing a single homogeneous product with two factors, there seems to be no reason for decline in output with addition of employment. This is because output is maximised to the point where the productivity of the scarce factor – capital – is maximum and as long as the marginal productivity of labour is positive, every increment in labour inputs causes a rise in output. However, this does not ensure that with increments of labour units, output–capital ratio will also increase. In other words, labour intensity might be accompanied by more use of scarce factors per unit of output. Furthermore, neither the input nor the output is homogeneous and hence capital and labour should be weighed according to their shadow prices in the process of aggregation.[21]

Measuring factor intensities in that case implies relative cost of the specific factor with respect to the total cost of production. This implies that it is the share of income that has to be redistributed and a mere increase in the number of people employed would hardly solve the problem. In countries such as India, we find a growth in informal activities that employ the larger segment of the workforce. Most of this growth is attributed to outsourcing and subcontracting which is associated with lowering the wage rate as well as worsening of working conditions. This relates to the issue of factor substitution because lower price might increase the use of that factor, but it does not necessarily mean a rise in the share of expenditure on that factor. In other words, reduction in wages might result in growth of employment, but since in developing countries, the elasticity of substitution of factors is close to zero, a rise in employment might not lead to a higher share for wage-earners.

The average growth of capital intensity in manufacturing has also affected employment outcomes of developing countries, particularly in the context of relocation. The relative cheapening of investment goods was much sharper in advanced countries than in the developing world. The reason behind this was that for developing countries commodity intensity of investment goods basket is relatively higher while the weight of information and communication technology

---

[20] Ibid.
[21] For a detailed discussion, see Morawetz (1974).

capital and that of machinery has been relatively low.[22] As a result, production structures that show high elasticity of substitution of capital for labour experienced faster replacement of labour by capital. On the other hand, for production structures where elasticity of substitution was low, were offshored to developing countries in search of cheap resources, particularly labour. Therefore, manufacturing activities that were offshored from the North record low substitutability between labour and capital. Now if the elasticity of substitution had been higher for those offshored to capital-scarce economies, the likely response would have been substitution of capital by cheap labour. But if tasks offshored from the North show low elasticity of substitution, the resulting change in the composition of manufacturing may increase capital share in developing countries. This simply boils down to the fact that manufacturing activities offshored to developing countries might be considered labour intensive according to advanced economy standards, but they would be actually capital intensive given the average factor proportions of manufacturing in developing countries.[23] This can be empirically substantiated by the fact that sectors which are more globally integrated, as measured in terms of foreign value added share in gross exports, are relatively capital intensive and involve higher skills and technology.[24] Global integration in case of India has been more in sectors such as computer, electronic and optical equipment, transport equipment, electrical machinery, motor vehicles, trailers and semi-trailers, fabricated metal products, chemicals and non-chemical mineral products, coke, refined petroleum and nuclear fuel. The degree of integration has been far less for textile and textile products, food and beverage, tobacco or leather products which are considered to be labour-intensive industries in India.[25] Therefore, depending on manufacturing exports as a preferred route to employ unskilled labour at least with the given export composition does not seem to be really promising.

Given the nature of changes that the manufacturing sector is undergoing and will undergo in the near future due to the use of new technology, it is not reasonable to assume that growth of manufacturing will resolve the problem of delinking growth and employment. In fact, studies reveal that labour productivity shows 'unconditional convergence' across countries towards the global technological frontier in the case of organised manufacturing regardless of policy and institutional determinants.[26] In the next section, we discuss that certain

---

[22] IMF (2017b: 129).
[23] Elsby, Hobijn and Şahin (2013).
[24] Discussed in greater detail in Chapter 3.
[25] Roy (2019a).
[26] Rodrik (2011).

services do show similar features as well. Therefore, if the larger segment of employment in developing countries happens to be in these segments and activities, one can think of possibilities of convergence in income across countries as well. However, what has happened in the recent decades in India is the opposite. It is the low-productivity, low-skill segment of both manufacturing and services that accounts for the largest share of absorption in the course of structural change.

## A Misplaced Debate

Early development theories, particularly those which focused on relations between growth, per capita income and sectoral composition, did not find any significant relationship between per capita income and share of services in national product.[27] In fact, services used to be defined negatively as activities that are non-tangible and non-commodity, involving a large range of amorphous and heterogeneous activities. Classical political economists often made a distinction between productive and unproductive labour and some of the elements of those debates might throw some light on the futility of the current discourse on manufacturing versus service.

The common thread in Smith and Marx was the notion of unproductive labour which is not producing surplus and is not exchanged against capital, receiving instead payment from revenue. However, Adam Smith was categorical in defining productive labour:

> A man grows rich by employing a multitude of manufacturers: he grows poor by maintaining a multitude of menial servants ... the labour of the manufacturer fixes and realises itself in some particular subject or vendible commodity.... The labour of the menial servant, on the contrary, does not fix or realise itself in any particular subject or vendible commodity. His services generally perish in the very instant of their performance.[28]

Therefore, activities without a material existence are to be considered unproductive. Services were also characterised as highly perishable and they seldom leave any trace of value behind them.

J. S. Mill, however, redefined the boundaries of productive and unproductive labour and opined that materiality should not be the defining principle of whether an activity is productive. Instead, the effect of such activities on the object or human being should be taken into account in defining productive

---

[27] Kuznets (1957).
[28] A. Smith (2003 [1904]: 422–23).

labour.[29] In that context, education and health services should be considered as productive as it enhances human capabilities. But Mill went further to define government services as productive as they also have an indirect impact on labour productivity.

Marx's notion of productive and unproductive labour was a departure from Smith in the sense that materiality was not a defining principle in his analyses. Marx argues that productive labour in capitalism is not defined by the quality of its use and it is immaterial whether it takes the form of a good or service; what is important is whether such activities are performed by labour that are exchanged with variable capital and whether they produce surplus value or not. In *Theories of Surplus Value I*, Marx says,

> For example Milton, who wrote *Paradise Lost* for five pounds, was an unproductive labourer. On the other hand, the writer who turns out stuff for his publisher in factory style is a productive labourer. Milton produced *Paradise Lost* for the same reason that a silkworm produces silk. It was an activity of his nature. Later he sold the product for five pounds. But the literary proletarian of Leipzig, who fabricates books ... under the direction of his publisher, is a productive labourer.... A singer who sells her song for her own account is an unproductive labourer. But the same singer commissioned by an entrepreneur to sing in order to make money for him is a productive labourer.[30]

The notion of unproductive in Marx does not in any case mean that such labour is not useful. Rather, it underlines the peculiarity of capitalism as a system that recognises labour as useful only when it produces surplus value. In *Capital II*, Marx also discusses the circulation process within the circuit of capital. The process of circulation involves activities that do not actually produce surplus value, but create preconditions for the accumulation process to continue. Stephen Resnick and Richard Wolf analysed the Marxian notion of fundamental class process and subsumed class process where the former involves direct labour power and the capitalist producer, while the subsumed class process involves merchants, financiers, suppliers, banks, and so on, who create preconditions for the fundamental class process.[31] There is no hierarchy of importance in these two processes and each constitute the other. The difference is that labour employed in the fundamental class process is paid out of variable capital and they produce surplus value that is appropriated by the capitalist owner while services involved in subsumed class process are paid out of the surplus value.

---

[29] Mill (1852: 57).
[30] Marx (1963: 401).
[31] Resnick and Wolff (1987).

Marx also discussed how transportation can impact the turnover time of capital and hence the realisation of surplus value and profit rate.[32] Therefore, whether labour produced goods or services was immaterial in Marx's analyses. The defining feature of productive activity in capitalism is how it directly produces or indirectly contributes to the creation of surplus value. And the same activity can be considered as productive or unproductive depending on the context of production relations in which the labour is being used. Commodity production as the defining form of productive activity does not, however, mean that the commodity has to have a physical bodily existence as 'goods'. It can easily be non-tangible services since commodity is essentially a conceptual category that captures a social relation where something is produced for sale.

In more recent literature, T. P. Hill emphasises transactions as the key notion behind commodities which could be both goods and services. Hill says, 'A service may be defined as a change in the condition of a person, or of a good belonging to some economic unit which is brought about as the result of the activity of some other economic unit with the prior agreement of former person or economic unit'.[33] It, therefore, says that a service is enacted on some person or on a good owned by the person who receives the service. If it affects the person as it happens in the case of services such as education or health services or music and entertainment services, it is categorised as 'services affecting persons'. On the other hand, services such as maintenance, cleaning and hairdressing are activities that impact a good owned by some other person or economic unit and these are termed as 'services affecting goods'. It is also argued that services are not necessarily perishable as Smith suggested. Rather, services such as education and health have a longer term impact mostly of a permanent nature while services such as hairdressing are of a temporary nature. Despite the fact that it is hard to separate production and consumption of services, it does not mean that they are physically consumed in the sense of being extinguished. Hill was of the view that instead of assuming a dichotomy between goods and services, it would be more meaningful to categorise goods and services that act upon goods and those on persons. The Material Product System of accounting practised in erstwhile socialist countries adopted this categorisation in measuring and categorising output.

The intrinsic quality of manufacturing as conceived in the Kaldorian framework that manufacturing assumes the role of the engine in the growth process emerges from the fact of high-productivity growth being possible in manufacturing. Growth of manufacturing output leads to growth of productivity

---

[32] Marx (1957).
[33] Hill (1977).

in manufacturing, primarily attributable to static and dynamic scale economies relating to plant size and cumulative learning experience.[34] The impact of manufacturing on output growth also stems from spillover effects on other sectors through technical progress. However, many of these features are visible in services particularly as a result of transport, communication and information revolution. Some services have become tradable as well. In fact, modern services such as financial intermediation, computer services, business services, communications and legal and technical services show faster growth with rise in per capita income. In India, relative prices of services did not increase, but productivity has increased faster than manufacturing.[35] Moreover, the growth of services in India is primarily driven by private final consumption expenditure and exports. It is often argued that the growth of services in India is attributable to 'splintering', where services activities are increasingly contracted to separate enterprises to reduce costs.[36]

Barry Eichengreen and Poonam Gupta[37] have shown that the share of value added in services accounted for intermediate demand arising from industry and agriculture declined from 40 per cent and 5 per cent, respectively, in 1991 to 31 per cent and 2 per cent, respectively, in 2007. This basically shows that the growth of services is driven by its own demand. The most important aspect could be the degree of labour absorption. In this count, they show that for low-skilled workers, employment elasticity is negative for manufacturing as well as for various categories of services. But for high-skilled labour, sectors such as finance, communication and business services as well as hotels, wholesale trade and transport show higher employment elasticity than manufacturing. Therefore, neither manufacturing nor services are capable of absorbing the huge number of unskilled labour and put them into a higher productivity path as assumed to be the generic capacity of manufacturing in development literature.

Studies suggest that there are two waves of service growth relating to per capita income of a country. In the initial phase, service sector share of output increases with a decelerating rate until it levels out at roughly US$1,800 per capita income (in 2000, US purchasing-power-parity dollars). In the second wave, at roughly US$4,000 per capita income, the share of the service sector begins to rise before eventually levelling off.[38] Since 1990, there has been an upward shift in the second wave of services growth indicating that the second

---

[34] Kaldor (1966).
[35] IMF (2018: 13).
[36] Bhagwati (1984).
[37] Eichengreen and Gupta (2010).
[38] Eichengreen and Gupta (2009).

wave starts at lower levels of income compared to what it was before the 1990s. The second wave of services growth, however, is driven by the growth of modern services, mainly financial services, communication and business services. But all these facts suggest that there are certain services demand which increase at higher per capita income and they show higher productivity. They do not, in any case, suggest that these productive sectors are actually providing the larger share of employment within the service sector as a whole. On the contrary, the major absorption in the service sector happened to be in traditional services. Gaurav Nayyar has shown that the larger chunk of new employment in services in India has been in the traditional, unorganised, free-entry segment as domestic servants, other personal services, sewage and refuse disposal, sanitation and other similar activities.[39] The average per capita output in most of these services is less than that of agriculture which, of course, increases due to urban 'infrastructure shock' and hence attracts more people from the agricultural sector with higher expectation of income. But eventually, due to crowding and congestion, productivity in urban informal services declines while productivity in agriculture increases due to people shifting away from agriculture. Therefore, contrary to the Lewisian trajectory where people were supposed to move from low productivity to higher productivity segments, a vast mass of people in India are actually moving within the low productivity segment across rural and urban regions, across sectors such as agriculture, informal manufacturing and informal services.[40]

## Real Cause of Worry

Rather than manufacturing *per se*, it was perhaps the way manufacturing evolved in early industrialising countries and the late industrialisers of East Asia, particularly Japan, Korea and China, that provides answers to the real problem. Manufacturing emerging to be the driving force of economic growth has much more to do with distribution of income and inclusivity rather than achievements in productivity. Hartmut Elsenhans[41] discusses this as a civilisational process, analysing the distinction between the tributary mode of production in Asia and the rise of industrial societies in Europe. Technological superiority of Asia over the European world continued till the end of the eighteenth century and Europe used to import luxury goods from Asia, particularly from China and India. European goods were considered inferior and, in fact, the presents of courtesy

---

[39] G. Nayyar (2012).
[40] Roy (2008).
[41] Elsenhans (2015).

that Vasco da Gama offered to the sultan on reaching Calicut were taken as an insult because of the clumsiness of the goods.[42] Industrialisation refers to a civilisational process that attaches greater importance to standardised products rather than producing luxuries for the rich. It involves an economic as well as cultural and institutional process that prioritises mass production instead of catering to the elite. Britain could outcompete Flanders and, later on, France, Venice and Italy despite the latter having advanced industrial techniques primarily because it specialised in cheap goods. It could marginalise the Asian producers who relied on elite customers and could sustain itself on the basis of a skewed distribution by appropriating rents. Early specialzation of Europe in cheap products consumed by people who did not care for distinction and were interested only in the use of the product was the defining feature of capitalist industrialisation. It is also important to note that peasants in Western Europe were well-off to buy products produced by craftsmen and the proto-industry. For late industrialisers, the transformation was a calibrated process of maximising the ratio of inputs of labour to inputs of cooperating factors in successive phases of industrialisation. It was related to the choice of technology which is generally decided at the level of enterprises, but with a long-term view of increasing the efficient use of labour rather than that of scarce factor capital. This defined the path of East Asian industrialisation where utilisation of labour and their gradual upgradation to higher skills defined the calibration of technology choice. What is perhaps common in both these trajectories is a relative restraint imposed by the structure of incentives, institutions and culture of these societies in responding to elite demands and attributing priorities to the process of diffusion that creates mass market.

In sum, the engine can carry the economy forward only when it remains linked with the bogies. Otherwise, the engine will move faster, but will not drive the economy along with it. Higher income stimulates new demand and new industries come up in response, employing more people. These industries expand their scale of operation and introduce new technologies as a response to rising competition, leading to a decline in the relative prices of products. In this process, income increases because of new employment as well as for the real income effect of cheap goods. This makes goods accessible to the masses, income increases and once again new demands arise. If the gains of higher productivity are not diffused as gains in terms of income, manufacturing output will also take a turn towards capital-intensive production that caters to the demands of a few. And in that case, virtues of manufacturing-led growth may not materialise.

---

[42] Ibid., 38.

In fact, satiation of demand has a causal relationship with structural change in an economy.[43] Generally speaking, household expenditure on a particular good reaches an upper limit beyond which expenditure ceases to rise in response to rise in income. As more and more people reach the satiation level for a commodity or group of commodities, the demand for such commodities tends to decline while that of other goods increases. If income inequality increases, implying that few have high incomes whereas the large majority lacks adequate earnings, then the cycle of satiation is short circuited as a few people can buy those goods and the majority cannot, even if their demand is not satiated. Therefore, higher the diffusion of income, higher would be the demand for manufacturing goods. Otherwise, resources would shift early to other products or services that show higher income elasticity. The diffusion pattern of most goods resembles an S-shaped curve which shows demand growing slowly in the beginning, then faster and eventually levelling off.[44] Countries that are more unequal show a lower rate of diffusion.[45]

Growth of manufacturing in a developing economy primarily depends on the growth of the middle class, real wage growth and share of compensation of employees in GDP, diversification of domestic consumption and capacity to respond to changing demand. Rise in inequality, on the other hand, leads to weakening of middle income demands, causing shrinkage of standardised demand for goods and services. Rather, the minority rich with rising income share demand more luxuries mostly imported or produced with the use of capital-intensive technology. At the other extreme, demand for non-standard, low-cost, low-quality goods increases as the poor tend to compromise in quality with declining income.

The number of people belonging to the middle class is assumed to have grown in India, but it is far less than the share of people belonging to a comparable income stratum in China. Defining middle class by $2–$13 per day, the absolute number of middle class increased from 17.3 million in 1990 to 24.1 million in 2005 and, during the same reference years, the absolute number of people belonging to the middle class in China went up from 15.3 to 61.8 million.[46] Using a broad measure of $2–$20 per day as used by the Asian Development Bank (ADB), the share of people having more than $4 per day increased from 12 per cent in 1993–94 to 18 per cent in 2004–05 in India and from 18 per cent to

---

[43] Pasinetti (1981).
[44] UNIDO (2017).
[45] Ibid., 85.
[46] Ravallion (2009).

70 per cent during the same reference period in China[47]. A more recent estimation suggests that less than 3 per cent of Indian households have all five items: car or scooter, air conditioner, fridge, television and computer. There are 200,000 millionaires and 101 billionaires in India and these counts increased in recent times, but 300 million adults who earn more than the median income, but less than the top 10 per cent have captured only 23 per cent of increment in GDP since 1980. In China, this layer of middle class records 43 per cent share of growth increments during the same period.[48] Lucas Chancel and Thomas Piketty's[49] long-period study spanning 1922–2015 using household survey national accounts data and income tax data suggests that the richest Indians listed in *Forbes*' Indian Rich list accounted for 2 per cent of the national income in the 1990s. This increased to 15 per cent in 2000 and to 27 per cent in 2008–09 before the financial crisis. The top 0.1 per cent earners captured 8.2 per cent of national income in 2014–15. Such a high level of wealth concentration is very close to the peak reached in pre-independence India when, in 1939–40, the same rich segment accounted for 8.8 per cent of the national income. The bottom 50 per cent, on the other hand, records a drastic decline in their share in national income from 23.6 per cent in 1982–83 to 14.9 per cent in 2013–14.

The composition of consumption demand also provides explanation for a stagnating manufacturing sector in India. It is primarily the demand for durable consumer goods that contributes to the growth of the manufacturing sector. The growth and composition of private final consumption expenditure in India estimated from the National Accounts Statistics shows that the average annual growth of consumption of durable goods during the period 2000–01 to 2009–10 was 9.9 per cent which increased to 11.4 per cent for the period 2010–11 to 2017–18.[50] Hence, there has been a rise in demand for consumer durables during this period. The growth of services demand during the two reference period marks a decline from an average annual growth rate of 9.7 per cent to 8.8 per cent. The demand growth of semi-durable goods also declined while the demand for non-durable goods grew faster in the second period compared to the first decade of the 2000s. The important fact, however, is the share of durable goods in an average Indian's consumption basket. It was 3.2 per cent during the period 2000–01 to 2009–10 and 3.3 per cent in the subsequent period 2010–11 to 2017–18. The share of services in the consumption basket increased from 35.8 per cent in the first period to 48.7 per cent in the second reference period. The average

---

[47] ADB (2010).
[48] *The Economist* (2018).
[49] Chancel and Piketty (2017).
[50] Author's calculation from National Accounts Statistics available at www.mospi.nic.in.

growth of private final consumption expenditure was 7.2 per cent during the second reference period and it is expenditure on health, education, transport and miscellaneous goods and services that recorded a much higher growth rate than the average growth of consumption. This is primarily not an effect of higher per capita income reaching a level where demand for manufactured goods declines and that of services increases, but simply because of increased privatisation of these services resulting in a rising share of expenditure. According to the 2011–12 NSSO survey on monthly per capita consumption expenditure on durable goods by fractile classes of rural and urban areas, the bottom 90 per cent of the population together spend close to half of what is being spent by the top 5 per cent in buying durable goods.[51] Moreover, the expenditure on durable goods for the 12th fractile class is 6.5 times and 7.8 times higher than that of the 10th fractile class in urban and rural areas respectively. Since the growth of the middle class market is not large enough and the demand for consumer durables is highly skewed, favouring the top two consumption expenditure fractile classes, the domestic demand for consumer durables continued to remain concentrated within a few.

The stagnation in the share of manufacturing in domestic demand can further be explained by the fact that the share of wages in value added in the organised manufacturing sector declined from 29 per cent in 1970–71 to 12.2 per cent in 2015–16. On the other hand, share of profits in value added increased from 30.6 per cent in 1974–75 to 40.3 per cent in 2015–16.[52] The declining share of wage income has a negative impact on domestic demand for manufacturing because wage-earners seem to have a higher propensity to consume from their incremental gains in income compared to profit-earners.

In developing countries, it is generally held that domestic demand is supposed to have a higher contribution in domestic value added while reliance on foreign demand in domestic value added increases in advanced countries. Domestic demand constitutes 95 per cent of domestic value added in manufacturing for least developed countries, 67 per cent for the advanced countries and 84 per cent is the world average.[53] In fact, the largest share of domestic demand for manufacturing is accounted for private final consumption expenditure followed by gross capital formation and expenditure made by governments and non-profit organisations. The growth of gross capital formation in India dwindled in the recent past since 2012–13, it picked up in 2014–15, but declined thereafter and

---

[51] National Sample Survey Organisation Report on Household Consumption of Various Goods and Services in India available at www.mospi.nic.in.

[52] Author's calculation from the Annual Survey of industries, various years.

[53] UNIDO (2017: 66).

then recovered again in 2017–18.[54] The composition of manufactured exports also did not change much in India. Resource-based products continue to be the most important group in India's export basket, although some shift has taken place in terms of share from textiles to engineering goods and chemical products. The share of engineering goods increased from 17.3 per cent in 1999–2000 to 19.7 per cent in 2012–13 and 25.9 per cent in 2017–18.[55]

It is important to note that global manufacturing value added at constant 2010 prices more or less doubled during the period 1990 to 2016. During the same period, the share of developing and emerging industrial economies increased from 21.7 per cent to 44.6 per cent. In 2016, China accounted for 54.6 per cent of manufacturing value added in developing and emerging industrial economies group while India's share turned out to be only 7.7 per cent.[56] Because of the restructuring in global manufacturing value added, developing countries could have increased their individual share in the external sector. But this depends on the capabilities of respective economies in responding to rising demand. Otherwise, rise in domestic demand would be leaked as rising imports and, hence, gaining from rising share of global manufacturing exports remains unfulfilled. A summary measure of such capability indicator based on performance is the competitive industrial performance index (CIP) estimated by the United Nations Industrial Development Organization (UNIDO). The ranking of countries in terms of this indicator remains more or less stable in the short run but in the long run, changes in ranking capture the cumulative learning capability and technological deepening and upgrading of the manufacturing sector of the economy. UNIDO gives CIP rankings of 148 economies of the world. According to the 2015 ranking, China is the third after Germany and Japan and India's rank is 39.[57]

## Synergies between Manufacturing and Services

In today's world, it is simply meaningless to consider manufacturing and services as two mutually exclusive set of operations, giving rise to goods and services separated from each other and their relative demand shows a sequential pattern relating to increasing income stages. There is no denying that demand for services

---

[54] Author's calculation from National Accounts Statistics available at www.mospi.nic.in.
[55] Author's calculation from the RBI (2019) *Handbook of Statistics on the Indian Economy*, available at https://www.rbi.org.in/scripts/AnnualPublications.aspx?head=Handbook%20 of%20Statistics%20on%20Indian%20Economy (accessed 9 September 2019).
[56] UNIDO (2017: 160).
[57] Ibid., 182.

and share of employment in services is higher in advanced economies. Nevertheless, the share of services in household expenditure increases at a much lower per capita income than it used to be earlier. It is precisely because of the interdependence between manufacturing and services. Services are embodied in the manufactured good itself in various stages involving licensing, construction, design research and development (R&D), customs services, environmental clearance in the pre-manufacturing stage followed by handling of raw materials, testing, maintenance, health and safety of workers during the manufacturing stage. The post-manufacturing stage involves services such as packaging, transport, installation, advertisement, marketing, branding, quality control and after-sales services including repair, inventory and warehouse services, legal services, insurance and so on. Besides the fact that services embodied in manufactured goods increases the complementarity between manufacturing and services, there are services embedded in the manufacturing process and use of the good. For instance, a cellphone is a manufactured good, but it is usable only when telecommunication services are added to it which allows the user to further download apps that provide an array of services. In a Nokia N95 phone, only one-third of the value is related to manufacturing while the rest goes to services, some of which are done in-house and some outsourced. The share of embodied services in global manufactured exports amounts to 34.8 per cent in 2011.[58] Therefore, what seems to be emerging is more of a symbiotic relationship between services and manufacturing both due to the rising significance of embodied services as well as with the expansion of embedded services related to the manufacturing process. This is also why the demand for services takes off at a low peak of manufacturing share in GDP.

Besides increasing complementarity between manufacturing and services, certain kinds of services show higher demand in developing countries. According to the International Labour Organization (ILO), 7 per cent to 8 per cent of the labour force in Brazil and 9 per cent of that in Egypt are estimated to be employed in domestic services. The corresponding figure for Germany is 0.7, 0.6 per cent in the USA, 0.3 per cent in England and 0.005 per cent in Sweden.[59] The fact that Brazil has at least 10 times higher share of domestic servants than US or Egypt records 1,800 times the share of domestic servants compared to Sweden does not imply that more rich people stay in Brazil and Egypt. Rather, it is the availability of low-paid domestic servants that increases such employment. In other words, in developing countries, low-paid, low-productivity services account for the larger share of people employed in this sector. But in advanced economies,

---

[58] Hallward-Driemeier and Nayyar (2018: 146–47).
[59] Chang (2010: 31).

services that are close to the technology frontier mostly related to telecommunication, finance and business services account for the larger share of service employment.

The real question, therefore, is how to generate demand for standardised manufactured goods and services. The creation of surplus relates to appropriation of unpaid labour whether involved in manufacturing or in services and, therefore, there is as such no hierarchy attached to the relative importance of sources of growth. In fact, there is nothing wrong if the surplus created in productive activities is too high to sustain an expanding array of workers who are paid out of that surplus. The relevant point could be how to distribute the created value added such that it generates demand for goods and services involving higher productivity and quality rather than reproducing a scenario of higher inequality which gives rise to a sort of polarised demand. The few rich demanding luxuries which are either imported or produced using labour-displacing technologies and the impoverished vast majority on the other side mostly employed in low-end manufacturing activities in the informal segment or in low-paid service activities as security guards, domestic servants, cleaners, construction workers, serving in retail shops and so on can consume only low-valued, low-quality goods and services. In such a scenario of skewed distribution, growing manufacturing productivity or dynamic service activities that show features similar to that of manufacturing can hardly trigger a virtuous growth path of higher productivity, greater diffusion, higher demand, higher employment and wages and diversification of demand, because such productivity growth caters to elites' demand rather than being diffused as goods and services for mass consumption.

Early development literature primarily focused on changing income elasticity of demand and the resultant structural change in the economy. It talked less on price elasticity of demand that declines with fall in prices. It is not only income elasticity of demand that drives satiation, but considerable fall in prices had significant impact on demand. This is important because if the use of new technology and rising productivity affects segments where demands are unmet for the large majority, then even the labour-displacing effect of technology can be offset by rising demand due to declining prices caused by higher productivity. On the other hand, if the use of technology remains confined to catering to segments where price elasticity of demand is already low, then such technologies would cause a fall in employment. Demand curve, in fact, expresses a distribution of the uses of a good at different prices and such uses change at various price levels. A particular use of a good may lose its relative importance as income increases, but that does not necessarily mean that it would not be used at all. The same good may have different uses and can be demanded by new people as prices fall. At the higher tail of the distribution, price elasticity of demand is high as there are many unmet demands, but as price falls substantially making it accessible to all, price elasticity of demand also declines. Therefore, growth of productivity will increase employment only when the product demand is sufficiently elastic. In other words, employment increases when equilibrium demand increases faster than the fall in prices due to rising productivity. Therefore, at low per capita income levels, if the distribution is skewed, satiation of demand for some consumption is attained for the few quickly. However, since purchasing power of the vast masses continues to be low, the effects of high price elasticity of unmet demand could not be fully utilised and hence use of technology is likely to cause fall in employment.

# 3

# Global Production Network

## India and Developing Countries

The current phase of globalisation entails interdependence between spaces and regions of productions at a much higher scale compared to earlier phases of expansive growth realised through trade and commerce. The significant feature of the current phase is the breaking down of production tasks into multiple phases and the international division of labour is no longer based on the average factor intensity of final products. Instead, comparative advantages of production location are driven by factor intensity of particular components or intermediate inputs. The regime of production appears to be inclusive as it offers greater opportunity to developing countries in becoming a part of global production structures. It is no longer necessary to build a single-nation supply chain producing a final product for export. Instead, the process of industrialisation can be short-circuited by specialising in the production of particular inputs or assembling a final product. Hence, it is possible for a country to export a technology-intensive final product while contributing to only a labour-intensive task required for that particular product. This is often termed as 'second unbundling' of production. The first one relates to spatially separating spaces of consumption and production facilitated by steam-power and the use of railways and steamships. This separation soon became inevitable because of scale economies and comparative advantages derived from a particular factor intensity matching the abundance in factors of a region.[1] Such division of labour that emerged in the early nineteenth century facilitated increased global trade and migration due to fall in transportation costs, but it also led to concentration of production in certain regions in the form of clusters and industrial districts. The dual trend existed as coordination costs increased with the dispersion of production sites. The 'second unbundling' was caused by the information and communication technology (ICT) revolution as ICTs allow the coordination of production from a distance. Hence, the spatial scale of production is no longer fixed and networks of production span beyond national boundaries with simple or complex architecture of transactions.

---

[1] Baldwin (2012).

The change in the organisation of production has altered the pattern of global trade. Today, almost 60 per cent of world trade consists of intermediate goods and services that are incorporated in global production networks. This has given rise to a wide divergence between a country's export figures and its actual contribution in adding value. Average import content of exports was roughly 20 per cent in 1990, rose to 40 per cent in 2010 and is likely to touch 60 per cent in 2030.[2] What is even more significant is that two decades ago, 60 per cent of world trade was between developed nations (North–North), 30 per cent involved developed and developing nations (North–South) and only 10 per cent was between developing nations (South–South). It is estimated that within a few years, these three patterns of global trade are likely to have equal share.[3] The OECD report in 2012 further indicated that between 1990 and 2010, the share of BRICS economies in the exports of parts and components increased from 0.78 per cent to over 14 per cent. Non-OECD, non-BRICS Asia more than doubled their share in the same time period, recording a rise from 4.6 per cent to over 9 per cent in 2010. OECD countries' share, at the same time, declined from over 92 per cent of all exports of parts and components to 70 per cent in 2010.[4] There has been a significant shift in the geography of production toward the developing world in recent decades. However, one should not lose sight of the fact that even though China is the single largest country in terms of manufacturing value added, high income countries still account for 69 per cent of manufacturing value added and 17 per cent of global employment in manufacturing. Even in low-skill, labour-intensive tradeables, seven of the top ten exporting countries belong to the high income group and who do not show any revealed comparative advantage on these segments.[5]

The dispersion in production articulated through global production networks comes with a huge concentration of monopoly power and control that multinational corporations (MNCs) and transnational corporations (TNCs) enjoy. The top 500 companies account for 35–40 per cent of world income and the top 100 corporations have shifted 60 per cent of their production and global sales to foreign affiliates.[6] Intra-firm trade involving outsourcing and subcontracting operations account for roughly 40 per cent of global trade. The current regime involves a process of 'new nomadism' where production facilities are shifted from one place to another, giving rise to immense power for MNCs

---

[2] UNCTAD (2013).
[3] Gereffi (2018).
[4] OECD (2012).
[5] World Bank (2018: 50).
[6] Wise and Martin (2015).

vis-à-vis their regional suppliers as suppliers are always under threat of being delinked from the global network. It also offers greater flexibility in addressing detailed and diverse forms of demands as the life cycle of designs are shortened nowadays and a coordinated structure of 'mass customisation' helps fulfilling changing markets.

The externalisation of production has also caused a shift in the sources of corporate profit. In a traditional oligopoly, the power of the producer in charging a higher price emerges out of its control over the product market. In a global value chain, the role of the multinational buyer is more of an oligopsony and the power is driven from its control over the production process. The global production network (GPN) literature underscores the fact that relocating production is primarily driven by the opportunity to take advantage of global labour arbitrage. It is a matter of reducing production costs by choosing locations that offer cheap labour and cheaper natural resources. McKinsey Global Institute estimates that offshoring reduces the cost to the firm by 40 to 60 per cent.[7] Hence, distribution of production across the chain is not only geographically dispersed, but embedded in the larger structure of asymmetry that reproduces income inequality across and within nations. The next section will focus on the contesting and evolving perspectives on global production network followed by a discussion on the mode of integration in case of India in a comparative perspective. The fourth section discusses the gains from such integration and how asymmetries are reproduced in the outcomes as well. Finally, the chapter takes a look at how integration with global networks impacts employment and wages in India.

## Perspectives on Production Networks

Externalising production through outsourcing and subcontracting, in a sense, de-centralising production together with increased concentration of ownership and control is what defines the new regime of the global production network. There are two interlinked processes that might have resulted in the change in production organisation. One relates to the relative cost of sharing information and knowledge as against the cost of moving people. Since the mid-seventeenth century, when monitoring of production and sharing of knowledge became difficult in the existing home-based work, large-scale production in factories involving workers drawn from diverse places emerged as the dominant mode. In the current phase, the opposite happened. The relative cost of sharing information and knowledge vis-à-vis the cost of moving people fell drastically because of the

---

[7] McKinsey Global Institute (2003).

communication revolution and that, in turn, facilitated the externalisation of production. In Coasean terms, internalising production is a result of minimising transaction costs and the firm as an institution emerges more efficient than the market. But such reduction of transaction costs is also determined by the nature of the market that exists between the buyer and seller at various levels. For instance, if the suppliers or sellers attain a monopolist position in the input market, then internalisation would be cost-reducing. On the other hand, if there is competition between suppliers, a market-linked arrangement of externalisation would be more efficient. The network organisation facilitates competition between producers of components pitting one country against the other, supplier against supplier and worker against worker in a global scale. Hence, enhancing 'efficiency', as it is assumed to be, by extending specialisation to the level of components[8] is primarily a result of the asymmetric structure articulated through the process of globalisation. It destroys local monopolies, facilitates competition between suppliers located in various corners of the world, and the 'race to the bottom' for suppliers is actually a source of huge profit for a few oligopsonic multinational buyers.

The literature on the global value chain or its recent incarnation as global production network originates from the tradition of the world system theory, particularly the dependency argument that the structure of the capitalist system reproduces hierarchy and inequality through unequal exchange. T. Hopkins and I. Wallerstein (1986) define commodity chain as 'a network of labour and production process whose end result is a finished commodity'.[9] The exchange viewed originally as embedded in an asymmetric structure was gradually redefined conceiving global value chain as a distinct phase of capitalist industrialisation instead of seeing it as a heuristic device to analyse the concrete nature of the core and periphery relationship playing out in world capitalism. In course of time, the trajectory of value chain literature takes a serious turn, relying more on the empirical details of meso level or sectoral dynamics and firm level upgrading strategies rather than analysing capitalism as a system using political–economic categories.[10] Henceforth, value chain analyses remain restricted as a heuristic framework to understand the details of various stages of production and sometimes even narrowed down to a managerial perspective of supply chain analyses.[11]

The theoretical mould of global production network as laid down by Gary Gereffi and Raphael Kaplinsky largely draws from the Schumpeterian notion of

---

[8] Arndt and Kierzkowski (2001).
[9] Hopkins and Wallerstein (1986).
[10] Blair (2005).
[11] Porter (1985, 1990).

rent.[12] Chains are primarily repositories of economic rents that emerge out of scarce assets created through innovation or derived from privileged access to resources. In other words, the creation of rent at various nodes of value chains through a continuous process of upgrading and innovation defines the premium over and above the average rate of profit. Once the innovation is diffused through competition, the producer's rent gets converted into consumer's surplus. Gereffi identified three major dimensions of value chain analyses: physical input–output flows; territoriality and governance structure. Governance and upgradation are the two most fundamental concepts of value chain analyses. Governance is about the relative positioning of power across the chain and upgradation is about how participants can increase their respective shares by moving up the value ladder. T. J. Sturgeon and Jeffrey Henderson et al. later developed the notion of global production network to broaden the scope of chain analyses going beyond verticality of relationships and incorporates at certain levels the social process of reproduction of knowledge, capital and labour power mediated through hierarchical layers of networks and participants.[13] In fact, a large volume of case studies evolved in the recent past unravelling the maze of interdependence between economic actors engaged in exchange relationships in various sectors and regions.

Two interesting dimensions of global trade and interdependence demands further attention in this context. One is the rising share of low-income countries in US imports compared to imports from other countries and, second, import price deflation recorded in sectors that have both technological and value chain characteristics. Import price fell in sectors such as computers, electrical and telecommunication products while in the case of clothing, footwear, textiles, furniture, miscellaneous furniture and chemicals, the price deflation has been to the tune of 40 per cent during the two decades of 1986–2006.[14] Developing countries increasingly face declining terms of trade for manufacturing exports vis-à-vis the European Union. All these facts once again bring to the fore the Prebisch–Singer thesis in explaining emerging unequal exchange. In the twenty-first century, developing countries which export labour-intensive manufacturing products or are involved in the assembly of imported inputs face a declining average return in barter terms of trade with increase in exports.[15] In fact, expansion of manufacturing capacity in a single country makes sense, but when every other country follows the same strategy and creates production capacities

[12] See Gereffi (1994, 1999, 2001) and Kaplinsky (1998, 2000)
[13] Sturgeon (2001); Henderson et al. (2002).
[14] Milberg (2007).
[15] Kaplinsky (2007).

which remain unutilised, it provides greater leverage to oligopsonic lead firms to reduce supply price. Hence, from the global lead firms' perspective, creation of new capacities and new entrants in global production structure serve the purpose of reducing supply price. One perspective with regard to potential benefits could be that despite a low share in value added and declining unit supply price, if the absolute amount of value added increases, it generates employment and, hence, promotes development.

Dev Nathan[16] argues that development policies can be designed in a dynamic framework that increase benefits for both labour and capital in vertically specialised industrialisation through moving up the value chain. Firms can move from low-value earning, repetitive, labour-intensive tasks to multiple functions of 'full-package supply' and then further to high-value earning, designing and innovation. In developing countries, labour involved in global production chains receives higher wages than what it would in alternative possibilities of employment. Capital also gets access to the global market and, hence, attains a higher scale of operation compared to domestic markets even if the rate of profit is taken as the same in both cases. We will discuss the impact on labour at the end of this chapter, but for now, take note of the fact that such employment would only have a very limited multiplier effect as a larger part of the surplus generated in the process is transferred to foreign buyers. And it is also important to weigh such gains against the subsidies usually offered to producers by their governments to attract foreign investment.

## Global Integration: India and China

Production structure in today's world is far more interpenetrative than in the earlier phase of expansive growth in capitalism. Goods and services that cross national boundaries have a significant share of intermediate goods that enter into various stages of production in different countries, finally giving rise to the final product. It is because of this fragmentation of production into different stages that trade data does not capture the actual contribution of particular countries in the process of production. Components can be imported and then, with specific value addition, can be exported to other countries. It can again be re-imported from the third country after some value being added there and then, after performing the next stage of production, can be exported to a fourth country. In other words, there can be several phases of incoming and outgoing of goods and services which cannot be captured through figures of gross exports of a country.

---

[16] Nathan (2018).

OECD Trade in Value Added database allows us to understand the value addition in different stages of production across national boundaries. But this decomposition does not allow us to untangle firm-level interactions within a particular country. Moreover, the principal indicators of the TIVA database for the year 2018 provide the broad trends at the aggregate level till 2015, but the STAN indicators which give trends at a sectoral level are available till 2011. Hence, even if the broad trends are discussed for the period 1995–2015, the disaggregated data and participation indexes are computed for the period 1995–2011.

Figure 3.1 shows the percentage deviation of domestic value added in gross exports from gross exports, recorded for the world from 1995 to 2015. It shows that world gross export figures are inflated due to multiple counting and if we see the domestic value added contribution which enters the foreign final demand, the deviation from exports figures for the world as a whole has increased over time. It actually manifests increased integration of production across the world over time. Higher the deviation between figures of gross exports and domestic value added for particular countries, higher would be the level of integration of that country into the global production network. Countries such as Saudi Arabia and Colombia have deviations of less than 10 per cent while Korea, Malaysia, Chinese Taipei, Singapore, Ireland and the Czech Republic have deviations higher than 40 per cent. This implies that the latter set of countries are more integrated in their backward linkage compared to the former. Since 2012,

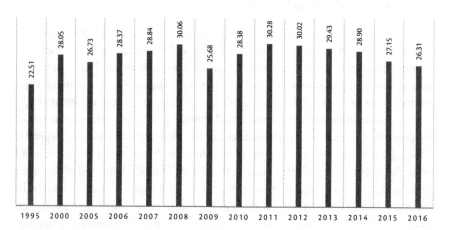

**Figure 3.1** Percentage of deviation of domestic value added in gross exports from gross exports, world

*Source*: Author's calculation from OECD-TIVA database.

however, we find that the deviation between these two figures declined which indicates shrinking of value chain as a response to the global financial crisis. If we compute the shares of various sectors in gross exports and domestic value added for the world, we find that the share of manufacturing and industry as a whole in gross exports is higher than their shares in domestic value added totals (Table 3.1). While in agriculture and allied activities, services and construction, the shares in terms of domestic value added is higher compared to what it is in terms of gross value of exports. Therefore, if we go by gross export figures, manufacturing and overall industry seem to be overvalued and in cases of agriculture, services and construction, export figures actually undervalue their contributions in output. The reason is these activities might have been considered as part of manufacturing value added even if they are actually not so. In case of finance, real estate and business service, the difference between two shares is the highest because a large part of these activities enter into the output of other activities, mostly manufacturing, and have not been accounted as independent services inputs.

The share of domestic value added in gross exports has declined for most of the developed and developing countries from 1995 to 2015. Table 3.2 shows the changes across countries during the reference period. It has marginally increased in the case of UK and the USA among advanced countries, and declined in cases of Japan and Germany. It is interesting to note that only in the cases of China and Hong Kong, the domestic value added share in gross exports increased during the reference period. The decline in domestic value added share has been higher in cases of Korea, India, Chinese Taipei, Thailand, Vietnam and Luxemburg during the period 1995 to 2005. In many counties, including India, domestic value added share in gross exports increased from 2010 to 2015.

**Table 3.1** Shares of sectors in terms of gross export (GE) and domestic value added in foreign demand (DVAFD)

|  | DVAFD | GE |
|---|---|---|
| Agriculture, hunting, forestry and fishing | 3.47 | 2.02 |
| Total manufactures | 31.06 | 56.05 |
| Industry (mining, manufactures and utilities) | 45.27 | 65.02 |
| Total services including construction activities | 51.26 | 32.96 |
| Construction | 1.03 | 0.55 |
| Total services | 50.23 | 32.41 |
| Wholesale, retail, hotels, restaurants, transport | 27.32 | 21.33 |
| Finance, real estate and business services | 19.56 | 9.37 |

*Source*: Author's calculation from OECD-TIVA database.

**Table 3.2** Share of domestic value added in gross exports during the period 1995–2015 for select countries

|                              | 1995  | 2010  | 2015  |
|------------------------------|-------|-------|-------|
| France                       | 82.69 | 77.92 | 78.64 |
| Germany                      | 85.12 | 78.49 | 79.01 |
| Japan                        | 94.39 | 87.84 | 86.77 |
| United Kingdom               | 81.75 | 82.55 | 84.92 |
| United States                | 88.54 | 88.95 | 90.52 |
| Brazil                       | 92.17 | 90.40 | 87.48 |
| China (People's Republic of) | 66.62 | 78.92 | 82.68 |
| India                        | 90.64 | 76.35 | 80.91 |
| Russian Federation           | 86.74 | 90.31 | 89.20 |
| South Africa                 | 86.83 | 81.33 | 77.41 |

*Source*: Author's calculation from OECD-TIVA database.

In Table 3.3, we see sector-wise trends in the share of domestic value added in gross exports in the case of India and China. The share of domestic value added in gross exports in 1995 was much higher for India (90.6) compared to China (66.6), but in 2011, it declined to 76 per cent for India while China's share increased marginally to 68 per cent. During the period 2011 to 2015, the share of domestic value added for India increased to 80.9 per cent and for China, it increased to 82.7. The sector-wise figures suggest that in manufacturing and for industry as a whole, the decline is about 23 percentage points while China's share in manufacturing increased by 8 percentage points (Table 3.3). Considering services in total or in various sectors, we see that the share of domestic value added in gross exports declined in almost all sectors for both India and China. At a more disaggregated level, it is seen that in almost all manufacturing activities, excepting wood products, other non-metallic mineral products and basic metals, the domestic value added share in gross exports increased for China and in the case of India, the share declined for all manufacturing activities and for all services except health and social work. These trends suggest that at the aggregate level, India is far less integrated into the global production network compared to China, but at the same time in the context of manufacturing, China has been able to increase its domestic contribution in exports over the years while there is a sharp declining trend in India.

In Table 3.4, we see the industry-specific contribution to domestic value added that enters into exports from India. The trends suggest that for manufacturing and industry as a whole, there has been a decline in contribution

**Table 3.3** Domestic value added share of gross exports, India and China during 1995–2011

| India | | | | | | | |
|---|---|---|---|---|---|---|---|
| | 1995 | 2000 | 2005 | 2008 | 2009 | 2010 | 2011 |
| Agriculture and allied | 97.15 | 97.38 | 95.95 | 95.95 | 96.51 | 96.35 | 95.93 |
| Manufacturing | 87.42 | 84.75 | 74.84 | 65.7 | 68.42 | 66.29 | 63.89 |
| Industry | 87.75 | 85.02 | 76.11 | 67.01 | 69.53 | 67.43 | 64.7 |
| Construction | 88.34 | 83.46 | 79.66 | 78.05 | 79.7 | 78.42 | 75.95 |
| Total services | 94.31 | 92.67 | 88.98 | 88.16 | 89.31 | 89.03 | 87.9 |
| Wholesale, retail, hotel | 94.48 | 93.1 | 90.02 | 87.7 | 89.47 | 89.22 | 88.56 |
| Finance RE and BS | 93.05 | 89.72 | 86.84 | 88.1 | 88.48 | 88.12 | 86.01 |
| Total | 90.64 | 88.72 | 82.53 | 77.34 | 79.03 | 77.69 | 75.9 |

| China | | | | | | | |
|---|---|---|---|---|---|---|---|
| Agriculture and allied | 92.99 | 92.23 | 89.94 | 90.16 | 91.32 | 90.18 | 89.85 |
| Manufacturing | 51.88 | 49.37 | 51.96 | 60.39 | 60.87 | 59.83 | 59.88 |
| Industry | 52.42 | 49.9 | 52.29 | 60.54 | 60.98 | 59.93 | 59.97 |
| Construction | 94.1 | 92.52 | 88.61 | 87.95 | 89.59 | 88.4 | 87.91 |
| Total services | 96.6 | 94.99 | 94.1 | 93.38 | 94.37 | 93.69 | 93.64 |
| Wholesale, retail, hotel | 96.71 | 95.14 | 94.77 | 94.24 | 95.23 | 94.76 | 94.7 |
| Finance RE and BS | 96.63 | 94 | 90.12 | 88.93 | 89.93 | 88.18 | 88.06 |
| Total | 66.62 | 62.72 | 62.57 | 68.23 | 69.18 | 68.00 | 67.84 |

*Source*: Author's calculation from OECD-TIVA database.

in domestic value added. Considering aggregate services, the contribution in 2011 is higher than that of 1995 levels but on looking closely, one finds that services contribution reached its peak in 2005 and then remained more or less unchanged. Within services, the contribution of finance real estate and business services records a steep rise from 5.9 per cent in 1995 to 12.4 per cent in 2011.

This can also be seen in a different way. Service inputs in various sectors of output have increased over time. One reason is the definitional change of productive activities. Those service activities which were earlier accounted on the head of manufacturing output as in-house components are contracted out and separately considered as services inputs. There is also a relative price effect, in the sense that prices of manufacturing goods decline faster than that of services because of higher productivity growth and, hence, values of the same manufacturing activity tend to decline over time, resulting in higher relative valuation of services. As a result, share of service inputs in manufacturing and other activities tend to rise. Table 3.5 only captures the share of domestic services

**Table 3.4** Industry share in domestic value added contribution to gross exports in India, 1995–2011

|                                     | 1995  | 2000  | 2005  | 2008  | 2009  | 2010  | 2011  |
|-------------------------------------|-------|-------|-------|-------|-------|-------|-------|
| Manufacturing                       | 47.89 | 42.91 | 34.98 | 31.66 | 33.73 | 33.17 | 31.93 |
| Industry                            | 49.99 | 44.16 | 38.18 | 34.03 | 35.95 | 35.26 | 33.31 |
| Services                            | 36.25 | 41.73 | 42.18 | 40.87 | 40.84 | 39.85 | 40.13 |
| Construction                        | 0.35  | 0.49  | 0.55  | 0.57  | 0.54  | 0.53  | 0.53  |
| Wholesale and retail trade          | 17.61 | 15.12 | 11.98 | 10.78 | 11.67 | 11.14 | 11.24 |
| Hotel and restaurants               | 2.22  | 2.43  | 1.65  | 1.26  | 1.45  | 1.33  | 1.31  |
| Transport, storage and communication | 6.83 | 9.45  | 11.05 | 10.65 | 10.51 | 10.35 | 10.49 |
| Financial intermediation            | 0.3   | 0.51  | 0.71  | 0.73  | 0.68  | 0.68  | 0.69  |
| Real estate and business service    | 5.62  | 8.94  | 11.96 | 12.52 | 11.81 | 11.69 | 11.68 |
| Community and personal services     | 3.67  | 5.28  | 4.83  | 4.93  | 4.71  | 4.66  | 4.71  |

*Source*: Author's calculation from OECD-TIVA database.

contributing to gross exports of various sectors of India during the reference period.

The share of domestic services value added in gross exports of India has increased from 44.5 per cent in 1995 to 47.5 per cent in 2011. It is, however, interesting to note that services contribution to total manufacturing exports has fallen from roughly 24 per cent in 1995 to 21 per cent in 2011 and a similar decline is visible for the industry as a whole. The decline in domestic value added share in gross exports has not, however, affected adversely the export performance of countries. In fact, gross exports as a share of GDP have increased for all countries in the world excepting Canada. In India, there has been a rise of about 13.2 percentage points in the share of gross exports to GDP during the period 1995 to 2011, but during this period, share of domestic value added as share of gross exports declined by 14.7 per cent. For almost all countries in the world, gross exports as share of GDP has increased and for most countries barring a few such as Canada, Norway, Netherlands, China and Philippines, the share of domestic value added in gross exports shows a decline. Philippines recorded the highest rise in share of domestic value added in gross exports. In the case of China, the gross exports as share of GDP increased by 7.2 percentage point during the reference period while the share of domestic value added as share of gross exports increased by 1.2 percentage points.

Table 3.5 Domestic services value added in gross exports of various sectors in India, 1995–2011

|  | 1995 | 2000 | 2005 | 2008 | 2009 | 2010 | 2011 |
|---|---|---|---|---|---|---|---|
| Agriculture, hunting, forestry and fishing | 5.31 | 6.39 | 7.63 | 6.44 | 6.42 | 6.43 | 6.47 |
| Mining and quarrying | 5.64 | 6.99 | 8.43 | 7.68 | 8.32 | 7.4 | 6.81 |
| Total manufactures | 23.69 | 24.8 | 24.65 | 20.6 | 23.58 | 21.83 | 20.88 |
| Industry (mining, manufactures and utilities) | 23 | 24.35 | 23.56 | 19.95 | 22.87 | 21.22 | 20.48 |
| Construction | 60.87 | 59.9 | 57.87 | 58.11 | 59.26 | 59.03 | 57.87 |
| Total services | 81.18 | 80.37 | 79.95 | 79.66 | 80.67 | 80.75 | 80.47 |
| Wholesale, retail, hotels, restaurants, transport | 81.22 | 80.43 | 78.25 | 76.8 | 78.39 | 78.65 | 78.94 |
| Finance, real estate and business services | 80.3 | 77.38 | 81.13 | 82.14 | 82.74 | 82.46 | 81.08 |
| Total | 44.5 | 49.05 | 50.01 | 47.1 | 48.89 | 47.41 | 47.46 |

*Source*: Author's calculation from OECD-TIVA database.

## Foreign Value Added and Net Gain

The decline of domestic value added in gross exports implies a rise in the share of foreign value added. Production structures are laid down crossing boundaries of nations through vertical, horizontal and diagonal networks coordinated by MNCs and TNCs. Phases of production have become commoditised and price competitions determine the geographical location of particular phases of production. Therefore, some regions and locations specialise in particular tasks and if the preceding stages can be procured at lower costs, it would be imported from other countries. However, there can be back and forth movements unilaterally or multilaterally and, therefore, possibilities of re-import and re-export exist. Foreign value added in gross exports has increased for all 61 major countries reported in the OECD-TIVA database. Luxemburg records the highest share of foreign value added in gross exports and Saudi Arabia has the lowest share in the year 2011. Countries that export oil or primary commodities record a relatively low share of foreign value added for obvious reasons. If we rank the countries in ascending order in terms of their share of foreign value added and divide them into three groups of roughly 20 each, then the group which shows a low share of foreign value added comprises developing countries such as Brazil, South Africa, Russia, Argentina and Indonesia and advanced countries like the USA, UK, Switzerland and Japan. In the middle group, we find both

*Contours of Value Capture*

**Table 3.6** Share of foreign value added in gross exports, India and China over the years

| India | 1995 | 2000 | 2005 | 2008 | 2009 | 2010 | 2011 |
|---|---|---|---|---|---|---|---|
| Industry (MMU) | 12.25 | 14.98 | 23.89 | 32.99 | 30.47 | 32.57 | 35.3 |
| Manufacturing | 12.58 | 15.25 | 25.16 | 34.3 | 31.58 | 33.71 | 36.11 |
| Services + construction | 5.75 | 7.44 | 11.16 | 11.96 | 10.84 | 11.11 | 12.27 |
| Construction | 11.66 | 16.54 | 20.34 | 21.95 | 20.3 | 21.58 | 24.05 |
| Total services | 5.69 | 7.33 | 11.02 | 11.84 | 10.69 | 10.97 | 12.1 |
| WTHRT | 5.52 | 6.9 | 9.98 | 12.3 | 10.53 | 10.78 | 11.44 |
| FREBS | 6.95 | 10.28 | 13.16 | 11.9 | 11.52 | 11.88 | 13.99 |

| PRC | 1995 | 2000 | 2005 | 2008 | 2009 | 2010 | 2011 |
|---|---|---|---|---|---|---|---|
| Industry (MMU) | 47.58 | 50.1 | 47.71 | 39.46 | 39.02 | 40.07 | 40.03 |
| Manufacturing | 48.12 | 50.63 | 48.04 | 39.61 | 39.13 | 40.17 | 40.12 |
| Services + construction | 3.44 | 5.03 | 5.96 | 6.7 | 5.7 | 6.38 | 6.43 |
| Construction | 5.9 | 7.48 | 11.39 | 12.05 | 10.41 | 11.6 | 5.9 |
| Total services | 3.4 | 5.01 | 5.9 | 6.62 | 5.63 | 6.31 | 6.36 |
| WTHRT | 3.29 | 4.86 | 5.23 | 5.76 | 4.77 | 5.24 | 5.3 |
| FREBS | 3.37 | 6 | 9.88 | 11.07 | 10.07 | 11.82 | 11.94 |

*Source*: Author's calculation from OECD-TIVA database.
*Notes*: MMU: manufacturing, mining, utilities; WTHRT: wholesale trade, hotels, restaurants, transport; FREBS: finance, real estate and business service.

India and China along with Mexico, Greece, France, Germany and Sweden. The top 20 countries in terms of share of foreign value added in gross exports comprises developing and developed countries such as Korea, Malaysia, Vietnam, Thailand, Denmark, Finland and Hungary.

Table 3.6 shows the sector-wise share of foreign value added in gross exports for India and China during the period 1995–2011. In case of India, the share of foreign value added in gross exports of manufacturing roughly trebled during the reference period increasing from 12.6 per cent in 1995 to 36.1 per cent in 2011. The increase is similar in case of industry as a whole. In case of services, foreign content in domestic exports more than doubled from 5.7 per cent in 1995 to 12.1 per cent in 2011. Within services, both in the cases of trade and hotels as well as activities related to finance, real estate and business services, there has been a sharp rise in share of foreign value added in gross exports.

In the case of China, share of foreign value added in manufacturing exports declined from 48.1 per cent in 1995 to 40.0 per cent in 2011. In cases of services, however, there has been a rise from 3.4 per cent to 6.4 per cent during the same reference period. It needs mention that the share of foreign value added in gross exports of manufacturing in China had been much higher than that of India, almost four times in 1995. However, over the past one-and-a-half decade, this share declined for China while it increased for India. In the case of services exports, foreign value added content was higher in the case of India compared to China in 1995, but this share shows a rise in both the countries over the reference period.

The TIVA database gives data for various sectors within broad industry categories over the years. Table 3.7 shows the share of foreign value added in gross exports for various sectors in India for 2011. The sectors are grouped according to their respective shares in ascending order. We see that real estate activities record the lowest share of foreign value added in gross exports and coke, refined petroleum products and nuclear fuel industry, record the highest share of foreign value added in gross exports. Roughly, service-related activities and manufacturing activities such as leather, textile and wood products show shares of foreign value added content in gross exports as less than 20 per cent. Manufacturing activities related to computer equipment, electrical equipment, transport equipment, motor vehicles, machinery, metals and chemicals industry record foreign value added content of gross exports higher than 30 per cent.

The pattern broadly suggests that manufacturing products that are of higher value, more technology-intensive and capital-intensive account for a higher share of foreign value added in gross exports. If we see the rise in this share over a period of time, sharp increases are visible in chemicals and metals where the rise has been more than 20 percentage points. Nevertheless, textiles and leather footwear, which are relatively labour intensive, also record a rise in the share of foreign value added in exports to the tune of more than 10 percentage points during the reference period.

The important question, however, is how a country gains out of participation in the global production network. The domestic value added content of gross exports have declined for almost all countries in the world and, obviously, foreign value added share increased barring very few exceptions. One argument could be that although domestic value added as share of gross exports had declined, the absolute amount of domestic value added matters because the larger its value, the higher would be the potential of a particular economy to create jobs. So, even if the share of domestic value added in gross exports declines, if the absolute amount increases, it would be beneficial for a country. However, a similar argument would be that higher the foreign value added content of gross exports, the higher is the loss of potential jobs. In order to comprehend the gains and losses through participation in the global production network, it is necessary to measure participation rate and net gain.

Table 3.7 Industry-wise share of foreign value added in gross exports in India, 2011

| < 10% | > 10%–20% | > 20%–30% | > 30% |
|---|---|---|---|
| Real estate activities (1.54) | Community, social and personal services (10.37) | Electricity, gas and water supply (23.05) | Computer, electronic and optical equipment (31.19) |
| Education (2.55) | Other community, social and personal services (10.38) | Construction (24.05) | Other transport equipment (31.49) |
| Wholesale and retail trade; repairs (3.55) | Hotels and restaurants (11.06) | Other non-metallic mineral products (25.54) | Transport equipment (32.00) |
| Agriculture, hunting, forestry and fishing (4.07) | Food products, beverages and tobacco (12.14) | Wood, paper, paper products, printing and publishing (24.82) | Electrical and optical equipment (32.47) |
| Wholesale and retail trade; hotels and restaurants (4.4) | Total business sector services (12.33) | Pulp, paper, paper products, printing and publishing (25.27) | Motor vehicles, trailers and semi-trailers (32.48) |
| Financial intermediation (5.62) | Health and social work (12.84) | Rubber and plastics products (27.13) | Machinery and equipment, nec (32.46) |
| Computer and related activities (7.53) | Real estate, renting and business activities (14.47) | Chemicals and chemical products (28.56) | Electrical machinery and apparatus, nec (33.96) |
| Mining and quarrying (7.87) | Transport and storage (18.73) | Electricity, gas and water supply (23.05) | Fabricated metal products (34.72) |
| Renting of machinery and equipment (8.1) | Transport and storage, post and telecommunication (18.84) | Construction (24.05) | Total manufactures (36.11) |
| | Wood and products of wood and cork (19.46) | Other non-metallic mineral products (24.54) | Basic metals and fabricated metal products (40.22) |
| | Textiles, textile products, leather and footwear (19.83) | | Basic metals (42.11) |
| | R&D and other business activities (19.90) | | Manufacturing nec; recycling (42.37) |
| | Post and telecommunications (19.92) | | Chemicals and non-chemical mineral prod (44.32) |
| | | | Coke, ref petroleum products and nuclear fuel (56.57) |

*Source:* Author's calculation from OECD-TIVA database.

Participation rate of a country is measured by participation index computed as follows. The OECD dataset gives figures of foreign value added embedded in exports which capture the backward linkage and domestic value added embedded in foreign exports measuring forward linkage of a country in the production network. Now for a particular country, if we add the two absolute figures and compute the share of a particular country in the aggregate of individual sums, we get the participation rate index for that country. This index gives a measure of how the country is integrated with the global production network and if the value of the index increases over time, then the participation of the country has increased during the reference period. On the other hand, the ratio of domestic value added embedded in foreign exports to foreign value added embedded in a country's gross exports gives a rough measure of net gain out of participation. If the value is less than 1, there is net loss and the higher the value over one, the higher would be the net gain.

We see that for advanced countries comprising OECD countries, the USA and UK taken together, the foreign value embedded in their gross exports has declined over time and domestic value embedded in foreign exports for the group as a whole has also declined during the reference period (Table 3.8). This suggests that for advanced countries, both backward and forward linkage have shrunk over time. In the case of BRICS taken together or for India and China separately, both foreign contribution to their gross exports and their contribution to foreign exports have increased over time. It implies that developing countries have increased their participation in the global production network, but the level of integration has been undoubtedly much higher for advanced countries compared to developing countries in any particular year. The participation rate index for countries such as the USA, UK, Italy, Japan and Germany has declined during the period 1995 to 2011. For developing countries, the participation rate has increased during the reference period. Comparing the net gain index, the UK, USA and Japan are among the select developed countries that record net gains, having the index value greater than one while Italy and Germany record a net loss. Considering developing countries, we see that Brazil, Russia and South Africa record net gain and India and China show a net loss due to increased participation. Comparing figures of 1995 and 2011 in case of India, the participation rate index shows a five-fold increase. However, it recorded a net gain in 1995 whereas in 2011 it shows net loss.

In Table 3.9, we map the matrix of 62 countries showing rankings in terms of participation index in the vertical axis and net gain/loss ratio of countries grouped according to their rankings in the horizontal axis. If the ranking is 1, then it shows highest participation rate or gain/loss ratio. The ranking for net gain/loss ratio is taken in terms of absolute value. Here, interpretation in terms of the ratio

**Table 3.8** Backward and forward linkages for select countries, 1995–2011

| OECD+UK+USA | 1995 | 2000 | 2005 | 2008 | 2009 | 2010 | 2011 |
|---|---|---|---|---|---|---|---|
| FVC in GE | 53.35 | 49.63 | 45.98 | 45.75 | 42.92 | 41.68 | 42.31 |
| DVC in FX | 64.12 | 58.48 | 52.99 | 47.45 | 49.20 | 46.90 | 44.97 |
| **BRICS** | | | | | | | |
| FVCin GE | 2.396 | 2.676 | 3.518 | 4.600 | 4.316 | 4.894 | 5.251 |
| DVC in FX | 4.263 | 4.569 | 6.772 | 8.082 | 7.082 | 8.215 | 8.843 |
| **India** | | | | | | | |
| FVC in GE | 0.359 | 0.422 | 1.078 | 1.649 | 1.840 | 2.253 | 2.366 |
| DVC in FX | 0.521 | 0.686 | 1.203 | 1.415 | 1.550 | 1.906 | 1.879 |
| **China** | | | | | | | |
| FVC in GE | 4.658 | 6.586 | 11.611 | 11.453 | 12.932 | 13.815 | 13.644 |
| DVC in FX | 1.328 | 1.904 | 4.121 | 6.043 | 6.155 | 6.582 | 6.630 |

*Source*: Author's calculation from OECD-TIVA database.
*Notes*: FVC in GE: Foreign value contribution in gross exports; DVC in FX: Domestic value contribution in foreign exports.

**Table 3.9** Mapping of net gain/loss and participation rate index

| | | | Net gain/loss ranking | | |
|---|---|---|---|---|---|
| | | | 1–21 | 22–40 | 41–62 |
| P | R | 1–20 | US, Japan, UK, Russia, Saudi Arabia, Switzerland Australia | Germany, France, Italy, Spain, India | China, Korea, Chinese Taipei, Mexico |
| A | A | | | | |
| R | T | | | | |
| T | E | | | | |
| I | | 21–40 | Netherlands, Norway, Brazil, Indonesia, Hong Kong, South Africa, Chile | Sweden, Poland, Austria, Denmark, Finland | Thailand, Ireland, Czech Republic, Turkey, Hungary, Luxemburg, Vietnam |
| C | R | | | | |
| I | A | | | | |
| P | N | | | | |
| A | K | | | | |
| T | I | 41–60 | Philippines, Argentina, Romania, Colombia, Brunei, New Zealand | Israel, Greece, Lithuania, Croatia, Iceland, Cyprus | Slovak, Portugal, Slovenia, Estonia, Costa Rica, Cambodia |
| I | N | | | | |
| O | G | | | | |
| N | | | | | |

being higher or less than 1 is not taken into account. However, countries showing ranking above 21 have the value of the ratio less than one and hence they experience net loss. Therefore, the first column figures are the countries who record net gain by participating in the global production network and the rest actually record a net loss. The top left group of countries comprise those who rank high in terms of net gain and they are also the top 20 in terms of participation rate in the global production network. Barring Saudi Arabia, which has specific resource advantage, the rest are advanced countries. The UK, USA and Japan belong to this group of top gainers while Brazil, South Africa, Philippines, Indonesia, Argentina and New Zealand are gainers among developing countries though their participation rate is relatively low. The third column comprises mostly developing countries and transitional economies and they are the worst losers with varying degrees of participation. China falls under the top right group. China records top ranking in terms of participation rate, but this results in higher net loss. India shows net loss, but its participation rate is less than China's.

Offshoring of manufacturing to countries such as China or India is much higher compared to offshoring in services, considered as share of total services activity in the USA.[17] However, the worrying fact is the declining unit price of exports from developing countries. The decline in the relative price of manufacturing in the past three decades has been attributed to rapid industrialisation and export from East Asia, especially China. The barter terms of trade in manufactures between developing countries and the European Union suffered a decline.[18] 'Immiserising growth' implying falling returns with increasing economic activity is reflected in a decline in unit price of exports specially in cases where countries rely heavily on simple assembly of imported inputs.[19] In fact, it once again brought to the fore the unequal exchange of labour embodied in manufactured goods and services produced by developed countries with that of labour involved in the production of light engineering and assembling jobs as well as standardised services. Ming Ye et al. propose a stylised smile curve with reference to distribution of value added (Figure 3.2). This provides a rough framework of the distribution of value added depending upon the nature of activities and the geographical location of specialisation.[20]

The smile curve above suggests that higher gains are attributed to activities related to conceptualisation, R&D, design and commercialisation of production mostly located in advanced countries. The other gainful activities relate to

---

[17] Liu and Trefler (2008).
[18] Maizels et al. (1998).
[19] Kaplinsky (2007).
[20] Ye, Meng and Wei (2015).

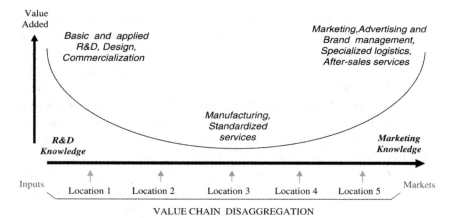

**Figure 3.2** Smile curve and the distribution of value added in the global production network
*Source*: Ye, Meng and Wei (2015).

marketing, advertisement, brand management and after-sales services. These activities are largely managed by the parent companies of MNCs and TNCs located in developed countries. The least share of gains account for activities related to manufacturing and standardised services are largely undertaken by the developing South. If we compare similar smile curves over a period of time, we find that over time, the smile has deepened at the bottom implying a relative increase in difference in value share between the bottom and the top two edges of the smile curve.[21] In other words, the participation of developing countries has increased over time and higher the participation, lower has been the gain in relative terms.

## Impact on Labour

Externalisation of tasks through offshoring is driven by factor cost differentials across regions, particularly when instructions are instantaneously communicated and intermediate outputs can be moved easily and cheaply. Hence, trade in tasks affect the labour market outcomes in both the host and originating country. However, the decision regarding the choice of tasks to be outsourced depends on the nature of tasks and the trade-off between ownership and control that the multinational parent firm faces. It is also important to note that substitutability of factors particularly between labour and capital in a particular line of production,

---

[21] World Bank (2017).

availability of technology complementary skills and exposure to routinisation of a task determines the decisions of offshoring. Assuming that realistic production functions would have elasticity of substitutions at varying degrees rather than the extreme cases of Walras–Leontief–Harrod–Domar assumption of constant input coefficients or Cobb–Douglas function implying a unitary elasticity of substitution between labour and capital, the constant-elasticity-of-substitution allows divergence in structure of production and trade between countries. [22] The choice of offshoring as well as the impact on different segments of labour has not been uniform. Rather, it depends on varying factor intensities and elasticity of substitution between labour and capital. Noteworthy is the fact of coincidence of declining labour's share in value added at the macro level for both advanced and developing countries in a phase of greater integration of production as well as of relative cheapening of investment goods. This also raises questions about the standard assumption of labour share remaining constant over a longer period in macro level analyses.

Labour's share declined for 19 advanced countries which account for 78 per cent of the aggregate GDP of advanced economies and for 32 developing countries accounting for 70 per cent of total GDP of developing economies. The median labour share for OECD countries declined from 66.1 per cent in the early 1990s to 61.7 per cent in the late 2000s. The ILO also underlines the fact that global networks accounted for 20.6 per cent of employment in 2013 and the expansion was higher in developing countries. However, growth of employment fell sharply in the post-crisis period because exports were hit particularly in sectors such as transport equipment and machinery which involve larger chains of tasks and also some countries opted for 'in-sourcing' by undertaking activities that were earlier imported. It has also been reported in several studies that the decline of labour's share has not been uniform. The middle-skilled workers are hardly hit despite their share in total employment remaining more or less unchanged. The low-skilled workers are uniformly affected across countries primarily because of change in the composition of workforce in favour of educated workers. It is only the high skilled workers who could increase their share in the new regime of global production.[23]

The global production network embedded in a regime of free flow of capital opens up access to huge labour force, particularly in China, India, Indonesia, Thailand and ex-Soviet countries. According to IMF, the 'export weighted global work force' derived by multiplying the numerical growth of the workforce by the growing ratio of export to GDP found that effective global workforce

---

[22] Arrow et al. (1961).
[23] IMF (2017b: 127).

quadrupled between 1980 and 2003.[24] New labour was added to the global workforce with very little additional capital, resulting in a declining bargaining power for labour as a whole. More specifically for advanced countries, there has been a cheapening of investment goods, which was not so sharp in the case of developing economies, and that led to substitution of labour by capital. This substitution is often such that even if the cost of capital declines, capital's share increases in value added. With the declining demand for labour, the bargaining power of existing workers also weakens which further adds to the declining wage share. The more a factor is exposed to routinisation, the higher is the substitutability of labour by capital and greater the possibility of that work being automated. Therefore, if the elasticity of substitution between labour and capital is higher than one, because of the cheapening of investment goods, automation is the preferred choice for capital. Tasks for which the substitutability of labour by capital are low, are the tasks that are to be offshored to developing countries where wage costs are relatively low. But such tasks which might be labour intensive according to advanced country standards happen to be relatively capital intensive in a developing country scenario and hence reduce the share of labour in developing countries. ILO studies show that there are positive impacts of global production networks in terms of labour productivity in developing countries and hardly any impact in terms of wage levels.[25] Hence, with rising productivity together with wages remaining stagnant, the wage share in value added declines. An empirical estimate of the World Bank suggests that participation in global value chain has exerted strong negative impact on labour share in income for both advanced and developing economies. An increase in intermediate goods imports of 4 per cent of GDP is likely to result in a decline of labour share on an average to the tune of 1.6 per cent, but much higher impact is estimated for developing economies.[26]

Two important employment trends in India in the recent past is indicative of how entrepreneurs responded to achieve competitiveness in a globally integrated production process. One is the rise in employment in the organised manufacturing sector with rising share of contract workers and the other is increased fragmentation in the unorganised manufacturing segment. Both of these trends contributed to a weakening of labour's bargaining power vis-à-vis employers or buyers of intermediate goods. During the period March 2014 to July 2015, there was an addition of 0.32 million workers in organised manufacturing while the share of contract workers of newly employed in organised manufacturing went

[24] IMF (2007: 162, fig. 5.1).
[25] ILO (2015: 143).
[26] IMF (2017b: 135).

up to 85 per cent. In the case of unorganised manufacturing, the only segment that recorded growth in employment is the Own Account Manufacturing Enterprises (OAMEs) which are basically one-person enterprises or the self-employed who do not hire any labour and mostly employ unpaid family labour.

According to the NSSO survey on Unincorporated Non-agricultural Enterprises (excluding construction), the total employment in unregistered manufacturing increased from 34.8 million in November 2010 to 36.04 million in 2015–16, an increase of 1.24 million in five years.[27] The rise has been higher in OAMEs to the tune of 1.84 million, while employment declined in establishments that are relatively larger within the unregistered segment that employ one to ten hired workers, have employed 0.67 million less workers during the same period. Therefore, the rise in employment in the organised manufacturing sector was driven by contractualisation and in the unorganised segment employment increase was accompanied by fragmentation of productive activities. It is also important to note that the growth of one-person enterprises is visible more in the tradeable segment of the manufacturing sector. In 1989, informal tradeables accounted for 6.2 million workers, that is 19 per cent of total manufacturing employment, and 24 per cent of establishments involved in manufacturing activities. In 2010, employment in this segment rose to 16.4 million workers which is 39 per cent of manufacturing employment, and accounts for 55 per cent of manufacturing establishments. In total, informal tradeables recorded 166 per cent and 193 per cent growth in employment and establishments, respectively, across the two decades.[28] The dynamics of employment in the formal sector also suggests that employment on the basis of contract increased faster in relatively capital-intensive sectors compared to labour-intensive sectors.[29] This might be because sectors such as chemicals, auto-components, motor vehicles, metals, computer equipment, etc., which are increasingly integrated to the global production network, are struggling to remain buoyant in global competition by taking advantage of the availability of cheap labour.

Excessive focus on reducing wage levels, however, does not work beyond a point. The reason is that competition is largely driven by unit labour cost which is a composite index measured as a ratio of product wage per unit of labour productivity. Unit labour cost is the wage paid to the worker measured in terms of output price with respect to the monetary value of output produced per unit of labour. It is evident from the relation that if the productivity of the worker increases keeping the wage unchanged or if the productivity increases faster than

---

[27] NSSO (2017).

[28] Ghani, Kerr and Segura (2015).

[29] Kapoor and Krishnapriya (2019).

the rise in wages then unit labour cost also declines. It can be shown that unit labour cost is directly related to real wage and the ratio of price of wage goods to the price of output and inversely related to labour productivity. Therefore, there can be various ways of reducing unit labour costs and pushing down wages is not the only option. One can argue that if the wage goods are subsidised or cheapened by imports or through various household or community diversification strategies, then *ceteris paribus* unit labour cost may decline. The East Asian strategy was primarily of increasing productivity through investment in fixed capital together with a strategy of 'subsidised learning'. India, however, relied largely on cheapening of wages that is likely to have a negative impact on productivity in the longer run.

# 4

# Financialisation in India

## Emerging Trends in Corporate Sector

Diffusion of capital in the realm of global production structures as well as in financial mediations seems to be the defining feature of the current phase of globalised capitalism. Capital relations tend to make every economic activity of the world subservient to the imperatives of global capital. It imposes a monitoring structure ensuring financial transactions and various forms of mediations between supply of inputs, production and sale commensurate to the norms defined by the global architecture of finance. Production and finance often appear to be separated and financial returns accrue to 'monied' capital operating at a distance from production, but profit in any case originates in productive activities that transform and enhance use-values. The relative importance of circulation, as blown out of proportion, and the relative shift of profit share moving away from productive activities to financial transactions is typical to the current phase of capital accumulation.

Notable is the fact that growth of profit seems to move faster than the growth of investment and a trade-off between growth and profitability constrains the decision-making process of an individual firm. It has wider ramifications, giving rise to a puzzle at the macro level which is that profit-making gets increasingly disconnected from production and, as a result, accumulation occurs without commensurate increase in productive employment. A profit growth being increasingly delinked from production and employment inevitably leads to asymmetric distribution and rising inequality in income that ultimately affects the economy's demand structure. But financialisation also permeates household income and savings by creating liquid asset markets which can be readily transacted at reasonable values. Therefore, instead of holding idle money, economic agents will be willing to direct their income to accumulate productive assets. The financial accelerator generates income that is supposed to have a positive feedback on demand for both consumption and investment and hence expected to take care of the widening demand gap emerging out of unequal distribution. In fact, the relative dominance of finance in the current phase of capitalism has been appreciated as nothing new. It happens to be the feature emerging in every systemic cycle of accumulation in the long history of capitalism.[1] Financial expansion relates to the matured phase of the systemic cycle of accumulation where capital takes its abstract form after a phase of material expansion and the matured moment of financialisation is seen as a precursor to a terminal crisis supposed to be followed by a new cycle of accumulation.[2] The notion of systemic cycles, however, fails to see capitalism as a class process and attributes production and finance as separate domains articulated only through nation state-finance nexus. The current phase of financialisation, on the contrary, needs to be analysed as an organic process emerging out of a peculiar accumulation regime in the neoliberal age that subverts productive activities.

Finance has an important role to play in the process of growth and development in capitalism. The two major 'frictions' in the market that financial instruments are assumed to ease off are transaction costs and information costs. It is argued that development on the financial sector impacts growth through capital accumulation and technological innovation.[3] Finance primarily reduces liquidity risks and allows mobilising savings of dispersed owners for investments in projects having long gestation periods. Savers may not be interested in holding illiquid assets and the financial market allows steady conversion of assets into liquid purchasing power. The trading of assets allows the owner to convert stocks into money, but since the share continues to be owned by someone else, the money mobilised by the firm can be used for long-term projects. In other words, the financial market facilitates trading, hedging, diversifying and pooling of risks. However, the impact of greater risk-sharing and more efficient allocation of capital on savings is ambiguous and, hence, is not very conclusive regarding impact on growth.[4]

The other important role of the financial market is to reduce information cost. A fund-owner may not be able to easily access information on the assets s/he might be thinking of investing in. If access to such information involves a fixed cost to every new investor, then a layer of intermediaries may pool resources to gather information and share it with investors. Stock markets aggregate and disseminate information through prices of stocks. Joseph Stiglitz,[5] however, argued that since information is largely captured in terms of share prices and since such information has a good public character that is accessible to all, an

---

[1] Braudel (1980).

[2] Arrighi (1994). Arrighi identified four systemic cycles of accumulation in the long history of capitalism: Geonese cycle spanning 220 years, Dutch cycle of roughly 180 years, the British cycle of 130 years and the present US cycle is continuing for 100 years.

[3] Levine (1997).

[4] Obstfeld (1994).

[5] Stiglitz (1985).

economic agent would put very few resources for actual research on the firm. Besides reducing information costs *ex ante* through financial markets and instruments, the owners also try to monitor corporate managers' performance and acquisition of information *ex post*. There can be intermediaries who share the responsibility of monitoring a firm's performance on behalf of the owners. Financial arrangements can be made in terms of rewards that help align managers' interest with those of the owners. Moreover, threats of hostile takeovers in a well-developed stock market put indirect pressure on managers who could lose their jobs after takeover due to underperformance.[6] The other important contribution of financial market is assumed to be mobilising funds for technological innovation. As transaction cost reduces, facilitating exchange, specialisation, innovation and growth are assumed to be positively affected. But studies also show that financial markets actually do not contribute to new innovations, but facilitate expansion of 'on-the-shelf' technologies that are economically attractive.[7]

The typical patterns of higher levels of financialisation, albeit not without exception, are linked with higher per capita income and productivity. It is also very difficult to capture financialisation as a process of increased mediation between transactions of various forms of money and credit as loanable capital are diffused through various debt instruments and securitisation. These mediations usually do not manifest as a structural shift in output or employment. Expansion of the financial sector and compositional changes in sources and use of finance at the aggregate level only provides certain indicators to locate the sectoral shift in profit realisation. Financial transactions, in any case, are flows and assets amassed as stocks of financial companies do not follow usual profit-augmenting channels. Enhancement of values in assets in this case does not depend only on the motivation of the owners of such stocks only. Rather, it is conditioned by many other economic and non-economic factors that are beyond the scope of a particular owner. Also, features of financialisation of a particular country depend upon variations in concrete institutional and cultural endowments developed historically. In the context of advanced economies, the literature on varieties of capitalism often categorises countries as 'liberal market economies' represented largely by the Anglo-Saxon model typical to the USA and the UK. The other category is 'coordinated market economies' referring mainly to Germany and

---

[6] The new institutional economic models suggest that shareholder value orientation should be supplemented by stock markets that facilitate hostile takeovers and market-oriented remuneration. Such institutional architecture would compel managers to focus more on current shareholder value and hence the principal–agent problem is resolved.

[7] Greenwood and Smith (1997).

Japan. The symptoms of financalisation differed in these two groups of countries contingent upon historical evolution of financial relations in particular countries.[8] The US case was triggered by a housing bubble while in Germany there was no such indication. Surajit Mazumdar, while commenting on the Indian context, argues that evolution of Indian capitalism as Third World capitalism does not fit into the broad classification set out in the varieties of capitalism literature and also the parameters of categorisation do not factor in the particularity of the Indian case, namely its colonial background and the fact that it could not overcome its agrarian barrier.[9] Hence, features of financialisation differ within the group of advanced economies and expectedly between advanced and developing countries.

In this chapter, we intend to focus on the extent of financialisation in India and see how it is different from advanced economies. Given the heterogeneity of trends and perceived impacts across these economies, it seems a challenge in identifying tractable empirical features that characterise financialisation in developed countries. In the case of India, we use such features as reference points and particularly look through the corporate sector in analysing the evolving nature of financialisation in India.

## Contesting Perspectives and Identifying Trends

Financialisation as a process is defined by G. A. Epstein: '... financialization means the increasing role of financial motives, financial markets, financial actors and financial institutions in the operation of the domestic and international economies.'[10] This definition seems to be analytically vague because it primarily articulates expansive mediation of finance without problematising the process itself. G. R. Krippner identifies the process of financialisation with reference to emerging distribution of accumulation. 'I define financialisation as a pattern of accumulation in which profits accrue primarily through financial channels rather than through trade and commodity production. "Financial" here refers to activities relating to the provision (or transfer) of liquid capital in expectation of future interest, dividends or capital gains.'[11] It refers to a particular type of accumulation that accrues not through the act of production, but in the realm of circulation by way of owning properties distantly linked to production. The perspectives on financialisation are largely related to the way one appreciates the

---

[8] Hall and Soskice (2001).
[9] Mazumdar (2010).
[10] Epstein (2005).
[11] Krippner (2005).

particular nature of accumulation accrued to distant proprietorship. The underlying common feature of Keynesian and neo-Keynesian theories belonging to the heterodox tradition is that profits accrued to 'absentee owners' tend to sabotage productive activities in the real economy and offer a premium on idle capital which are owned by financial intermediaries. On the other hand, neoclassical theories see financial instruments as vehicles to transform current consumption to future investments. The problem of macro economy in this case is viewed as an intertemporal optimisation problem where representative agents maximise their utility function by finding an optimal combination of current and future consumption over their life cycle. More importantly, traders who are absentee owners, at a distance from the industrial community, by way of purchase and sale of stocks make new information about economic fundamentals accessible to everyone and hence reduce the gap between 'intrinsic' values and actual prices. In this frame, the more observers are distant from real production, the more effective their intervention would be in arriving to a convergence between actual price and economic fundamentals. In spite of the fact that these two contesting perspectives, particularly Keynesian and post-Keynesian models on the one hand and the 'efficient market hypothesis' as representative of market efficiency-based models on the other hand, hold opposing views on the impact of the rising importance of financial intermediaries vis-à-vis the real sector, both assume the real and financial sectors of the economy as separated.

There is another view, derived largely from Marx's analyses on money and finance and extended to the contemporary, which offers a more integrated view of the real and financial sector. The argument is the following. It is not because profitability in the real sector stagnated that capital moved out from productive activities and opted for relatively more profitable ventures of speculation in the financial sector. Rather, it is the explosion of finance driven by the monopolised accumulated profit's increased demand for securitised assets.

The 'efficient market hypothesis' which is considered to be a benchmark in the analyses of modern finance, basically applies the Ricardian idea of comparative advantage in asset markets. The only difference is that for asset markets, the comparative advantage is not derived from productivity differences between producers. Rather, differences in information held by investors decide comparative advantages. The premise of the hypothesis is that at any point, there is some fundamental information regarding the underlying entities of financial securities which, although relates to present economic condition, captures the experiences of the past and future prospects.[12] Hence, if the information is not publicly

---

[12] See Fama (1965, 1970).

available, meaning that it is not reflected in prices, then a rational economic agent would take advantage of the mispricing and derive individual gains. However, the information available publicly is close to economic fundamentals and through instantaneous adjustments in the market, the missing information gets incorporated in financial asset prices and consequently reduces the possibility of gains due to comparative information advantage. Hence at the limit, the actual price of a security is a good estimate of its intrinsic value. It is notable that this argument does not deny the possibility of a discrepancy between actual and 'intrinsic' prices, but only suggests that such discrepancies are random and not systemic in character because any systemic discrepancy would be the source of benefit for someone and so prices would immediately respond to correct such deviations. The notion of instantaneous adjustments in efficient asset markets comes close to the 'random walk hypothesis' where it is assumed that successive price changes of assets are independent. It simply implies that a series of stock price changes have no memory. This means that past series will not predict future prices in any meaningful way.[13] It is only when prediction of future prices on the basis of information contained in past series of prices becomes impossible, that one can think of an ideal state where comparative information advantage ceases to exist. The question that, therefore, arises is why rational traders would invest in gaining information if the market itself was informationally efficient? S. Grossman and J. Stiglitz argued that it would make no sense to spend money if the prices perfectly reflect all the available information because such investments and costs would not be compensated by gains. Hence, either random walk hypothesis does not hold or representative agents are irrational.[14] The rejection of the instantaneous adjustment hypothesis and the related random walk hypothesis gave rise to a plethora of mainstream ideas largely derived from behavioural psychology that once again tried to reconcile the proposed hypothesis with the notion of rationality. This strand of literature anchors to the idea of 'bounded rationality' where individuals are goal-oriented and pragmatically process limited information restricted by cognitive ability and use heuristic shortcuts to achieve optimal solutions. But heuristic behaviour is against the notion of random walk and, therefore, possibilities of mispricing and of deriving gains out of that prevails.

The predominant macro perspective within the mainstream also presumes that the behaviour of a representative rational individual converges to what has been predicted by the model derived from the 'rational expectation hypothesis'.[15]

---

[13] LeRoy (1989).
[14] Grossman and Stiglitz (1980).
[15] Lucas (1987). For detailed discussion and critique, see Arestis and Sawyer (2004).

The problem is primarily conceived as an inter-temporal optimisation of utility by allocation of resources for current and future consumption over the life cycle. Firms maximise present value and, hence, act as a transforming vehicle for the household in converting current income into future consumption through investment. The underlying assumption is there is no default and financial markets are efficient and, in any case, the government or the central bank is in no better position than the market to assess bubbles and excess leverages. Therefore, it is always better to restrict intervention in this complex financial market.

Mainstream models of financial markets relying on the rational behaviour of representative agents could not, however, ultimately ignore the fact that rationality is only commensurate with investment decisions based on the mispricing of financial assets. And instead of processing huge information assumed to be publicly available, individual agents apply the rule of thumb, based on second-order-observation derived from cognitive behaviour. Keynes was categorical that such second-order observations and related speculations, if left to market forces, lead to financial instability and sub-optimal allocation of resources. In fact, investment decisions of firms are not always driven by the strict condition of equality between marginal efficiency of capital and the interest rate. Marginal efficiency of capital largely depends on the expectation of yield and the current cost of capital assets, while it is really difficult to predict future yields in a world of uncertainty. Keynes, therefore, argued that it will not be wise to think that current and future consumption or consumption and investment are determined by similar factors. The act of investment at the minimum should require two conditions: there must be expectation of profit and mobilisation of resources or access to sufficient finance to execute a project. In most of the cases, the entrepreneur's investment is not based on calculations of maximising profit, but driven by an expectation of positive reasonable profit which may not be the maximum. Therefore, the concrete nature of conflicts between various groups and the related institutions actually influence investment decisions.[16]

The changes in the structure of business, how the financial sector impacts the real economy, its growth and distribution have been the major focus of post-Keynesian theories on financialisation. The distinction between financial capitalism and entrepreneurial capitalism in Keynes was further dealt in post-Keynesian literature. Post-Keynesians[17] talked about the owner–manager conflict emerging in large corporations primarily as a manifestation of the growth–profit trade-off within the firm. The shareholders insist on immediate gains while the managers and workers would be more concerned about

---

[16] Keynes (1973 [1936]).
[17] Crotty (2003); Dallery and Van Treeck (2008); Stockhammer (2005–06).

accumulation and long-term growth of the firm. Higher dividend payouts, together with the shrinking space of mobilising resources through new stocks as new issues, tend to reduce existing share prices of the company and managers are constrained with regard to investment in capital stock. They rely more on leverage and in order to restrict the manager's likely intent to invest and hence use resource inefficiently, there has to be a share market that keeps in check such moves through persistent threat of hostile corporate takeovers. It is further supplemented by market-linked remunerations for managers so that the manager's preferences converge with that of shareholders. Eckhard Hein[18] argues that this has caused a marked shift of traditional managerial policy of 'retain and invest' to 'downsize and distribute'. The decision of the firm regarding levels of investment is determined by the finance frontier which shows the minimum profit rate to finance the desired accumulation rate in an incomplete capital market and the expansion frontier that relates profit rate attainable from a particular growth strategy. The equilibrium level of investment is given by the intersection of the finance frontier and expansion frontier. In other words, firms are primarily interested in a profit rate to ease the financial constraint and the accumulation rate would be less than the maximum level. Empirical trends suggest that there has been a rise in net-dividend payments and interest as a share of operating surplus in the US economy while corporate taxes as a ratio to net operating surplus declined since 1960, but much sharply after 1980.[19]

The second major implication of financialisation is the rise in opportunities of wealth-based and debt-financed consumption expenditure by households. Expansion of credit instruments as well as shareholder's asset value impacts the consumption expenditure. Robert Boyer[20] provides the first comprehensive framework to analyse the wealth-based financial regime. While privileging share-holder value, it also alters employment contract to increase profitability. A household's consumption depends more on equity holdings and public expenditure is restrained. The wealth-effect of financialisation on the real economy is not uniform. The analysis suggests, first of all, a complementarity between firm governance, household behaviour and employment relation. Second, the successes of finance-led growth depends on the degree of dependence of households on equity-based income. Economies depending more on wage-led income can experience opposite effects as compared to economies that are more equity-based. The positive wealth effect in Boyer's model is based on the assumption of high propensity to consume from rentier income. However, it can

---

[18] Hein (2009).
[19] Ibid.
[20] Boyer (2011).

give rise to a contractionary regime as well if the impact on consumption out of wealth effect is low.

The third important feature of financialisation as shown in post-Keynesian literature is the declining share of wages in aggregate income. As the interest burden increases, the share of interest on net operating surplus increases and the response of the entrepreneurs would be to push down the share of labour income. The declining share of wages, however, requires dismantling or at least weakening of the protective labour institutions such as trade unions, minimum wage laws and so on. This is precisely why net profit share increases despite rise in the share of interest income. However, the declining share of wages is likely to have a negative effect on aggregate demand which gets compensated to an extent by the wealth effect of financialisation. In economies where financialisation of household income is high, the wealth effect will be stronger to facilitate wealth-based and debt-driven consumption even though wage share declined. This wealth effect positively impacts demand as rising debt transfers purchasing power from consumers having low propensity to consume to those with high propensity to consume. But as interest burden increases, Thomas Palley[21] argues that once again there is a reverse flow of resources from the poor to the rich. Hence, from consumers with high to low propensity to consume. Therefore, the stimulation of aggregate demand through debt-financed consumption becomes unsustainable beyond a point. Amit Bhaduri[22] also argued along similar lines saying that stock market wealth is purely 'virtual wealth' and borrowing-based purchase increases due to financial deregulation. But it only adds to private indebtedness as interest burden increases and the expansive effects of wealth-based consumption die down.

The Marxian perspective, however, sees this development of the financial market as consequential to the growth of inequality in the real economy. Hence, the assumed dichotomy between the real and financial sector that runs through different versions of heterodox non-Marxian perspectives is inappropriate to Marxian analyses. The current crisis in financial sectors that spilled over to the economy as a whole is explained by most of the commentators as a regulation failure caused by reckless lending of banks and financial institutions at various layers. However, these are only proximate causes of a deeper problem which the current phase of neoliberal capitalism faces with rising inequality. Capitalism draws in all goods and services as well as resources in the realm of commodity production. And the huge concentration of wealth in the hands of the few, together with a declining share of the majority of the people, might not always

---

[21] Palley (1994, 1996).
[22] Bhaduri (2014).

get reflected in the form of realisation crisis, or crisis of over production as it used to be in earlier situations when the financial market was less developed. In the current scenario, firms and individuals put their amassed surplus back into the system to secure claims on future income stream created by the rest and that, in turn, creates huge demand for securitised assets.[23] But in order to have a developed financial market as a part of the process, securitised assets were standardised, consequently reducing the issuing of such assets. Once the pent-up demand for securitisation significantly crossed the supply of such assets, pressures were built up to create structured credit instruments which may not follow existing market standards. Hence, the enhanced demand for securitised assets as a result of rising concentration of wealth is the root cause for mounting pressure in issuing non-standard financial instruments that ultimately led to subprime mortgage crisis and consequently, a global financial meltdown.

Though it is difficult to arrive at features of financialisation that are universally applicable from existing empirical literature, a large majority of which is focussed on advanced economies, it would be plausible to identify at least some that might be used as pointers for the Indian case taken up in the following sections. Financialisation causes suppression of long-term investment growth with increasing concern for short-term investment and of maximising shareholders' return. Corporates, with increasing retained profits and because of constraints in issuing new stocks, rely more on internal funds and less on banking resources. Banks, on the other hand, increasingly move away from conventional banking activities and target household income as well as other non-banking returns. Commissions and fees emerge to be the growing source of income often manifested in declining share of interest income in banks' resources. In most advanced countries, household savings declined together with rising asset-based and debt-financed consumption and for corporates, the debt to equity ratio increased causing mounting pressure of interest burden over time.

There are institutional complementarities between financial and labour markets. Variations in interactions between these two markets were considered as important markers to differentiate 'Liberal Market Economies' and 'Coordinated Market Economies'. It had been the case that if capital markets were deregulated, then they had to be matched with a deregulated labour regime and often, the focus on long-term growth has been visible in capitalist models where investments are coordinated and the labour market is regulated. But deregulation of finance comes with deregulation of the labour market because with rising interest burden due to rising debt, rising profitability can only be

---

[23] Lysandrou (2011).

ensured by repressing wages, requiring a flexible labour regime. Finally, as expected in theory, finance would flow from low profitability segments to high profitability areas both in terms of sectors and regions and, hence, capital movements across the globe would ensure efficient allocation of resources. In the next two sections, we try to assess the extent of financialisation in India using the above-mentioned trends as reference points that featured mostly in the context of advanced economies.

## Financialisation: Macro Trends in India

The growth of GDP in India has been quite impressive in the past two decades accompanied by a consistent rise in the share of finance, insurance and business services.[24] It almost trebled since Independence and compared to the 1980s, this sector's share in GDP more than doubled (Figure 4.1). The share increased faster in the post-liberalisation period, mostly driven by the growth of banking and insurance services as compared to the rest of business services.

The growing share of this sector in GDP is a broad indicator showing the rising importance of finance in the economy. But what is more significant is an emerging trend of weakening link between capital formation and growth. The share of gross fixed capital formation (GFCF) in GDP declined from 34.3 per cent in 2011–12 to 30.9 per cent in 2015–16 and more than half of the GDP (55 per cent) is accounted for private final consumption expenditure. Notable is the

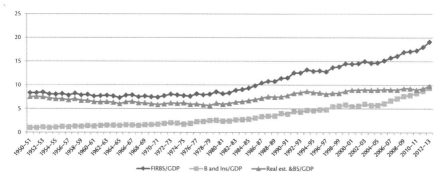

**Figure 4.1** Financial sector as share of GDP

*Source*: National Account Statistics.

---

[24] Murthy and Ranganathan (2013) show that share of manufacturing in non-government paid-up capital almost halved during the period 1991 to 2009–10 and the major gain was recorded by finance, insurance, real estate and business services.

fact that the share of investment in agriculture, mining, manufacturing, public utilities and construction declined since 2011–12. The share of investment increased in the case of services, particularly trade hotels and restaurants, and financial and business services. Business services account, on an average, for more than one-fourth of total gross capital formation. Interestingly, the share of investment in corporate sector surpluses declined since 2007–08 while the share of investment in household sector GDP increased during the recent period. Throughout the past few decades, the relationship between the growth of GDP and capital formation was consonant to each other. Since 2004–05, we see a declining trend of growth of investment while growth of GDP continues to rise.

Besides the broad trends of weakening links between growth and investment, the financial landscape in India is undergoing change evincing early signals of growing importance of non-banking financial entities, non-banking activities of banks, increased resource mobilisation through capital markets and the bank's increased focus on household financing. The scheduled commercial banks account for more than half of the total financial assets in India, but their share has declined from 61.3 per cent to 58.5 per cent during the period 2010–17. The share of public sector banks declined almost by five percentage points during the reference period both in terms of share in total assets or in percentage of GDP. This decline of public sector share is being largely captured by private sector banks although the share of foreign banks in terms of share in total assets declined during this period. Along with public sector banks, the share of regional rural banks and cooperative credit institutions declined during the past decade. The rise in the share both in terms of GDP and with respect to total financial assets was quite significant for non-banking financial companies and mutual funds. The share of non-banking financial companies in terms of GDP increased from 7.7 per cent to 11.6 per cent during the reference period and in terms of total assets, their share increased from 5.7 per cent to 8.3 per cent. The share of mutual funds in total financial assets increased from 5.1 per cent to 7.5 per cent. Insurance companies and other financial institutions also increased their respective shares during the period 2010–11 to 2016–17. Market capitalisation as percentage of GDP both in BSE and NSE increased sharply during this period. However, the turnover ratio that implies total value of shares traded during the period divided by the average market capitalisation for the period declined, indicating that the amount of shares traded per unit of market capitalisation declined during this period.[25]

Figure 4.2 shows the sectoral shares of non-food credit of commercial banks. The share of industry in non-food commercial credit declined from 43.1 per cent

[25] For details, see Roy (2019c).

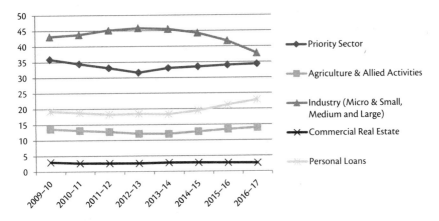

**Figure 4.2** Sectoral shares of non-food credit of commercial banks

*Source*: RBI, *Handbook of Statistics on Indian Economy*; author's calculation.

in 2009–10 to 37.8 per cent in 2016–17. The priority sector, which is redefined, also accounts for a marginal decline in share while the share of personal loans increased from 19.3 per cent to 22.8 per cent.[26] This primarily shows the shifting importance of banking sector activities where banks are more and more into household finance. Credit relating to consumer durables, credit card outstanding and vehicle loans increased by more than 2.5 times during 2009–10 to 2016–17. Credit on account of education loan almost doubled. The biggest increase is, however, accounted by other personal loans which grew by more than three times during the period. These facts primarily indicate the increasing importance of household finance in banking operations. Financial indicators for the scheduled commercial banks indicate that the ratio of liquid asset to total asset increased from 2011 to 2017 while the ratio of net interest income to gross income sharply declined from 22.2 to 13.2 (Table 4.1). It is indicative that the share of the non-interest component of income increased during this period. It is also important to note that non-performing loans as percentage of total loans increased from 2.4 per cent to 9.6 per cent during the reference period which is quite a significant

---

[26] This is in complete contrast to the situation prior to bank nationalisation in India when the share of bank credit to industry and commerce was 87 per cent in 1965, with agriculture accounting to only 0.2 per cent and it candidly reflected the merger of bank and industrial interest as noted in S. K. Goyal, H. K. Manmohan Singh, V. B. Singh and S. C. Gupta authored report titled 'Banking Institutions: A Critical Review' in Goyal (2014: ch. 10, 153–234).

**Table 4.1** Select banking sector financial indicators

| | 2011 | 2012 | 2013 | 2014 | 2015 | 2016 | 2017 |
|---|---|---|---|---|---|---|---|
| Leverage ratio (tier 1 to total asset) | 7 | 7.3 | 7.5 | 7.1 | 7.6 | 8 | 7.9 |
| Leverage ratio regulatory capital/total asset | 9.9 | 10 | 10.1 | 9.2 | 9.5 | 9.9 | 9.5 |
| Non-performing loans/gross total loans | 2.4 | 2.9 | 3.4 | 4.1 | 4.6 | 7.8 | 9.6 |
| Net interest income to gross income | 22.2 | 19.1 | 18 | 17.8 | 12.5 | 12.8 | 13.2 |
| Trading and fee income to gross income | 7.2 | 5.9 | 5.7 | 5.8 | 3.9 | 3.9 | 4.6 |
| Liquid asset to total asset | 15.2 | 14 | 14.8 | 13.5 | 13.6 | 13.1 | 20.5 |

*Source*: IMF (2017a: 38).

increase, a part of which might be due to the definitional change adopted in conformity with Basel norms.[27]

One of the major features of financialisation in advanced countries in general and the USA in particular is the declining household savings over time. In case of India, we find a contrasting scenario where net savings as share of disposable income consistently increased in the past few decades. The share was 9.3 per cent in the mid-sixties and continuously increased, reaching a peak of 29.1 per cent in 2007–08 and declining thereafter, but hovering around 23–24 per cent during the current decade. In a similar reference period, the decline in household savings rate in the USA was 5.6 per cent in 2010, reaching a peak of 7.6 in 2012 and declined to 3.1 in 2017. Hence, unlike advanced countries, India did not experience a decline in household savings as share of disposable income. However, there has been a rise in household debt as percentage of GDP during the recent past. It was 10.1 per cent in 2007 and declined to 8.6 per cent in 2012 and then again increased to 10.2 per cent in 2017.

The composition of household savings also undergoes a change (Table 4.2). The share of deposits in household savings declined from 58 per cent to 44 per cent, a 14 percentage-point decline in five years, although deposits still account for the largest share in India's household savings. The share of shares and debentures increased from 1.8 per cent to 2.8 per cent during the reference period and there has been a significant increase in the share of claims on government. For insurance funds, the share marginally declined from 21 per cent to 18 per

---

[27] Das and Rawat (2018).

**Table 4.2** Distribution of household financial savings

|  | 2011–12 | 2012–13 | 2013–14 | 2014–15 | 2015–16 |
|---|---|---|---|---|---|
| Deposits | 57.95 | 56.97 | 56.01 | 49.93 | 43.77 |
| Shares and debentures | 1.77 | 1.60 | 1.59 | 1.55 | 2.73 |
| Claims on government | -2.35 | -0.67 | 1.94 | 0.08 | 4.40 |
| Insurance funds | 20.98 | 16.91 | 17.17 | 23.33 | 17.57 |
| Provident and pension funds | 10.26 | 14.71 | 14.93 | 14.72 | 18.28 |
| Gross financial savings of HH | 100.00 | 100.00 | 100.00 | 100.00 | 100.00 |

*Source*: RBI, *Handbook of Statistics on Indian Economy*; author's calculation.

cent while the share of provident and pension funds increased from 10 per cent to 18 per cent in the five-year reference period.

The share of compensation to employees as percentage to total expenses declined generally across the world and particularly more sharply in the case of India during the period 1999–2013. In India, there has been a consistent fall in the share of compensation to employees in total expenses. In 1974, it was 23.4 which came down to 8.1 per cent in 2013 despite the world average and labour share in advanced countries being much higher even after the decline.[28] Figure 4.3 shows the share of wages, profit and interest as share of gross value added for the period 1970–2016 in the factory sector that constitutes the organised component of the manufacturing sector in India.[29] The share of wages in value added in the organised manufacturing sector declined from 29 per cent in 1970–71 to 12.2 per cent in 2015–16. On the other hand, share of profits in value added increased from 30.6 per cent in 1974–75 to 40.3 per cent in 2015–16.

It is worth noting that there has been a consistent decline in the share of wages in value added during the entire period although the fall was much faster since the late eighties and there was a marginal upward trend since 2010–11. In the case of share of interest in value added, it reached its peak of 28.4 per cent in 1991–92, came down to 9 per cent in 2006–07 and then increased to 14 per cent in 2015–16. The share of profits in value added declined from 30.6 per cent to 9.5 per cent in 1987–88 and then showed a sharp upturn, reaching a peak of 53.8 per cent in 2007–08 and then it declined to 40.3 per cent in 2015–16. The upturn of the share of profit curve roughly coincides with the period showing downturn of the share of interest curve given that the wage share curve continued to decline during the same period. Hence, in the backdrop of continued squeeze

---

[28] For labour share trends in advanced and developing countries, see IMF (2017b: 122).
[29] Computed from *Annual Survey of Industries*, CSO (various years), Government of India.

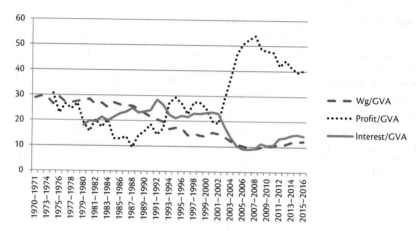

**Figure 4.3** Share of wages profit and interest in GVA in factories
*Source*: Annual Survey of Industries, various years, EPWRF.

of workers' share in value added, the share of interest has declined since 1991 and that could be because of easy availability of credit as the cost of credit declined or because of declining dependence on borrowed funds that might have reduced the share of interest in value added. As a result of any one of the two or both happening together, the share of profits in value added increased sharply during this period.

## Changing Nature of Corporate Finance

The growth–profit trade-off discussed in literature in the context of financialisation becomes relevant while analysing the investment pattern of the corporate sector in India. Since rewards to managers increasingly get linked to firm performance measured in terms of share-holder value, the choice of investment decisions are largely in favour of short-term gains rather than favouring long-term real investment. As a result of such change in the investment portfolio resulting in a stagnation or decline in the growth of gross fixed capital formation, the firm's profitability, at least in the short run, gets delinked from real investment growth. This happens through two channels. Increased financial investment and financial profitability crowd out real investment due to change in the incentive structure that favours short-term profitability. On the other hand, increasing recourse to financial investment and borrowings that lead to increased payment liabilities in the financial market means reduction in the availability of funds from internal resources to fund real investment.[30] S. K. Goyal and C. Rao[31] discussed extensively how inter-corporate investments, aiming to increase the share of group companies in marketable securities, have negatively affected profits and savings of large enterprises in India during the nineties. The ratio of interest payments to total costs increased while investments suffered because of rising interest costs together with low returns from investments and loans to group companies. Due to stifling internal resources, debt to equity ratio increased for Indian corporates. In a more recent study, Sunanda Sen and Zico Dasgupta[32] analysed the aggregate corporate sector trends using CMIE Prowess database till 2011–12. The study identified the changing nature of corporate investment in India with the share of industrial securities showing a marked decline while that of financial securities sharply increased during the period 2002–03 to 2011–12. It also shows that gross fixed asset formation to total corporate use of funds declined sharply during the same reference period.

In this section, CMIE Prowess database was used to see the changes in eleven select parameters related to corporate finance for 554 financial and non-financial companies operating in the manufacturing sector in India. It also uses performance indicators of non-government, non-financial (NGNF) private limited and public limited companies as well as that of non-government, non-banking financial and investment companies reported in the *RBI Bulletin* for various years. The RBI sample covers 292,308 NGNF private limited companies, 16,923 NGNF public limited companies and 18,225 non-government, non-banking financial and investment companies.

The distribution of assets as reported by the Securities and Exchange Board of India (SEBI) shows that in India, the largest share of assets, more than one-third, has been accounted to foreign portfolio investment. Insurance and mutual funds are the second and third in terms of asset holdings in India. The share of the corporate sector in total assets declined from 1.45 per cent in 2010–11 to 0.95 per cent in 2016–17. The growth of operating profit on an average has been higher in financial companies compared to non-financial companies. Since 2008, the growth of profit for both these categories of companies more or less shows a consistent decline and growth rates of operating profit have been negative since 2012. Only in 2015, the profit growth of financial companies taken together turned out to be positive, but the growth rate continued to be negative for non-financial companies. Taking the non-financial sector as a whole which comprises a panel of 747 companies that include manufacturing companies, we

[30] Organhazi (2006: 125).
[31] Goyal and Rao (2002).
[32] Sen and Dasgupta (2015).

*Contours of Value Capture*

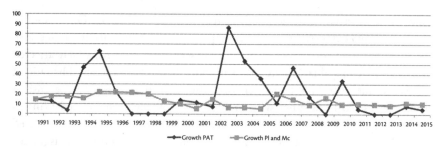

**Figure 4.4** Growth of profit after tax, plant and machinery in corporate manufacturing
*Source*: CMIE Prowess; author's calculation.


see similar trends for operating profit growth in financial and non-financial companies. As the trends suggest, there was a sudden collapse of profit growth for both sets of companies immediately after the financial crisis. It recovered in 2010 but suffered a secular decline in subsequent years, slipping to negative growth rate in profit. It is also important to note that the growth rate of assets was much faster than the growth of capital for manufacturing companies taken together for the reference period. The phenomenon of declining investment in real physical capital is clearly evident in the corporate sector. Figure 4.4 shows that since 1991, the growth of plant and machinery in the select sample of manufacturing companies reached its peak of 22.1 per cent in 1995 and then dropped to 5.5 per cent in 2001. It once again increased to 20.4 per cent in 2006 and then declined to 10.3 per cent in 2015.

Surajit Mazumdar[33] has showed that since 1990–91, the share of GFCF as a percentage of GDP largely manifests a rising trend for the private corporate sector and registered manufacturing. In fact, the share reaches its peak before the financial crisis and then declines. There was a high degree of fluctuation in corporate and manufacturing investment since the economic reforms and they mostly manifest similar trends as much of corporate investment is still in manufacturing. Figure 4.4 shows the growth of plant and machinery in corporate manufacturing as well as the growth of profit after tax. Growth of plant and machinery in the recent past reached the 20 per cent mark only in 2006 and since then, it has declined. During the period 1995–98, growth of investment in plant and machinery was consistently higher than 20 per cent. The growth of profit in manufacturing shows very high fluctuation for the entire period, but since 2004 and 2005, the growth of profit after tax in corporate shows a declining trend.

---

[33] Mazumdar (2015).

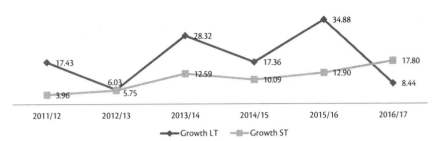

**Figure 4.5** Growth of short-term and long-term investments in the corporate sector
*Source*: CMIE Prowess; author's calculation.

Therefore, it is evident that growth of profit has, on an average, been higher for financial companies compared to non-financial companies; second, there has been a decline in the growth rate of investment in plant and machinery of corporate firms, particularly in the manufacturing sector and the growth of profit also declined in corporate manufacturing.

The financial structure in terms of resources and liabilities of the corporate sector is also undergoing change. Overriding concern for shareholder returns led to short-term gains rather than a long-term increase in productive capacity. The change in the nature of corporate investment is captured in Figure 4.5 that reports the growth of long-term and short-term investment during the period 2011–12 to 2016–17. It shows that the growth rate of long-term investment in 2011–12 was 17.4 per cent and it declined to 8.4 per cent in 2016–17. On the other hand, the growth of short-term investment was 4 per cent in 2011–12 and it went up to 17.8 per cent in 2016–17. Notable is the fact that the share of bank borrowing to total borrowing declined from 56.6 per cent in 2012–13 to 51.5 per cent in 2014–15.

One of the important parameters indicating financial health of companies is debt-to-equity ratio. In the case of NGNF private limited companies, the ratio of total borrowings to equity was 86.3 per cent in 2013–14 and increased to 87.6 per cent in 2015–16. The group of companies having annual sales between 250 million rupees to 1 billion rupees actually recorded the highest value of the ratio. Table 4.3 shows the total borrowing to equity ratio by industry for NGNF private limited companies. The ratio is above 100 per cent for mining and quarrying, textiles, iron and steel, construction, transport storage and communication and real estate. Total borrowing to equity ratio increased during the period 2013–14 to 2015–16 for iron and steel, construction, services, wholesale and retail trade, real estate and computer and related activities out of 15 industry groups. The

**Table 4.3** Total borrowings to equity ratio of NGNF private limited companies by industry

|  | 2013–14 | 2014–15 | 2015–16 |
| --- | --- | --- | --- |
| Mining and quarrying | 114.1 | 93.7 | 106.7 |
| Manufacturing | 95.6 | 91 | 85.1 |
| Food products and beverage | 100.3 | 97.8 | 99 |
| Textiles | 145.4 | 137 | 134.7 |
| Chemicals and chemical products | 69.6 | 64.3 | 60.5 |
| Iron and steel | 135.2 | 150.9 | 161.2 |
| Machinery and equipment | 55.7 | 55.8 | 52.7 |
| Electrical machinery and apparatus | 91.2 | 80.9 | 69.6 |
| Motor vehicles and other transport equipment | 125.8 | 112.6 | 97.6 |
| Construction | 179 | 192.4 | 200.7 |
| Services | 64.7 | 64.8 | 68.6 |
| Wholesale and retail trade | 45.8 | 45.3 | 50.6 |
| Transport storage and communication | 119.9 | 110.9 | 117 |
| Real estate | 135.8 | 147.6 | 165 |
| Computer and related activities | 29.3 | 33.6 | 31.5 |

*Source*: *RBI Bulletin*, 2016.

ratio was highest in the case of construction that crossed 200 per cent in 2015–16 followed by real estate and iron and steel. It is evident that the construction boom in India was largely debt-driven and, hence, highly vulnerable to fluctuations in the financial market.

Figure 4.6 summarises the change in corporate finance, particularly with reference to the private corporate sector. It shows that debt to equity ratio for private limited companies increased from 20.6 per cent in 2007–08 to 53.8 per cent in 2015–16. The interest coverage ratio consistently declined since 2007–08 from 4.2 per cent to 2.7 per cent in 2011–12 followed by a rising trend, reaching 4.2 per cent in 2013–14, and then it declines. What emerges from the above trends is that the corporate sector is increasingly becoming vulnerable to financial fluctuations and consequently, increased vulnerability and rising liability to external sources reduces the space to increase investment in real physical assets. According to RBI reports, roughly 10 per cent of 292,308 companies are vulnerable. That is, they have a debt to equity ratio of more than 200 per cent and interest coverage ratio of less than 1 per cent. These companies, however, accounted for more than 41 per cent of the total debt of the select group and 39 per cent of the total borrowing from banks accounted for this select group.

Figure 4.7 shows the changing composition of funds for the period 2007–08 to 2015–16. Total borrowings and reserves and surplus show a rising trend for

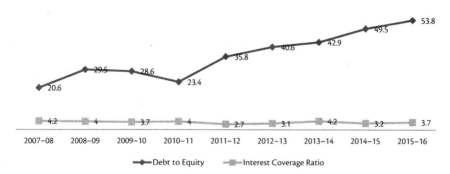

**Figure 4.6** Debt to equity ratio and interest coverage ratio for private limited companies
*Source*: *RBI Bulletin*, various years.

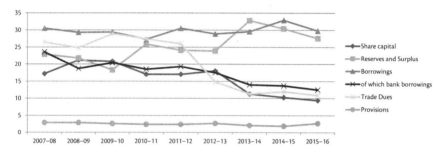

**Figure 4.7** Shares of various sources of funds in NGNF private limited companies
*Source*: *RBI Bulletin*, various years.

the reference period. Provisions' share remained more or less the same with marginal rise in 2015–16. Out of total borrowings, borrowings from banks declined sharply and trade credit also declined since 2012–13. Share capital for private limited companies declined from 17.2 per cent in 2007–08 to 9.4 per cent in 2015–16. This primarily shows that the corporate sector has not been able to raise funds from the capital market at the rate it could in 2007–08. It is important to note that bank borrowing as a source of funds declined from 23.6 per cent in 2007–08 to 12.5 per cent in 2015–16.

Figure 4.8 shows the uses of funds of private limited companies in gross fixed asset and plant and machinery during the period 2007–08 to 2014–15. It shows that expenditure share on gross fixed asset declined from 42.4 per cent in 2008–09 to 29 per cent in 2010–11 and then increased, reaching 48 per cent in 2014–15. However, the expenditure share on plant and machinery declined consistently from 28.4 per cent in 2009–10 to 7.8 per cent in 2012–13 and marginally

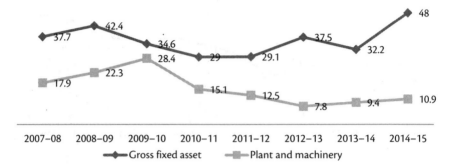

**Figure 4.8** Shares of gross fixed asset and investment in plant and machinery in uses of funds for private limited companies

*Source*: *RBI Bulletin*, various years.

increased to 10.9 per cent in 2014–15. The rising gap between the two trends since 2009–10 might be because the corporate sector invested in land and other tangible and intangible assets while investment in plant and machinery as a share of uses of funds declined during the reference period. The share of external sources in cases of private limited companies is as high as 82.6 per cent, but for public limited companies, it is relatively lesser, accounting for 66.1 per cent and for financial and investment companies, the share of external resources turns out to be 72.7 per cent. The summary ratio for Indian non-financial companies measuring the degree of financial mediation is given by equity capital weighted mean of debt to equity which increased from 40 per cent in 2001 to 83 per cent in 2012. This ratio for the corporate sector is higher in case of India compared to those of Brazil, Japan, Russia, China, United Kingdom, the United States and South Africa. [34]

Finally, regarding the sources of finance, it is also important to note that the corporate sector in India is increasingly exposed to external commercial borrowings (ECB), which increase as a share of total liabilities from 17.6 per cent in 2012 to 21.6 per cent in 2016 (Figure 4.9). In fact, ECB has emerged as the prime component of external debt and in March 2015, ECB accounted for two-thirds of India's external debt. Moreover, in the post-crisis period debt, flows such as bank lending and private capital have gained prominence over equity flows such as FDI.[35] A borrower opting for ECB compared to domestic loan,

---

[34] Linder and Jung (2014).
[35] Ray, Sur and Nandy (2017).

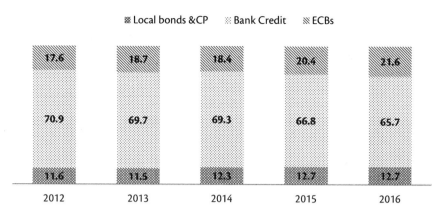

**Figure 4.9** Corporate sector's exposure to external commercial borrowings
*Source*: Bank of International Settlements, *Annual Reports*.

reduces interest rate roughly by 7.5 per cent. Moreover, non-financial corporations are involved in carry trade to take advantage of cross-country interest rate arbitrage. Ahana Bose and Parthapratim Pal[36] have shown that micro and small enterprises recorded a foreign exposure of 40 per cent on an average during the period 2010–2016. Most of these firms have negative net forex earnings as it had fallen sharply after the financial crisis and, therefore, hedging the currency risk becomes difficult for these firms. Increased exposure to external borrowing makes corporate balance sheets more vulnerable to external shocks. On the other hand, the ECBs are highly concentrated with one-sixth of total approved foreign loans going to 14 large conglomerates. With rising debt to equity ratio, therefore, corporate returns and the space for investment in long-term physical assets becomes increasingly conditioned by interest rate as well as exchange rate fluctuations.

## Profiteering through Wage Repression

The implosion of loanable funds, the various forms it takes in terms of financial assets, and the way it affects the real economy requires concrete determinations than abstract generalisations. The Indian story resembles many features of financialisation that are similar to that of advanced economies, but with significant

---

[36] Bose and Pal (2018).

differences both in terms of degree and direction of change. Growth rate of long-term investment shows a declining trend in India's economy, particularly the corporate sector. The relative weight of finance and business services in GDP increased manifold during the recent period. The share of public sector banks, regional banks in total financial assets declined while the importance of mutual funds and pension and provident funds are on the rise. The share of industry in non-food commercial credit issued by commercial banks declines while the share of personal loans, loans on consumer durables, credit card outstanding and vehicle loans within the category of personal loans increased. Bank borrowing to total borrowing fell sharply for non-financial companies and the debt to equity ratio for private limited companies increased quite significantly during the recent period. The operating profit of financial companies was consistently higher than that of non-financial companies, but it shows a declining trend since 2008 presumably because of the financial crisis. In terms of distribution, the decline in the share of wages in value added has been steeper in case of India and for many other developing countries, which is indicative of the class repression on workers that comes along with deregulation of finance.

These features are quite similar to the patterns of financialisation that the advanced economies have experienced in the post-War decades. But there are significant differences as well. The depth of capital market and the participation in stock market is still very thin compared to advanced economies. Despite shares of non-banking institutions in financial assets being on the rise, the largest share is still accounted for by commercial banks. It is also noteworthy that the larger shares of corporate finance have been external resources in case of India which has been distinctly different from the case of advanced economies, particularly the USA where internal resources emerge as the main source of corporate finance. The Indian case resembles more with Hilferding's formulation of finance with reference to the twentieth century rather than what emerges as the dominant feature of corporate finance in advanced economies.[37] The most significant difference, however, in the case of India vis-à-vis advanced economy trends relates to saving patterns of households and their reliance on financial assets.

---

[37] Hilferding provides a comprehensive analysis of the rise of finance capital. Finance capital was defined as the fusion of bank and industrial capital, they accelerate the inherent tendencies of concentration and centralisation in capitalism and MNCs or TNCs emerge as the symptomatic incarnation of such trends. Capital represents self-augmenting value and hence expansion of capitalist accumulation beyond the boundaries of nation-state is quite natural. But expanding capital needs resources and banks collect idle money to convert them into investment. They provide 'circulating credit' to meet short-term requirement of firms and also finance long term projects through 'investment credit'. Hence, expanding monopoly firms were dependent on external finance mobilised by banks (Hilferding 1981).

Though there are indications of a change in composition of personal loans, reliance on credit is on the rise and also a rising trend of debt-financed consumption expenditure. But unlike the USA, India's household savings as a share of disposable income increased over time. Indeed, it is also true that household debt as a percentage of GDP in India increased, but it is still far lower than what it is in the USA. The important point is that in the case of advanced countries, decline in aggregate demand caused by a declining share of wages was partially and temporarily mended by debt-financed and wealth-based consumption of the working class that are largely integrated with the financial market. In case of India, the slowing down of demand caused by a repression of wages together with not-so-higher degree of financialisation of household income can only be partially displaced through wealth-based and debt-financed consumption of the middle class.

In the process of financialisation, the firm opts for the profit-maximising point that is related to a lower rate of growth or accumulation as profitability or shareholders' return gain primacy over accumulation. But this argument raises the important question that if firms opt for a lower accumulation rate, how can higher profitability be sustained with a stagnant or declining investment rate at the macro level. Following is a plausible explanation. According to the national income accounting, net profit is equal to the sum of consumption out of profit income, net private investment, government deficit and external balance less of workers' savings. Workers' savings is workers' income net of workers' consumption. Now, in this macro equation, net profit would increase only if private investment, government deficit or external balance increases or workers' savings fall. In the current neoliberal regime, there are constraints in increasing government deficit as such signals of enhanced state expenditure is an anathema for global investors and hence inimical to policies that internalise inflation targeting through fiscal management norms.

In case of India, the external balance was negative throughout and the deficit in the external front shows an increasing trend in the recent past. Private investments also do not appear to be bullish as reflected in declining trends in the growth of GFCF. Therefore, given the macro identity, the only means to increase profitability is either to increase consumption out of profit income or reduce workers' savings. The growth in India is largely driven by consumption demand in the recent phase which may provide a clue to the riddle as to why we can have higher profitability despite slowing down of accumulation. Workers' savings may decline either because of fall in workers' income keeping the consumption level unchanged or because of an increase in workers' consumption keeping the income level same, or a result of both. In any case, there has been a massive decline in the share of wage income in value added, real wages more or less remained the same or increased marginally while consumption of the workers might have increased because of increased credit. However, the growth of debt after a point demands a return payment that increasingly puts limits to expanding consumption on the basis of debt.[38] Therefore, the way to increase net profit given the lukewarm response in terms of private investment and constrained government deficit together with negative external balance is to repress wages and financialise consumption of goods and services so that growth can be sustained on the basis of increasing consumption expenditure. Finally, exposure to global finance results in rising corporate debt. C. P. Chandrasekhar and Jayati Ghosh [39] noted that there has been a re-emergence of private sector debt after the global financial crisis. The rising dependence of the corporate sector on foreign private debt would contribute to financial fragility and balance of payment problems as inflows are highly volatile and sudden reversals in capital flow may cause huge depreciation of the rupee, resulting in rising debt burden and interest costs in rupee terms. Therefore, financialisation in India faces a conundrum. It necessarily relies on wage repression which has been much higher in India compared to advanced countries, but at the same time since the vast majority of the population is out of the financial system, the scope of addressing the problem of deficient demand caused by rising inequality through wealth- or credit-based consumption has been limited. It only triggered consumption among the middle class while private investment growth did not come to the rescue because of the narrow base of such a rise in demand.

---

[38] Bhaduri (2014).
[39] Chandrasekhar and Ghosh (2015).

# 5

# Hierarchies of Capital and the Architecture of Value Capture

The global edifice of capitalism is hierarchical in nature and the relative position of a particular capital in this structural hierarchy defines its returns. The returns are uneven as the development of capitalism pans out unevenly across the globe. Indeed, the positions of different capital are not fixed forever either in absolute terms or in relative measures. Hence, the relative development of positions in terms of 'catching up' or moving up the ladder has been the dominant discourse in various theories within the broad genre of development literature. Presuming the unreal world of perfect competition as the never-existing 'ideal', economic theory captures such unevenness arising out of concentration and centralisation of capital as sources of rents. Rents accrue to legal proprietorship of resource that is scarce. Capital and land become sources of rent not because they are scarce due to natural reasons, but because of the institution of private property that makes resources scarce. Hence, the distribution of property rights is fundamental to the accumulation of rents. If ground rent is the return to the landlord owning land, profit is also the return to the capital-owning class. Notably, in all sorts of property, income owners receive an extra return without surrendering the ownership of property altogether and simply the act of lending the resource fetches the owner a return in the form of rent. The absolute rent that emerges because of proprietary ownership of land and capital were termed by Ricardo as landowner's rent and capitalist's profit respectively. Ricardo, however, makes a distinction between landlord's income and capitalist's profit. Capitalists save and do not waste wealth by way of luxurious consumption. Hence, they create resources for investment assuming that all resources saved would be invested in the future. Also, the capitalist was considered to be 'internal' to the process of production as against a 'functionless investor'[1] because s/he manages the production process. But this distinction was meaningful so long as the separation of ownership and control in capitalist enterprise did not reach the level of

---

[1] For a detailed discussion on how Ricardo, Veblen, Keynes and Proudhon perceived the rent and interest accrued to absentee owner, the rentier or 'functionless investor', see Sotiropoulos, Milios and Lapatsioras (2013: 9–29).

joint-stock companies. Further, the proposition that supply of savings automatically creates demand for investment had not been challenged in theory as well as in the real world. Keynes was rather explicit in identifying the 'absentee owner', the parasitical 'third' class, the *rentiers* who thrive on returns that come without any genuine sacrifice.[2] The heterodox tradition that followed has been critical of the return appropriated by the 'functionless investor' such as landlords at one point of time or financiers at a later date. Dominance of finance facilitates the detachment of business enterprise from the creation of 'real' wealth and increasing dominance of such enterprise may, in turn, sabotage productive activities. The critical narrative seems to suggest that the problem of capitalism in the neoliberal phase arises because of the relative dominance of finance which tends to subvert productive capital. This relative shift in the share of return within the capitalist class from productive capital to finance assumes prime importance in analysing the slowing down of growth and investment in the current phase of financialised capitalism.

This chapter, while taking off from the earlier discussion on the global production network and financialisation, intends to focus on the integrated project of 'value capture' mediated through various layers of production and financial imperatives. Value produced by the use of labour involves a process of exploitation and expropriation which is hidden behind the neutral term 'value added'. But the value created at a particular stage of production need not be manifested as 'value added' in that specific stage. Rather, the larger portion of the appropriated surplus may be captured by big players in the hierarchical value chain. Using Marx's theory of distribution of profits among competing capitals, I argue that ignoring power relations as a systemic mechanism through which profits are actualised, would hardly allow us to see the actual limits of moving up the value ladder. The differential rate of exploitation exists in this globalised world and though such differences tend to reduce over time, convergence towards a uniform value of labour power across the world is a myth. In fact, such a process is being deliberately punctured by restrictions on cross-border movements of labour. This creates a peculiar asymmetry in the current scenario as profit rates across the world tend to converge because of free movement of capital while difference in wages continues to exist, giving rise to opportunities of labour arbitrage. On the other hand, globalisation also entails a change in the architecture of institutions that define property rights. And the differential returns are not only manifested as returns to labour located in the South, but also in terms of differential share in appropriated rents accrued to capital of the South.

---

[2] Keynes (1973 [1936]).

The world is actually not so flat as the ideological reification of capitalism seems to suggest. Therefore, the dominant perspective of the GPN literature and its prescribed path of industrialisation through participating and specialising in particular tasks in the global value chain is not without question. The problematic is quite complex and integrated rather than being confined into a particular stage of production or task.

It is also important to integrate the analyses of finance with that of production rather than viewing them as self-conscious, mutually exclusive, autonomous processes. The hierarchy of capital is mutually constituted by hierarchies that exist in the realm of production as well as in finance. The mythical separation between the two does not help us understand the class hegemony articulated and actualised through the integrated process of exploitation and expropriation. Merely suggesting that the shifting of accumulated surplus from production to finance is a matter of preference driven by considerations of profitability obscures the fact that extraction of surplus value from differentiated labour at an increased scale is mediated through finance. The decline of wage share in value added in the age of finance is not a mere coincidence; rather, financial repression contributes to the process of extraction of value from workers' income. In fact, the rise in inequality and accumulation of surplus value in a few hands has created enhanced demand for securitised assets with the promise to ensure a future income stream in exchange for current consumption. The claim for the future in an uncertain world is essentially what financial instruments offer, but the returns from these assets are actually driven by price formations influenced by speculative activities. It is also noteworthy that the financial architecture reinforces asymmetry between the North and the South and asserts norms that are conducive to augment returns for global capital.

The arguments made in this chapter follow from the core understanding of class process[3] where production, appropriation and distribution of surplus value are conceived of as an integrated whole and the realisation of this capitalist class process is actualised by multiple transactions occurring at the realm of production and circulation. The production of surplus value involves the fundamental class process where the direct producer or the worker and the owner of variable capital, the capitalist, are the prime actors. On the other hand, the subsumed class process entails those activities that create preconditions for the fundamental class process. The merchant capital, financers, managers, landowners, money-dealing capital, and so on, receive subsumed class payments for their specific roles in contributing to the class process. Returns to capital at various stages of production

---

[3] See Resnick and Wolff (1987).

as well as to those involved in the process of circulation emerge out of two fundamental interlinked processes: the law of value that asserts a socially sanctioned distribution of labour at a particular point in time and the effect of competition among capitals deploying differing technical composition. The value is realised in capitalism through the act of exchange manifested in money terms as price. Therefore, price and value are mutually constitutive of each other, but they are not the same thing. Appropriation of surplus value and its distribution as profit mediated through a maze of exchanges involving both production and circulation defines the trajectory of capital as expanding value.

## Labour Arbitrage

We begin with some concrete examples to foreground the problematic of 'value capture'. Contributions of various stages of production is generally measured in terms of 'value added', which is simply the difference between output price and input price. The output in this case might be an intermediate product of a particular stage of production or a final product before consumption. If the output price in a particular stage is reduced because of lower wages of workers involved in that stage, the input price declines as a result in the immediately next phase, reflecting a higher 'value addition' in the following stage even if the output price remains the same. This enhancement of value addition in the following stage is simply the result of the suppression of wage in the previous stage, other things remaining unchanged. However, the value addition is misconstrued as contribution of the latter phase. Therefore, it is easily understandable that wage difference, for a similar activity, between the workers of the South and the North makes much difference in measuring relative contribution of workers. The value added, as a measurement capturing the difference between input and output prices, is blind to the structural differences in wages and manifests low wage as a low value addition. For instance, Taiwanese-owned Foxconn Technology Group in China is the world's largest contract manufacturer of electronics supplying to Samsung Electronics, Hewlett-Packard, Sony, Apple, Microsoft, Dell and Nokia.[4] The production of Apple's iPods, in particular, involves 41,000 jobs worldwide including 13,290 in the USA and the rest distributed across outsourced centres. Only 30 of the US workers are production workers and the rest are retail, non-professional as well as professional workers. The ratio of wages at Foxconn China compared to similar production work in the USA is only 3.2 per cent and similarly in the case of retail and professional work these ratios are 6 per cent and 1.8 per cent

---

[4] Ngai and Chan (2012).

respectively. The number of workers employed in iPod-related activities was similar in the USA and China; yet the total US wage bill was $719 million and the total Chinese wage bill was only $19 million during the same reference year.[5] As a result of the low wages, the cost of production and hence the gross value of the output exported by China would appear to be low, resulting in a gross profit margin as high as 64 per cent accruing to Apple.[6] The gross profit is, however, shared between Apple, its North American distributors and the US government. Studies show that on an average, Chinese manufacturing wages remained fairly low at 2–3 per cent of US wages during the period 1980–2005. A more recent 2010 study suggests that whether it is Apple iPod or Apple iPhone, the Chinese labour cost is 2 per cent of the total value of output.[7] Despite the recent increase in the legal minimum wages in China, the Hokou system of household registration, student internship in factories and high labour intensity forced upon workers in large factory campuses help in maintaining low reproduction cost.[8]

A detailed study on the Nokia value chain reveals a similar story of value capture by the North. The Nokia N-95 smartphone is assembled in China for final sales in the USA. The final assembly, which is the main step in the physical incarnation of the product, accounts for only 2 per cent of the total value added, while EU-27 countries including Finland capture 51 per cent of the value added because they control the branding, development, design and management.[9] Nokia has significant intellectual property which it cross licenses to competitor firms. A new entrant without an intellectual property (IP) would have to pay 20 per cent of the cost of production while the assembly and manufacturing cost is only 2 per cent of the pre-tax sales price. It is evident that the licence fees cost much more than the assembly and manufacturing cost.

A study on the hard disk drive value chain shows that while the USA, Japan and Europe share 28.5 per cent, 0.9 per cent and 2.9 per cent of total employment in the industry respectively, they received 70.5 per cent in terms of wages. At the same time, South-East Asia offered 55.3 per cent of employment with 19 per cent of the wages.[10] In the case of garments, the mark-up captured by the US company on fast fashion t-shirts produced entirely in Bangladesh is 152 per cent over the manufacturing cost. This is even higher for a K P McLane polo shirt

---

[5] J. Smith (2012).
[6] Xing and Detert (2011).
[7] Kenny (2013: 20).
[8] Ngai and Chan (2012).
[9] Ali-Yrkkö, Seppälä and Ylä-Anttila (2011).
[10] Kenny (2013: 26).

retailed at US$175, pegged at a mark-up of 718 per cent, and the average mark-up for a Hermes polo shirt amounts to 1,800 per cent of the manufacturing cost.[11] A recent study provides detailed accounts of jeans produced in China for a French fashion house. The jeans were sold in France at a final price of €50, of which €31 account for distribution, marketing and advertising costs incurred by French companies, €6 are bagged by the French fashion house, and the manufacturers in China account for only €3.2.[12] Accessing internal Puma documents in 2004, a global rights organisation found that the Chinese worker was paid US$0.35 per hour and that the direct and indirect labour contribution for a pair of shoes was US$1.16. The total manufacturing cost on a shoe, including labour, was between US$3.41 and US$7.16 and Puma retailed it for US$70.82.

It is evident from the above facts that numbers capturing value added do not necessarily manifest the contribution of particular stages of production in the process of value creation. In any of the above cases, if wages in developing countries was close to that in advanced countries, the value share would have reflected with respect to costs and, therefore, value added would have altered significantly. Global asymmetry in distributing value added is, therefore, linked to the global asymmetry in wages which are being politically maintained by restricting cross-border labour flows. But what seems to be more challenging is how to analytically unveil the 'value capture' which remains hidden in value added figures. Also, it is not only about production of surplus value in low-wage segments of the world, but how this appropriated surplus value is distributed asymmetrically through the hierarchies of capital in the form of rents.

## Value Capture in Production Network

Rent refers to an economic return from a resource over and above the opportunity cost of the use of that resource. Generally speaking, it refers to a premium for owning a resource the supply of which is more or less fixed. Hence, as the demand increases, the market clearing price tends to rise, giving an additional return to the owner without the resource being depleted. There are also quasi-rents, which are temporary rents arising because of fixed supply of resource in the short-run, but in the longer run supply increases and with the diffusion over time the producer's surplus is gradually transferred to the consumer's surplus. The neo-Ricardian perspective of income inequality in general and of unequal returns in global production networks in particular draws heavily from the idea of cumulative creation of rents. The argument runs as follows. Each and every local

---

[11] J. Smith (2016).
[12] Kenny (2013: 30).

has certain specialities and endowment of resources and capabilities from which rent or quasi-rent can be derived. When all such locals enter a globalised market, the distribution of rents primarily depends on the creation of specific assets which include innovation in the sphere of technology, human resource, logistics, marketing and design. The quasi-rent, as temporary premium to a created asset, can be transformed into a perpetual rent through a process of cumulative dynamic specialisation. Therefore, integration into a global market may not necessarily lead to a convergence in income, but a rise in absolute income for all owners of resources across the world. It is also argued that for generic resources, the price is determined by supply and demand. Such prices act as opportunity costs for specialised resources employed, and the difference in return over and above the opportunity cost is perceived as rent. Hence, it is all about differential capacities in keeping a particular created asset away from competition. The asymmetry, in return, in a globalised world has to be explained by two related dimensions, namely differential capacities of creating specialised assets and a structural mediation of power articulated through institutions and regulation regimes that define property rights.

In fact, referring to Prebisch's thesis, Kaplinsky argues that the barter terms of trade of agricultural commodities vis-à-vis manufacturing declined only for generic commodities. In case of specialised niche agricultural products, barter terms of trade may be retained while the terms of trade for generic manufacturing products could decline over time. Therefore, the game is all about upgradation and improving governance and there is no intrinsic reason for a particular produce or a particular geography of the world to lose out.[13] The fact, however, does not support this optimistic scenario of equal probabilities of moving up the value ladder. Milberg and Winkler[14] suggest that 'strong absolute upgrading' occurs when value added per worker rises faster than the value of exports; 'weak absolute up-grading' is the case when average value added rises but is slower than the growth of exports; and when value added per worker grows at a pace lower than a quarter of export growth, then no upgrading is taking place. The logic behind this is that export value rises faster than the growth of value added per worker if the domestic value added content of exports declines or the number of workers associated with the same value added increases over time. Domestic value addition may decline because of the race to the bottom where developing countries compete with each other to reduce the offer price, including that of wage. The second effect could be because of more people being employed with diminishing returns. According to this study covering 30 developing countries in

[13] Kaplinsky (2005).
[14] Millberg and Winler (2010).

three continents for the period 1980–2006, none found to be recording strong absolute upgrading and only nine recorded weak absolute upgrading.

It is also important to note that despite there being significant relocation of manufacturing facilities towards developing counties in the recent past, the share of developing countries in global value added continues to be low.[15] The larger share of the value added is still captured by the advanced North primarily because these are the countries where the end-consumers are mostly located; additionally, the design/technology and brands are controlled by firms located in the North. The distribution of technology remained stable over the past 30 years with very few countries at the top of the pyramid reaching frontiers and a large concentration of countries continuing to remain stuck at the bottom. The top few achieved the fastest growth in terms of technological upgradation and the rest, despite small leaps back and forth, continue at the same level of sophistication as in 1971.[16]

In fact, the rent-centric approach focusing on a particular stage of production comprehends the process of distribution as a conflict related to the composite quasi-rents involved. Composite quasi-rents arise as return to specific resources when they are used in combination with each other. For instance, labour with specific skills and machine or a particular technology combine with each other to produce an output and their productivity increases in this process of combination. The distribution of such composite rent simply depends on the bargaining power of workers against employers who own the machines. It follows from a typical Ricardian framework where distribution is only considered to be a social process independent of the generation of surplus in the process of production. Marx was categorical in his critique of classical economists: 'All economists share the error of examining surplus-value not as such, in its pure form, but in the particular forms of profit and rent.'[17] In fact, Marx's critique of Ricardo's value theory rests on this crucial point. The production of surplus value is prior to its distribution as profit or rent and hence the origin of profit in a particular stage of production is related to the determination of the general rate of profit. The ontological priority of total capital and the prior determination of the general rate of profit in the Marxian scheme follows from the crucial insight that profit is accumulated as a class property in the first instance and not as individually determined gains of a particular enterprise. Hence, the average rate of profit determined for the economy as a whole is fundamental in the formation of prices that includes cost of production and profit accrued to individual capital in a particular stage.[18]

---

[15] As discussed in Chapter 3.
[16] Kemeny (2009).
[17] Marx (1963).
[18] Roy (2019b).

The neo-Ricardians, using the Sraffian system of determination of prices, argue that Marx's labour theory of value is superfluous. An observed configuration of physical inputs and outputs allows us to identify frontier uniform profit rates vis-a-vis uniform wage rates. The rate of surplus value or rate of exploitation in terms of labour values is of no use and the circuit of capital can be analysed by prices of production and distributional variables expressed in prices.[19] This actually undermines the fact that there is a regulation of social allocation of labour which is much more fundamental than immediate fluctuation of prices. In fact, a nuanced critique of single-structure theories of value evolves from Richard D. Wolf, Bruce Roberts and Antonino Callari revisiting Marx's 'transformation problem' from a non-essentialist framework.[20] Marx's theory of value and distribution is integral in nature where the system of values and that of prices are mutually constitutive. This double-structure is appropriate for Marx's object of analyses where the entry point is not distribution *per se*, but class process that includes production, appropriation and distribution of surplus value. Such a system of analyses allows identifying the deviations that arise between efforts and payments in concrete determinations in successive layers of production and circulation. Value and value-form are not equal but mutually constitutive and the social allocation of labour time includes the distribution of unpaid labour occurring in the process of circulation. A simultaneous determination of the price of production and value can only comprehend the redistribution of surplus labour time between industries and among capitals of varying organic composition of capital within a particular industry mediated through market prices.

There are three important dimensions relevant to the current discussion on price formation and differential returns to capital. The first relates to a scenario where we assume pure competitive capitalism, absence of monopoly as well as of any sort of reliance on pre-capitalist exploitation. The second aspect entails accumulation of rent as a result of monopoly power over certain resources and how the institutional structure influences realisation of such rents. Third are the realities of super-exploitation and primacy of labour arbitrage that make developing countries distinct from advanced capitalist countries in the current phase of globalisation.

When commodity production is the dominant form in capitalism, exchanges take place on the basis of a quantification of different qualities of labour as abstract labour, and the amount of such labour considered to be socially necessary to produce a particular commodity at a particular point in time determines its value. The cost price of the product is given by the sum of constant and variable

---

[19] See Steedman (1977) and Hodgson (1980); this was contested by Sheikh (1982).
[20] See Roberts (1987) and Wolff, Roberts and Callari (1984) .

capital advanced by the individual capitalist in a specific industry. And the price of production adds up the cost of production with the individual profit realised, which is given by the share of aggregate profit in proportion to individual capital advanced with respect to total capital. The profit component of the individual capitalist is, therefore, the product of the average rate of profit in that industry and the individual capital advanced. The average rate of profit in a specific industry, however, is determined by the normal capital in that industry that employs average technical composition of capital. The inflow and outflow of capital from various industries determined by the underlying value relations finally leads to a convergence towards the general rate of profit applicable for the whole economy. Therefore, the determination of the price of production as well as the difference from that to the average price are co-determined by the individual capital and the capitalist system of value relations as a whole. Value continues to be the regulator of the allocation of social labour and differential profits accrued to individual capitals are primarily the result of differences in the organic composition of capital. In other words, surplus value created in a particular stage of production is only potential profit and not the actual one while the actual amount of profit depends upon two kinds of transfer within the circuit of capital: one within a particular industry or intra-industry and the other between industries or inter-industry. One key insight that follows from this analysis is that if the average technical composition of a specific industry moves faster than the pace of innovation of a specific firm, the individual firm is likely to lose out even if upgrading takes place. This perhaps provides a better clue to understanding the 'technology gap' perpetually reproduced between developed and developing countries.[21]

So far we have assumed pure competitive capitalism and absence of monopoly or reliance on pre-capitalist oppression. Now we factor in differences in property rights on resources. Rent, that is, additional return over and above the average rate of profit, arises from the surplus value produced within the system, but it accrues to producers who either enjoy privileged monopoly access to certain resources or innovate or even evolve particular organisation of production that could be more productive than the average capital. But this is only a necessary condition for creation of rent. The sufficient condition for the existence of rent, as Marx argued, depends on whether that part of surplus value is taken aside from the process of equalisation of rate of profit.[22] Therefore, sources of rent should be protected from capitalist competition and this requires an architecture of property rights that deny access to specialised resources or assets. Here comes

---

[21] Kemeny (2009).
[22] Marx (1959).

the question of power, regulations and institutions that destroy certain monopoly rights and create others. Resources that are created in the North, such as knowledge and designing, are highly protected by patents, royalties and various other forms of property rights, while labour, that the developing South has in abundance, is made easily accessible to global capital.[23] As a result, in the spheres of labour-intensive manufacturing and standard services, capital from different centres in the South compete with each other and pull the offer prices further down, producing larger gains for MNCs and TNCs. This leads to a widening gap between the North and the South in terms of relative gains derived from global production networks as reflected in the deepening of the smile curve.[24]

The value of 'labour power' is determined the way values of other commodities are determined. It is determined by the amount of labour time considered to be socially necessary to produce the goods and services required to reproduce labour power as a future stream of supply. In a globalised world, one would, therefore, expect that there is a single value of labour power. Samir Amin argued that capitalism has been one and indivisible but it was never 'homogenising' at a planetary scale. Rather, it reinforced the asymmetry between dominant centres and dominated peripheries. But he argues that labour power has a single value which is associated with the level of development of productive forces taken globally[25]. However, this idea of a single value of labour power is too abstract and labour values are actually anchored to concrete determinations related to specific nations. This fundamental asymmetry and heterogeneity is maintained by keeping labour immobile, leading to differential rates of exploitation or unequal rates of surplus-value to exist in different parts of the world. James Heintz argues that developing countries face unequal exchange because they engage in exports that embody a greater amount of labour in exchange of imports that contain relatively less amount of labour.[26] This happens because profit rates are equalised across national boundaries owing to the mobility of capital while labour is the relatively immobile factor of production that allows differential wages and also differential rates of exploitation. Hence, developing countries that generally happen to be labour-surplus import goods at prices that have to accommodate both higher wages of industrialised countries and bound to equalise the rate of profit. But this asymmetry is hidden under the price structure. More importantly, if we arrive to some average value of labour power across nations, values of labour that are below such average and engage with global

---

[23] Also see Roy (2017).
[24] As discussed in Chapter 3.
[25] Amin (2010).
[26] Heintz (2006).

production processes can be considered to be undervalued. In Marx's discussion throughout *Capital*, labour power is assumed to be paid according to its value. The reason is that Marx was trying to explain the rise of profit and surplus value on the fundamental classical premise that exchanges take place on the basis of equivalence of value. Hence, even if the commodity labour power is bought at its full value, surplus value is generated and that was the major point of Marx's discussion. Therefore, the possibility of paying wages below the value of labour power was not included in the scope of the theory of surplus value. But as we see the realities of the world today, we come across not only exploitation but also expropriation where super exploitation by way of depressing wages below the value of labour power of respective countries has become the norm. Subcontracting and outsourcing tend to reduce both constant and variable capital while the surplus value increases and hence the rate of exploitation.

Not so surprising is the fact that increasing recourse to labour arbitrage has been ignored by many Western Marxists in analysing contemporary capitalism. The primacy of this super exploitation in the process of capitalist accumulation is rarely acknowledged on the ground that share of living labour's contribution to the total value of output has drastically declined due to increasing use of capital-intensive technology. The point highlighted is that such outsourcing and subcontracting and proliferation of arms-length transactions across nations gave rise to excess production capacities that put immense pressure on profit rate. John Smith[27] criticises David Harvey and Robert Brenner, who underplayed the critical role that labour arbitrage plays in the current process of capitalist accumulation and could see only dispossession as the source of capitalist growth. In fact, the displacement of the Global South is very much internal to the process of expanded reproduction of global capital. There is no denying that labour cost declines in the total value of output, but the more important point is that labour is the only source of surplus value and, therefore, using all opportunities to push down wages and pay the worker below the value of labour power has been a generic tendency of capitalism besides other cost considerations.

On the other hand, there seems to exist a very strong global narrative which views the Third World 'sweatshop' as something essentially different from the 'fair', 'humane', civilised labour practices of the North. This *orientalisation of exploitation* is problematic because it is as if capitalism of the North is separated and independent of the capitalist processes of exploitation and expropriation carried out in the Global South.[28] On the contrary, all these form of archaic, 'uncivilised' processes of exploitation feed into the accumulation of capital

---

[27] J. Smith (2016).
[28] Ercel (2006).

coordinated by MNCs and TNCs. Second, it tends to undermine the role of domestic capital that mediates between the class processes involving Third World labour and multinational capital. The direct employer involved in a subcontracting job actively presides over the super-exploitation. The owner of capital extracts surplus value from labour, but what is being received as his share of total profit would be less than proportional to its contribution in the total pool of surplus value created. This is once again because producers in developing countries are positioned at a lower level in the global hierarchy of capital as they often take recourse to labour-intensive technologies that represent low organic composition of capital.

A related issue could be how small enterprises integrated into the global value chain receive their share in value added. Valorisation in the case of small firms is not regulated strictly by average rate of profit of normal capital, but actually depends upon the means of subsistence required to reproduce the family business.[29] It is the sum of cost of production and the notional interest rate that can be derived on the liquidation value of productive assets that gives the minimum margin required for survival. However, whether such firms can continue in a global network of production depends upon the dynamics of normal capital in a specific industry. As the general level of productivity improves, the threshold levels of technology and scale of operation required to compete also tend to rise. As a result, it becomes difficult for small firms to remain integrated with the value chain without compromising the average rate of profit. It is quite possible that smaller capitals sell at a price which is greater than the minimum level required for survival, but less than the price of the average capital. In such cases also, it is the buyers from smaller capitals who benefit in terms of sourcing inputs at below-normal price because competition among the small enterprises eventually brings down the price at the minimum level. Hence, locating industries and integrating smaller firms of developing countries into the global value chain serves the purpose of deriving surplus profit out of competition among these players.

## Finance and Value Capture

Profit emerging in value chains and the cardinal role of labour arbitrage in a milieu of differential rate of exploitation has not been adequately appreciated in the broad spectrum of heterodox literature. The reason could be the underlying view that capitalist profit-making in today's world is largely delinked from

---

[29] Carrera (1998).

productive activity. Hence, the expropriation of surplus by predatory finance either by deriving absolute rents from financial assets or through extraction of income from workers' earnings should be the main focus of analysing neoliberal capitalism. Indeed, there has been a shift of profit from productive activity to financial mediation and this idea is further substantiated by the fact that rise of finance coincides at least for the West with episodes of crisis marked by stagnating profit rates and burgeoning unemployment in the realm of production. The problematic of financialisation, therefore, rests on the assumed divorce of capital from the realm of production and focuses on the sphere of circulation where financial mediations take place. Moreover, such separation is considered as indicative of a repressive regime for productive activities, often reflected in slowing down of investment in physical capacities and slow growth, ultimately making the neoliberal capital accumulation somehow dysfunctional. The circuits of capital which begin with money capital and end with augmented capital capturing surplus value as profit without being mediated by the phase of production (M-M') are considered to be separated from the normal capitalist circuits of capital (M-C-M') where surplus value is produced through the act of production. Therefore, capturing value in the circuits of capital of the former type through speculation and various forms of expropriation have been the mainstay of critical perspectives.

The notion of 'absentee owner' or functionless capital attaining relative importance within various factions of capital has been identified as the distinctive feature of contemporary neoliberal capitalism. But such analyses figuring factions of capital as distinct self-contained subjects is by far inimical to Marx. In *Capital II*, Marx discusses the general circuit of capital –that of 'industrial capital' – which does not refer to any particular sector or industry but explains the metamorphosis of capital in the process of self-augmentation.[30] It begins with money capital being transformed into productive capital in the form of variable capital and means of production, then undertaking the act of production and producing commodities, giving rise to commodity capital and, once sold, giving rise to augmented capital in money form. The general circuit of capital involves money capital, productive capital and commercial capital and phases of production and circulation. But these forms of capital do not emerge as self-conscious subjects in Marx. Rather, all these forms of capital are subservient to the prior existence of social capital and, hence, part of a concrete totality which are morphed into various forms in the capitalist circuit. The general circuit is, therefore, the social capital on the move for the sole purpose of creating surplus

---

[30] Marx (1957).

value by exploiting unpaid labour from the workers. Marx makes a distinction between commercial capital and money-dealing capital on the one hand and interest-bearing capital on the other. Commercial capital enters into the circuit in the beginning phase and also at the end of the stylised general circuit of capital, facilitating sale and purchase of inputs and outputs and remains entirely within the sphere of exchange. The role of commercial capital is to minimise the cost of conducting the circulation of capital as a whole. Money-dealing capital manages money within the circuit, safeguards deposits and transfers and also manages transactions between various money attached to different nationalities. Merchant capital, which includes both commercial capital and money-dealing capital, is remunerated according to the average rate of profit.

Interest-bearing capital, on the contrary, enters into the circuit and exits deriving a return which is not linked to the process of creation of surplus value.[31] This is spare capital which is leaked out of the circuit because of regular disengagement of value from the circuit. This disengagement happens to take care of various precautionary reserves, depreciation fund and temporarily unutilised profits that create the social foundation of credits. It constitutes the loanable funds and the interest rate is primarily determined by the supply and demand of such loanable funds. In other words, interest-bearing capital mobilises idle money emerging out of the spontaneous process of accumulation and reallocates them for capitals integral to the circuit. The interest-bearing capital, therefore, is created outside the circuit and earns a share of surplus value, but not on the same footing as merchant capital or industrial capital. It also reflects that the dynamics of interest-bearing capital is dependent on the idle money generated in the course of real accumulation. But more interestingly, Marx argues that generally the upper limit of the average interest rate is the average rate of profit. But in certain episodes of the business cycle, interest payments may peak to a level such that it erodes the profit and even the capital fund of the productive capital. Essentially, the determination of rate of interest has no profound relationship with the material basis of social reproduction. It is determined by the historical structures of credit institutions and expectations of profit at a particular point in time. This is precisely why Marx considers interest-bearing capital as a form of fictitious capital. The circuit of interest-bearing capital does not represent any particular faction of capital; it is not owned by 'monied' capital or rentiers as against productive capital. Instead, the most general form of capital, the mobilisation of idle funds owned by the capitalist class as a whole, is thrown into the circuit of industrial capital and taken back depending on the dynamics of

---

[31] Marx (1959).

capitalist accumulation. This, however, does not mean that interests can only be earned by lending money to capitalist borrowers who appropriate surplus value. It can be lent to workers for non-capitalist consumption as well and the money lent has to be paid back with interest independent of whether it has generated profit or not. This is why interest earning from usury existed in pre-capitalist societies as well. But with the emergence of the credit system and related institutions in capitalism, the supply, demand and return from money-lending is increasingly linked with the rhythms of capitalist accumulation.[32] In fact, Marx makes a distinction between interest and profit of enterprise.[33] The former is the part of revenue accrued as interest as a return for the money advanced while the latter is the return to the capitalist for the act of organising productive activity. If the former share increases, it is evident that profit of enterprise declines. But this conflict between return to finance and that of productive enterprise is not the whole story. Marx argues that the rate of profit of enterprise increases with leverage ratio so long as the average rate of profit is higher than the interest rate and it is also important to note that because of the use of finance, the profit of an enterprise goes above the average rate of profit.[34]

But to begin with, what explains return to interest-bearing capital? Money advanced as loanable fund in capitalism assumes an additional use value apart from its usual use value as money and that is its capacity as potential capital as a means of producing profit.

> Money – here taken as the independent expression of a certain amount of value existing either actually as money or as commodities – may be converted into capital on the basis of capitalist production, and may thereby be transformed from a given value to a self-expanding, or increasing, value. It produces profit, i.e., it enables the capitalist to extract a certain quantity of unpaid labour, surplus-product and surplus-value from the labourers, and to appropriate it. In this way, aside from its use-value as money, it acquires an additional use-value, namely that of serving as capital. Its use-value then consists precisely in the profit it produces when converted into capital. In this capacity of potential capital, as a means of producing profit, it

---

[32] For a discussion on differences between pre-capitalist usury and interest-bearing capital, see Itoh and Lapavitsas (1999).

[33] Marx (1959: ch. 23).

[34] Taking off from Marx's analyses in *Capital III* (1959: ch. 21), Costas Lapavitsas in *Profiting without Producing: How Finance Exploits Us All* (2003: ch. 6) extends the analyses relaxing the strict assumption adhered to by Marx that capital invested may not be all borrowed and partly be owned by the producer and then how profit of enterprise and interest rate relate to each other through leverage ratio.

becomes a commodity, but a commodity sui generis. Or, what amounts to the same, capital as capital becomes a commodity.[35]

It simply reflects a reward received by the owner of money for parting with his or her property for the time being with the general possibility of augmenting a sum of money through lending. Interest-bearing capital in the form of capital stocks gives rise to 'fictitious capital' emerging out of market capitalisation where every periodic income is viewed as flow of a capital which releases equivalent income at the ongoing rate of interest. The titles of such capital stocks create the illusion that they constitute real capital. Marx in *Capital III* discusses at length the relationship of price of such holdings of fictitious capital vis-à-vis rate of interest. As interest rate increases, the prices of such titles of fictitious capital falls.

In his *Finance Capital*, Rudolf Hilferding, within the Marxist tradition, explains the role of finance in capitalism and discusses its various forms and institutions which offer great insights in understanding contemporary finance.[36] Hilferding discusses derivatives as standardised future contracts in tangible commodities and argues that these derivatives deal with price risk. With reference to the processing industry, it was discussed how important it was for producers to get a grasp of future prices of raw materials. Future prices are purely speculative, particularly when commodities experience price fluctuations. Futures markets allow capitalists to calculate the future profit abstracting from potential risks. Business syndicates and monopoly combines can ease out future risks by setting high prices or by maintaining stable prices and, hence, can substitute risk trading. In a relatively competitive scenario where controlling price fluctuations at a global level becomes difficult, speculation, according to Hilferding, is the mechanism by which capital handles market fluctuations, rationalising them by creating 'smaller and more frequent oscillations'. Speculation is some form of arbitrage which is driven by a search for 'marginal profit' that arises because of price differences that occur over a period of time. It is essentially a zero-sum game where no profit is being created, but one speculator's gain is another's loss. Capitalists who specialise in these activities gain more when there is participation of a huge number of inexperienced traders in the market and their losses accrue as gains to big players. Notable in the context of current discussion is that Hilferding did not consider speculations and related 'margin business' as some distortion of an idealist image of capitalism. Rather, he considered such activities as the most legitimate offspring of the basic capitalist instinct of creating

---

[35] Marx (1959: ch. 21).
[36] Hilferding (1981).

exchange value. He went further, explaining how derivatives acquire 'moneyness' where derivatives emerge as pure embodiment of exchange value and become 'a mere representative of money'.[37]

Robert Pollin, while critiquing Giovanni Arrighi for not providing an adequate analytical framework of the theory of systemic cycles of accumulation, argues that financial profit emerges in three plausible scenarios[38]: First, because of redistribution of profits while total profits remain the same. This is financial expansion of some who are in the favourable side of the trade and losses are incurred by others. Second, financial profitability increases when concomitant to the process of pure financial dealings, the capitalist class as a whole can force a redistribution of income and wealth in their favour. For instance, in a corporate takeover, both buyers and sellers gain in the form of higher stock prices or dividends as the total profit increases since owners could reduce wages or tax burden by denying long-term commitments to workers or the community. It can also happen if governments squeeze the population to make payments for outstanding debts. The third source of profitability for finance is by way of enabling capital to move from less profitable ventures to more profitable activities of material production and exchange. Therefore, financial profit is an envelope term that consists of elements of surplus value as well as gains arising from redistribution of profit within the capitalist class and also because of a redistribution of income and wealth in favour of the capitalist class. It takes various forms accruing primarily to owners of loanable funds as a return from lending, holding equity and trading financial assets. Profits accruing to financial institutions relate to their role as intermediaries in the flow of loanable capital.

Profits relating to finance, hence, is a subsumed class payment out of the surplus value produced and appropriated in the fundamental class process. It is paid to contribute to creating the preconditions of fundamental class process. Hence, the sources of profit for finance originates in the realm of production and distributed in the process of circulation. The other sources of profit as described can be termed as 'profit upon alienation' and profit through expropriation which Marx mentioned in the later part of *Capital III* as secondary exploitation. Profit

---

[37] 'The commodities are equivalent to money; the buyer is spared the trouble of investigating their use value, and they are subject only to slight fluctuations in price. Their marketability and hence their convertibility into money at any time is assured because they have a world market; all that need be considered is whether the price differences will result in a profit or a loss. Thus they have become just as suitable objects of speculation as any other claims to money; for instance, securities. In futures trading, therefore, the commodity is simply an exchange value. It becomes a mere representative of money, whereas money is usually a representative of the value of a commodity' (Hilferding 1981: ch. 9).

[38] Pollin (1996).

upon alienation is limited to gains and losses within the sphere of circulation and, hence, a zero-sum-game. But profit on expropriation relates to direct transfer of value from workers' savings to lenders where money is being used as a means of consumption or in paying household debts. Such transactions could be in the form of mortgage or consumption loans to households relating to health or education services, fees for managing pension funds or mutual funds. Workers enter into such transactions to attain use values, but the financial institutions earn huge profits by rendering such services. These transactions are embedded in systematic asymmetry where lenders or financial institutions are much better placed in accessing information, organisation as well as in terms of social power. Expropriation assumes immense importance in financial profit these days as reflected in changing sources of revenue of financial institutions which is more towards consumer lending.

## Empire of Capital

The assumed dichotomy between capitals operating in the realm of production and that in finance presumes differentiated capital as self-conscious 'subjects' and ontologically privileges productive capital over finance. Sometimes, the predominance of certain factions of capital over others are historicised as particular phases in a sequence in the long period cycles of social accumulation of capital and dominance of finance is considered to be the autumn or terminal phase in a particular cycle.[39] But capital actually exists as a class dominance and performance of various fragments of capitals is nothing but the metamorphosis of the single entity of social capital. The surplus value produced in a particular act of production is only potential profit and is not appropriated immediately by the individual capitalist as profit. The appropriation of surplus value produced in different fundamental class processes are appropriated by the social capital and distributed thereafter in the form of ground rent, industrial profit, commercial profit and money-dealing profit. Therefore, it is not that capital moves out of the realm of production and settles in financial activities in search of higher profits. Rather, finance attained a relatively privileged position in the current conjuncture to obtain higher share of surplus value created in the realm of production.

Increasing concern for shareholder return is what constrains productive accumulation, but that does not mean that capital of a particular type dominates over the other variant. Rather, the needs of social capital are reified in the form of essential financial parameters. Within the production network, there is an

---

[39] Arrighi (1994).

increasing shift of capital towards high-valued activities involving 'knowledge production', logistics and coordination rather than in manufacturing. In order to maximise shareholder value and minimise risks, global players prefer to work with few big companies and hence a new spate of centralisation of capital is on the way.[40] In fact, some of the multinational manufacturing brands are not at all involved in any kind of manufacturing activity and it is really very difficult today to delineate the complex maze of circuits of capital involving productive or financial activities. Increasing importance of propertied knowledge and appropriation of rent therefrom as well as global coordination of production demand a governance structure to stabilise the hierarchies of capital. Moreover, with the collapse of Bretton Woods, fluctuations and differentials in exchange rate as well as in interest rate add to the uncertainties in profitability which global capital has to grapple with.

Finance or interest-bearing capital accruing gains out of 'profit upon alienation' or by expropriation assumes the form of fictitious capital. It is a fictitious or pure appearance form of capital which earns money out of money and not being mediated by any production of use values. Marx calls it fictitious, but also acknowledges it as the pure form of capital relations creating exchange values. Increased demand for securitised assets needs to be analysed as related to the imperatives of social reproduction of capital as a whole rather than as fractions of capital having generic qualities of augmenting value. The Marxian notion of fictitious capital attaining the quality of commodity *sui generis* implies that such capital is a reified form of appearance of social accumulation of capital. It is termed as fictitious not because it has a mystical power delinked from the material existence of capital relations, but because it is a fetishised reification of necessities of capital relations objectified in performance indicators of financial markets. Financial instruments commodify risks. Risk is defined as the probabilistic chance of realising a future price. But the subjective expectation of a particular future price and related risk emerges within a particular reification of capitalist reality. Expectations of profit presuppose availability of certain information, technical processing of such information and slicing and bundling of related risks in the form of financial derivatives. Commodification of risk does not make it immediately commensurable. Risks are generally specific in nature with their concrete realities. Derivatives and financial markets make them commensurable, giving rise to objective parameters of measuring risks.[41] This space of 'objectivity', if de-reified, foregrounds a social necessity of reproducing capital relations. A

---

[40] Milberg (2007).

[41] For a detailed discussion on commodification of risk, see Sotiropoulos, Milios and Lapatsioras (2013: ch. 8).

firm not able to tackle rising pressure on wages or not able to introduce technology to garner rents, not able to reduce product wage of workers, not able to break the supply barriers by forcibly acquiring land and many such qualifications defines the comparable information constituting profiles of companies. Therefore, preconditions for the reproduction of exploitation and expropriation that ensures a particular return in the future are reified as objective parameters of financial markets. Securitisation of risks and related financial architecture including rating agencies impose a systemic rhythm to the process of real accumulation. It is essentially a governance structure that oversees the individual capabilities of capital in abiding by a particular norm. The norms if violated manifest in a fall in stock prices. With rising inequality in the neoliberal regime, the demand for commodities is surpassed by the demand for securitised assets that promise to take care of future consumption. The rich want to ensure their stake in the future through financial assets. The poor and the middle class are increasingly drawn into financial markets by way of curtailing public provisioning of health, education, pension and other entitlements. Increasing fluctuations in exchange rate or interest rate force nation-states to accumulate reserve funds in the form of foreign assets that are pegged to a quasi-world currency. Commodification of whatever exists under the sky including perceptions about the future is the end game of capitalism and the rule of the game is articulated by a norm structure defined by financial markets. This is the governance of the empire of capital, a global architecture of regulation and accumulation regimes that intends to stabilise fluctuations in future profitability and defines returns of individual capital given their position in the hierarchies of global capital.

# 6

# Informality

## Regime of Accumulation and Discourse of Power

Binaries hardly capture the complexities of real life, particularly of the world of work in which human labour using brains and brawns creatively engage with nature, change its surroundings and realise their existence in the course of changing themselves. Indeed, it is necessary sometimes to break down and categorise a complex whole to understand the relationship between the simple categories conceptually created and the way they constitute the complex totality. However, the progress of conceptual categories rarely follows the time sequence of history; instead, it may indicate opposite movements. The way we understand informal–formal relationship is a case in point. Informality is an empirical category representing heterogeneous forms of unprotected labour. Petty-producers, street vendors, construction workers, home-based workers, domestic workers, contract labourers, sex-workers, delivery boys, ragpickers and a range of other activities that provide earnings to a majority of the workforce in urban space come under the rubric of informality. The category of informality is predicated on the notion of formal, but according to the sequence of history, 'informality' predates the 'formal'. Just as people were unemployed before being employed. It is only since a particular juncture of history, one could find that a human being is being employed by the other or a class of few propertied people who engage the large number of property-less in the services of the few. But informal is defined as a negation of formal and unemployed as the state of not being employed. Similarly, life had been wageless for the larger part of human civilisation. It is only in capitalism that wage labour emerges to be the predominant form of work relation and non-wage labour appears to be pre-modern or pre-capitalist. Paradoxically, what came later in the course of history, defined earlier forms according to its own image. Centring of capital relations reign our conceptual space and a false boundary, implicitly identifying capital relations with the 'formal', imparts violence to the informal in the realm of thought.

The politics of conceptualising categories, therefore, sometimes reverses the order of history. The primacy of the 'formal' in defining the informal in itself makes the informal seem as if it is something abnormal, weak, cannot stand on its own feet, a deviation from the norm, an unwanted appendage continuing from the pre-capitalist past that capitalism wants to get rid of. It further extends to identifying capitalism with the 'formal' work and 'informal' looks like the pre-capitalist 'other'. The message is clear and simple: capitalism thrives on the basis of equal exchange, an exchange on the basis of equivalence of value where labour power of certain value is exchanged against wages. Hardly any force is visible in this labour market. Capitalism offers jobs and it is a matter of choice whether the worker opts for employment at a given wage rate or not. There is no force involved in the process of engaging the worker and in a market, hardly any chance of exchange exists where a particular commodity fetches less than its value. It is the ideal world of freedom where labour is completely free. This narrative of 'free' labour somehow could not come to terms with the realities of the world, where people are forcibly dispossessed by others from their means of production to transform those means into capital, where wages are much less than the value of labour power, differential rates of exploitation continue to exist, a large mass of people are socially constituted who accept sub-human forms of work because they have no other option to make both ends meet. One of the ways of reconciling the fact with the assumed classical and neo-classical imagery of capitalism viewed as the pristine province of free labour is to demonise, devalue and criminalise the 'other' as pre-capitalist or informal. As if they are outsiders to the ideal world of capitalism and require policies and interventions for a reasonable cure. The category of informal continues to be unstable in the conceptual space. It is even more difficult to use it as a universal empirical category independent of society and history. It refers to size structures, counting employment and consumption of energy as against processes that characterise informality. It was earlier referred to as a sector, but it gradually became difficult ignoring the fact that informality is ubiquitous. This chapter, first of all, aims to historicise informality, see it as linked with a particular regime of accumulation in the larger context of combined and uneven development of capitalism.[1]

From the fifties till the seventies, there was huge migration of people pouring into the cities of poor countries in Asia, Africa and Latin America. The shanty towns and slums emerged as the site of assertion of the right to the city by the poor who were forced to move on for a better future in colonial settler countries or in plantation economies of the Americas. It was not waged work that featured this 'wretched of the earth' in squatter towns. Rather, it was petty production, and various forms of wageless life continued to exist and did not wither away with the magic wand of capitalist development. It persisted as a big, uncomfortable question mark to the narrative of free labour–formal wage employment combine

---

[1] Trotsky (1973).

defining the conceptual space of capitalism. In the early seventies, the British development economist Keith Hart was studying the Frafra migrants from Northern Ghana who had settled at the shanty town of Nima on the outskirts of the old city of Accra. It was the livelihood of the Nima slum-dwellers which typified the vast majority of working poor in urban Third World cities during that period, a life between wage employment and self-employment. This was co-opted by ILO and later developed as an important empirical category named 'informal sector'.[2] But this non-capital space is not delinked from the process of capitalist accumulation, it is not at all an appendage that clings to the body of capitalism as some unwanted part. It has a distinct role to play and has played a role throughout the history of capitalism. The notion of informality was later propagated with a positive connotation, not as a lack of something 'normal', but as alternative sources of employment also capable of producing surplus. It was a response to the dependency theorists who view informality as a national assimilation of a structural dependency where surplus created in the periphery is transferred to the core by means of unequal exchange[3]. Indeed, such a characterisation of informality as a space of 'dependent development' subordinate to the formal sector of the economy would be too simplistic. Informality is, first of all, not homogeneous. It cannot be equated to poverty and, of late, it ceases to be a feature of developing countries alone. But the benign characterisation of the informal sector needs to be problematised. It has to be located within the conflicts that arise between the development of productive forces in capitalism and its continuing form of relations of production. The combined and uneven development of capitalism does not manifest always as distinct geographical spaces of development and underdevelopment. Rather, it emerges as a complex process. For advanced economies, in the context of new technologies, autonomy of labour displaces wage–time measurement of value while in poor countries, emergent archaic forms of work, expropriation in the form of negating rules of equivalence of exchange assumes predominance.

   The next section discusses the changing nature of employment and the rise of precarious labour, followed by locating informality within the regime of accumulation. In the fourth section, we historicise the notion of informality and see the nature of uneven and combined development of capitalism in this context. Finally, it is argued that 'informality' is a discourse of power in the neoliberal regime where denial of rights for the vast section of the working poor and use of 'unfree' labour is being legitimised by categorising them as informal.

---

[2] Hart (1973).

[3] Dependency theorists viewed informality as structural. It was seen as a distinct feature of the countries in the periphery. See Bienefeld (1979), Bromley (1978) and Danies (1979).

## Employment and Precarious Labour

Wage and salaried employment accounts for only about half of the global employment today and in South Asia and Sub-Saharan Africa, the share is even less, roughly to the tune of 20 per cent. Fewer than 45 per cent of the wage and salaried workers are employed on a full-time and permanent basis.[4] The decline of standardised jobs is a trend which is not being limited to developing countries anymore, but pervaded the job markets of advanced countries as well. Production structure assumes a global character facilitated by innovation in communication technology and cross-border movement of capital. Changes in the mode of investment, production structure and the reallocation of production across the globe is accompanied by change in the relationship between labour, capital and the state. This technological change since the mid-eighties, together with a liberal regime adopted across the world, facilitated gains from huge wage difference existing between the North and the South. In fact, technology of the North was coupled with cheap labour of the South, giving rise to a division of the world between 'headquarter' economies and 'factory' economies.[5] This reorganisation of global production relies on advantages of new communication technology on the one hand and labour arbitrage on the other. This emerged as the preferred way of reducing labour turnover costs and wage costs at the same time. Access to the reserve army of labour of the South resulted in a massive shift of manufacturing from the rich North to low-wage segments of the South. Currently, 83 per cent of the world manufacturing workforce lives in the Global South.[6] The relative increase in the global supply of labour has largely reduced the bargaining power of workers, making them vulnerable in the face of extreme flexibility that capital enjoys through cross-border movements. Changes in labour regime is further facilitated by internal and cross-border migration, giving rise to a mix of labour market outcomes that are largely favourable to skilled workers while unskilled workers, particularly medium-skilled workers involved in routine work, seem to have lost their share in almost all countries.[7]

In the past three decades in India, there has been a huge shift in employment reflected by a decline in employment share in agriculture from 69 per cent in 1983 to 47.8 per cent in 2011–12.[8] The people who moved out of agriculture

---

[4] ILO (2015).

[5] Baldwin defines headquarter economies as countries whose exports contain relatively low share of imported intermediaries and factory economies as those having high share of imported intermediaries in their exports (Baldwin 2012).

[6] Data derived from ILO-KILM database quoted in J. Smith (2016).

[7] IMF (2017b).

[8] Various rounds of NSS reports on Employment and Unemployment Surveys.

were largely engaged in informal jobs. Within the non-agriculture group,[9] wholesale and retail trade and repairing activities account for the highest share of informal workers. In the rural area, 95.1 per cent of the workforce in this sector is informal while the figure is 93.6 per cent in urban areas. Accommodation and food service activities record a share of informal workers to the tune of 91.5 and 91.8 per cent in rural and urban segments respectively. In rural areas, 95.3 per cent of workers involved in real estate activities belong to the informal category while in the urban segment, the proportion is relatively less at 87.7 per cent. In manufacturing, the share of informal employment is 85.3 per cent in rural areas and 75.9 per cent in urban areas. Mining and quarrying, utilities and finance and insurance activities account for relatively low share of informal employment for obvious reasons. Wholesale and retail trade, repair of motor vehicles, motorcycles and activities related to accommodation and food services are the sectors in which more than 90 per cent of workers, both female and male, belong to the informal category.

One of the most striking features of India's labour market is the relative stability of the distribution of workforce by employment status. In the past three decades, the share of regular employment as a proportion to total employed increased by only five percentage points. The share of casual employment remained close to 30 per cent and there is a marginal decline in the share of self-employed. It is really worrying that in spite of high growth during recent decades, more than half of the workforce is self-employed and less than one-fifth of the population is in regular employment. The NSSO survey on unincorporated, non-agriculture (excluding construction) estimated that in 2015–16, there were 63.4 million enterprises in this segment. Of this, 84.2 per cent are own account enterprises i.e. who do not employ any hired labour. In manufacturing, the share is even higher accounting for 85.5 per cent of the enterprises. In terms of employment, 111.3 million are employed in unincorporated, non-agricultural activities excluding construction and 62 per cent of them are self-employed.

NSSO results also suggest informalisation of the formal sector as the proportion of regular and salaried workers who do not have any written contract has increased over the years. Currently, 65 per cent of the regular and salaried workers have no

---

[9] The 68th Round report on informal sector collected for both usual principal status workers and usual subsidiary status workers engaged in non-agricultural sector (industry divisions 05-99 of NIC-2008) and a part of the agricultural sector (industry groups 014, 016, 017 and divisions 02, 03 of NIC-2008). The industry groups/divisions 014, 016, 017, 02 and 03 are in the agricultural sector excluding growing of crops, plant propagation, combined production of crops and animals without a specialised production of crops or animals. These activities are referred to as AGEGC activities.

written contract of employment.[10] Half of the regular and salaried workers do not report any provision of paid leave and roughly 98 per cent of the casual workers do not enjoy any such right. It is evident from these facts that an increasing proportion of workers in all categories are being denied paid leave over the years. More than half the regular and salaried workers are not entitled to any social security provisions and the proportion has increased over time. Within casual employment, the share of workers having no social security provisions is as high as 93 per cent although this share is lower than what it was in previous rounds. It implies that the workers employed in enterprises that are categorised as formal by employment size and ownership criteria are increasingly denied the rights applicable for the formal sector. Informalisation facilitates a substitution of regular workers by contract and casual labour which not only directly reduces labour costs, but also reduces bargaining power of the existing formal workers.

The rise of the informal workforce including the rise of contract and casual labour in the formal sector is not independent of wage–profit relationship. NSSO figures suggest that roughly the wages of regular and salaried workers are 2.6 times higher than that of casual labourers. In rural areas, the regular/salaried wage is double the wage of a casual worker, while in urban areas, the difference is even sharper, close to three times. In the case of regular salaried workers, the male wage in the rural areas is 57 per cent higher than the female wage while in urban areas, male wage is about 27 per cent higher than female wage. On that count, for regular salaried workers, gender discrimination in terms of wages is higher in rural areas compared to the urban counterparts. In the case of casual workers, the trend seems to be opposite. In rural areas, the male wage is 43 per cent higher than the female wage while in urban areas, the male–female gap is roughly 55 per cent. The rural–urban wage gap is also quite significant. Average urban wage, considering all workers, is 1.7 times higher than the average rural worker. It is significant to note that for casual workers, the rural–urban wage gap is marginal while for regular/salaried workers, urban wage is 1.46 times higher than the rural wage. If we see the wage differences by enterprise, we find that in rural areas, workers employed in partnership and proprietary firms earn roughly 70 per cent higher compared to those engaged in household enterprises. In the urban areas, this wage gap by enterprise type is 68.6 per cent. Therefore, in both urban and rural areas, workers in household enterprises earn much less than those employed in proprietary or partnership firms. It, therefore, follows that informalisation signifies a process that ultimately reduces return to labour and weakens claims derived from established norms.

---

[10] NSSO (2014).

Services account for a large number of informal activities. It is not only about low wage capturing the vulnerability of this burgeoning workforce, but also about imposing a life without a 'shadow of the future'. Guy Standing moves beyond the binaries of formal and informal and defines the 'precariat' as a new class in the making, which is neither protected by the community nor by the enterprise in which they work. They are deprived of all sorts of state or private benefits, lack work-based identity, no career in jobs as jobs and employers keep changing, move around as packets of labour power that hardly anyone owes for long.[11] This is the lowest rung of class categorisation, different from the stable working class and the 'salariat'. They are beyond the frame of a social compact through which the organised workers come to terms with the state or employer in exchange for social security and welfare measures. They are like urban nomads, who migrate from one place to another, either guided by the contractor or by kinship and friends who moved out earlier in search of jobs. They are used as construction labourers, domestic workers, low-paid street sellers, service boys often undocumented and kept invisible in the 'formal–legal' space. They exist as labour, but have hardly been recognised as citizens and are denied most of the rights and entitlements because they are 'informal'. Undoubtedly, they constitute a large part of the urban labour force in developing countries and a rising proportion in advanced economies.

Samir Amin[12] makes a distinction between property-owners and managers, small business-owners, on the one hand, and the popular classes on the other. The popular class of wage-earners and non-wage, self-employed workers consists of two broad groups, one consisting of people who possess certain skills and can bargain with the employer on those grounds, often organised in many countries, and the other group features precarious labour, mostly unskilled, who lack political power to ascertain their collective rights. Half of humanity resides in cities and three-fourths of the urban population belongs to the popular classes of which, in centres of capitalism, the proportion of precarious labour is 40 per cent while the share is roughly 80 per cent in the periphery. This vast majority of unprotected labour is integrated with the circuits of global capital, but exist as non-capital, constituting the capital–non-capital complex of the world of capitalism.

## Informality as a Regime of Accumulation

Categorising informal as pre-capitalist or a feature of stunted development of capitalism typical to post-colonial societies does not explain the persistence and

---

[11] Standing (2016).
[12] Amin (2008).

expansion of this unprotected segment of the labour force. The imagery of capitalism is of a society of definite form of wage labour where contracts are well defined and exchanges take place in markets on the basis of equivalence of value, as a world of 'free labour'. Therefore, all sorts of 'un-freedom' and expropriation that we see around us are excluded from the conceptual boundary of capitalism is a position of convenience. Capitalism exists with wage employment, non-wage self-employment and other forms of underemployment and unemployment and the predominance of any one or more of these are context-specific and historically determined by class struggle. Unemployment was never a significant feature of capitalism in its early phase. Rather, it was seen as unanticipated incidents of shock that need to be insured by the state. For the first time, the crisis of capitalism in the 1930s brought to the fore mass unemployment as a perennial problem which had its obvious social and political implications. Keynesian proposition of demand management in a milieu of involuntary unemployment came as a temporary resolve and parts of advanced capitalism adhered to a social democratic welfare regime for about two decades. However, the intrinsic tendency of capitalism to have productivity growth driven by competition between capitalists tending to outpace the growth of labour force has continued to be the perennial destabilising factor. It was more or less settled, particularly in the context of late capitalism in post-colonial countries of the South, that underdevelopment of these countries is unlikely be followed by the kind of development that the advanced capitalism of the North achieved. More importantly, technology growth which was increasingly labour-displacing cannot be reversed. In other words, use of labour-intensive technologies that created enough scope for labour absorption in Europe in the course of its industrial development cannot be repeated once again in developing countries. Europe also benefitted from the mass migration of surplus population to the Americas, making dispossession almost invisible. Therefore, capitalism in any part of the world today cannot anymore be as it was in the initial phase of capitalism in some parts of Europe.

The centring of 'free' wage labour in the world of work as something typical to capitalism somehow idealises capitalism as a system of defined exchange between sellers and buyers of labour power. Marx sarcastically expressed this freedom as 'doubly free': one, she is free to dispose of her labour power as her own commodity and, second, has no ownership of any other commodity or means of production for the realisation of her labour power.[13] But real world labour market in developing countries does not necessarily resemble complete proletarianisation of the work force. Many a time, it could be that the worker is not the carrier and

---

[13] Marx (1958: ch. 6).

possessor of labour power at the same time. There can be innumerable overlaps in the world of work where workers do possess some tool or means of production – may be the worker and employer are the same, may be selling labour power through a contractor or playing the role of a contractor and, at the same time, working as a worker, working with different employers on part-time contract, involved as unpaid labour, selling a part of the produce beyond a threshold while working in some other field as wage labour and so on. These labour processes are neither free in the double sense nor can be considered as pre-capitalist. In fact, the notion of working class emerged in the nineteenth century and capitalism existed with slavery, petty-producers, subcontracted wage labour, labour by chattel, lumpen and various other forms of proletariat. On the other hand, wage labour existed before it was conceptualised in its modern form in Greece and Germany during the fourth and fifth centuries AD. It existed in China, Iran and Macedonia in military service and the current form of workers with stable wage were seen in Egypt where they were engaged in the construction of tombs.[14] Slave labour in capitalism was gradually substituted by wage labour because slave labour entails fixed costs of maintenance and they were not skilled enough to keep pace with the development of new tools. Particularly with the growth of commodity economy, capitalism not only created human beings whose labour is separated from their bodily existence and sold as labour power, but also, they get wage as exchange value. Hence, they are not only producers, but also consumers of goods and services. On the contrary, slaves only possess use value. In a world of commodities, it was needed to impart values of predictability in exchange, equality, freedom and justice for possessors of commodities and wage work got easily embedded in the logic of market. Hence, coexistence of different forms of labour, including wage labour, is not inimical to capitalism and it is only when slave labour became uneconomical with the rising supply of labour that it was substituted by wage labour. It, therefore, follows that the norm of capitalism is to push down the return to labour and enhance surplus rather than setting 'free' wage labour as the norm for the proletariat.

Persistence of the informal segment as a continuing form of production and labour process is often seen in the light of Marx's two very important categories, namely, primary accumulation of capital and 'reserve army of labour'. Capitalism, in its recourse to primary accumulation, transforms the means of production owned by the dispossessed into capital. But in the current conjuncture, it can hardly absorb all the dispossessed people as workers in factories. This has given rise to a peculiar scenario particularly in the post-colonial context, often referred

---

[14] For a detailed discussion on how labour forms existed and various forms of resistance in the history of work, see Van Der Linden (2011).

to as blocked development in the Gramscian sense. This is further characterised as complex hegemony where there can be contesting symbolic-cultural spaces and the notion of justice evolves through conflicts, negotiations and compromises, between conflicting claims of capital and non-capital, rather than capital destroying pre-capital altogether.[15] It further complicates the analyses of the informal because it not only rejects the view that fullest development of capitalism in due course would erase the curse of informality, but also opens up the radical possibility of the way the informal negotiates with the state regarding claims of resources.

Informality is often equated with the 'reserve army of labour' that helps in containing wages of workers in capitalism. Marx in *Capital* talks about three layers of the reserve army of labour which are as follows.[16] The floating layer is in close vicinity to the cities and contains industrial labour force that is temporarily excluded from the active labour force because of some crisis or fluctuations contingent to a particular situation. The second layer is the latent part consisting of people mostly from rural areas who lost their jobs because of adopting capitalist forms of agriculture and related mechanisation. They end up as potential urban workers. The third layer is the stagnant part consisting of sweatshops where workers work at low wages, the lowest segment of the domestic industry and the paupers. These segments particularly, as discussed in Marx, possibly resemble the unprotected workers of the present world but with an important caveat. They do not act as reserve for the capitalist production as and when required. Instead, they exist as a permanent unprotected and excluded labour force, condemned for ever, hardly getting any chance to be exploited in the formal capital relations.

The question, therefore, is how this informal segment helps the process of capitalist accumulation. Kalyan Sanyal[17] and Partha Chatterjee[18] see capitalism as a complex overdetermined space of capital and non-capital and in the realm of the political articulation, the divide has been conceived as between 'civil society' and 'political society'. According to this scheme, within capitalism there is a segment of 'accumulation economy' owned by capital/corporate who own capital and accumulate surplus. The other non-capital/non-corporate segment constitutes the 'need economy' which is unable to accumulate. In this analyses, while the process of accumulation undertaken by capital not only destroys non-capital which resembles primary accumulation, but also creates the non-capital. According to Sanyal, there is a flow of surplus from the accumulation economy

[15] For a detailed discussion, see Chatterjee (1988, 1993).
[16] Marx (1958).
[17] Sanyal (2007).
[18] Chatterjee (2011).

to the need economy by way of credit and other transfers which unites small producers once again with means of production. Sanyal calls it a reversal of primitive accumulation of capital or 'de-capitalisation'. And the reason to feed the non-capital or need economy from accumulated surplus, according to Sanyal, is only political – to maintain the stability of capitalism. In other words, the non-capital does not contribute to the process of accumulation. Neither is it required as a supplier of labour, but it overdetermines the class process as a part of a political process.

Though the Sanyal–Chatterjee scheme in a post-colonial context offers a robust theoretical structure to explain the persistence of capital–non-capital dualism and the political articulation of these segments, it grossly undermines exploitation and expropriation that characterises present-day capital–non-capital combine and reduces the entire relationship into an exclusion and rejection narrative. It is assumed that the vast majority of enterprises within the informal sector do not contribute in producing surplus, but exist only by depending on surplus flowing out from accumulation economy articulated through governmentality. The fact, however, is that either by self-exploitation or being forced to accept wages below the value of labour power and by competing with each other to realise their returns engaging through market, informal labour and enterprises generate surplus that is usurped by entities representing corporate capital. Ajit Chaudhury and his co-authors considered that the postmodern reading of the field of overdetermination does not recognise hierarchy or power relations that exist between capital and non-capital, but the constituting processes and elements are recognised only through difference. Chaudhury and others, therefore, propose a conceptual frame of overdetermination with hierarchy and call it a 'mimicry of overdetermination' through which the post-colonial 'other' engages with the core.[19] In this lineage, Anjan Chakrabarti and his collaborators further problematised the informal sector using the lens of class process, identified heterogeneous combinations of production and appropriation of surplus in a differentiated space of informality which is generally clubbed together as the homogeneous 'other' of the formal segment.[20] In a post-Lacanian sense, Chakrabarti sees hegemony as spectral and capitalism as 'delusional cosmology' which does not allow us to see the constitutive outside of the circuit of global capital. In this analyses, a part of the non-capital is seen as the foregrounded other, the assimilated other which is linked to the circuit of global capital. But there is also the foreclosed 'other' which is 'alive in action and dead

---

[19] Chaudhury, Das and Chakrabarti (2000).
[20] Chakrabarti and Thakur (2010).

in language', the 'world of the third' which is the constitutive outside of the circuit of global capital.[21]

It is not by design, therefore, that the informal simply exists to supply cheap labour and inputs for the reproduction of labour power that the core capital relations require in the process of accumulation. Instead of a functional relationship often assumed to explain the role of informality in capitalist accumulation, it would be wise to see it as a regime in totality where capital and non-capital not only engage, but mutually constitute and recreate each other. Taking advantage of informality as a repository of cheap labour is well documented, but it has its own limits as cheapening of wages comes along with declining productivity and, therefore, it is important to see how such wage depression helps in reducing unit labour costs. The use of cheap labour in the process of industrial subcontracting only partially explains the functional role of the informal segment. Subcontracting relationship between formal and informal may be the dominant reality in Latin American cities, but has not been similarly significant for other parts of the developing world. The structural function of the informal sector in supplying wage goods to the working class and thus containing the reservation wages is also not tenable, both empirically and analytically. In fact, cheapening of wage goods can be done better by introducing large-scale production that reduces average unit costs and by importing from other countries as was in Sub-Saharan Africa. It is not also empirically true that the larger share of wage goods originates from the informal segment of the economy.[22]

Capitalism is a totality in structure which always included different forms of labour and production processes. The non-waged labour, unpaid labour, self-employed worker, bonded labour, slave labour, archaic forms of production and labour processes and primary accumulation were actually very much endogenous to the process of capitalism. The typical 'factory worker' who mirrors the image of formal employment was not distinctive of capitalism before the Industrial Revolution. The early phase of capitalism continued with various forms of petty production, crafts and workmen often tied in putting out systems. The separation of the unit of consumption and that of production, that is, between household and production plant became complete only in the beginning of the nineteenth century. A decade before the First World War, the share of very small enterprises employing less than five workers was 95 per cent in Germany and 91 per cent in the United States. Majority of the workforce moved out from their home to work

---

[21] The concept of the 'world of the third' as distinct from 'the third world' is discussed in Chakrabarti, Dhar and Cullenberg (2012) and Chakrabarti, Dhar and Dasgupta (2015).
[22] See Schmitz (1982) and Wuyts (2001).

only since 1914.[23] The separation of household and production site became complete with the rise of modern factories. This significantly altered the work-leisure trade-off as hardly any trade-off continued to exist for the workers. In fact, workers are left with no autonomy, but to sell their labour power. There has been actually nothing 'informal' about this and the appropriate mix of all these labour forms and production processes defines the regime of accumulation in a particular juncture of history.

Michael Aglietta, in her theory of capitalist regulation, offers a nuanced perspective in understanding the dynamics of labour regimes.[24] Regimes of accumulation is a less abstract concept than the principle of accumulation. A regime of accumulation is a form of social transformation that increases relative surplus value under the stable constraints of the most general norms that define the absolute surplus value. Extensive regime of accumulation is that in which relative surplus value is obtained by transforming the organisation of labour. Intensive regimes, however, create a new mode of life for the wage-earning class by establishing a logic that operates on the totality of time and space occupied by individuals in daily life. The transformation of the production process and the process of reproduction of labour power was linked with the technicalities of production. For instance, Taylorism was a response to reduce the autonomy of labour, to homogenise the labour process through minute details, making human labour an appendage of its tools. Fordism is a stage that supercedes Taylorism. It denotes a series of major transformations in the labour process closely linked to changes in the conditions of the existence of the wage-earning class. It entails the formation of a social consumption norm and tends to institutionalise the economic class struggle in the form of collective bargaining. This also initiates a close articulation between the process of production and mode of consumption, it universalises wage labour and affects modalities of wage payment through mass consumption. It is the system of semi-automatic assembly line that reduced the mean time of transmission, drastically shrunk the possibilities of individual resistance and fixed workers to strict output norms. This was a response of capital when it faced the crisis of legitimacy. Workers, however, challenged the prerogatives of capital and capital responded through a compromise with organised labour. So, in exchange for full employment and rising wages in the post-War period, the Keynesian compromise allowed capital to make decisions on investments and also initiate changes in the production organisation. This compromise was embedded in a social compact that bridged the gap between production and consumption. Increased trade and competition during the 50s

---

[23] Castells and Portes (1989).
[24] Aglietta (2000).

and 60s, however, ended up in a crisis of over accumulation and a general squeeze in profits. In response to that crisis of profitability, capital took recourse to both spatial and technology fix, shifting production to low-wage segments of the world and also by newer technologies that reduce workers' bargaining power.

Neoliberal globalisation signifies changes in production structure with dual trends of concentration and monopoly-formation through TNCs mostly located in the North coupled with decentring of production through arms-length outsourcing and subcontracting in the low-wage South. Free movement of capital together with restrictions in the global movement of labour allow differential labour regimes to exist within national boundaries which, in turn, allows substitution of similarly skilled workers by way of shifting production from high-wage to low-wage segments. In other words, labour arbitrage becomes possible both internally as well as globally as global capital gets access to labour reserve. In this regime, production structures are altered in favour of capital, giving rise to a regime of accumulation that take advantage of not only improved technology and production organisation to increase relative surplus value, but also of unprotected labour that allows expropriation through devaluing the value of labour power and externalising the reproduction costs through subcontracting by which a part of consumption fund flows into the accumulation fund of capitalism.

## Systemic Crisis and Precarious Labour

One of the major features of contemporary capitalism is its declining requirement of direct labour with the rise in productivity. This is also accompanied by increasing wage inequality between skilled and unskilled workers across the world. Middle-level workers are worst hit because of declining relative wages caused by increasing substitution of routine jobs by new machines. In 1930, J.M. Keynes talked about 'technological unemployment' and roughly two decades later, Wassily Leontief could see the future of capitalism where more and more labour would be replaced by machines and that it would be hard to employ all job-seekers.[25] The pace of productivity becoming much higher than the growth of labour force is a structural problem within capitalism, giving rise to episodic crisis including that in the 1920s. Productivity grew much faster as a result of which employment fell short. Capitalism is only capable of recognising work as waged labour and wages are paid in terms of labour time. Therefore, people who are left out in the process of accumulation are also left out in the process of distribution as they could not sell their labour power. For obvious reasons, this

---

[25] Keynes (1930) and Leontief (1952).

leads to crisis of underconsumption or of realisation. The Keynesian solution to this perennial problem in the 1930s was two-fold: restrain the growth of productivity by shifting a sizeable share of social product or wealth towards waste production, namely military expenditure and consumerist culture, and institute a mode of distribution that does not necessarily depend on individual productivity, but is based on a social contract of classes that ensures a stable purchasing power of the working class. The crisis of realisation was temporarily displaced and capitalism could attain a managed balance between production and consumption, ensuring sustained growth for about two decades in the fifties and sixties when income inequality fell sharply. In the early seventies, the crisis of capitalism was, however, caused due to stagnating productivity manifested through state expenditure growing faster than the growth of the economy. It created the pretext for a class assault on working peoples' entitlements and protective institutions. The turnaround in productivity happened only in the late 1990s and that was largely facilitated by technology such as automation, robotics, artificial intelligence, and the internet of things. Once again, such production structures tend to reduce the need for direct human labour in capitalist production. Various studies suggest that in the next two decades, 47 per cent of jobs in the US and 57 per cent in the OECD are at risk of automation.[26] In other words, the development of productive forces has reached a level which is qualitatively different from earlier forms of production that employed large number of simple labour and returns to labour would be measured in terms of labour time. In fact, inequality in distribution increases as new productive forces require skilled labour whose relative returns have increased while on the other hand, routine works are either automated or transferred to low-wage segments of the world. In this context, the flow of surplus from the accumulation economy to the need economy or the distribution of 'social surplus' in the form of income transfer independent of individual contributions to production is a case in point. It is once again an attempt to restore balance between production and consumption, manage the crisis of legitimacy that capitalism is about to face in a much fierce manner compared to its earlier phases of crisis.

The system, therefore, requires more qualified and skilled labour to match new productive forces and that requires more 'free' time to be out of waged work. It also provides workers a certain level of autonomy as new skills are yet to be standardised to make them substitutable. The mean age of joining the labour force increases, retirement age declines and the concept of lifetime employment, with a strict sense of discipline based on defined tasks, is on the wane. With the

---

[26] Acemoglu and Restrepo (2017).

new machines, the role of direct labour recedes and skills refer to more of appropriation of general accumulated knowledge of science than individualised, immediate tasks.[27] Enhancement of productivity demands more of learning and commitment to performance than loyalty to a time frame of simple expenditure of labour. Wage employment and the determination of wage on the basis of labour time, therefore, increasingly becomes inappropriate to measure individual contribution to social production. The conflict has to be displaced either by an alternative mode of distribution that in some sense transfers purchasing power to people who are not called for work and restore the balance between production and consumption or by aborting the potential growth of new productive forces by way of taking recourse to old forms of production and labour processes wherever possible. In the context of neoliberalism, the first option is a remote choice. It actually blurs the distinction between work and non-work, it opens up the possibility where selling labour power seizes to be the only option to survive for a vast majority of people and that is unacceptable in capitalism. With a huge increase in unemployment that is likely to happen because of technology change, the reproduction cost of labour has to be borne by the state exchequer as a transfer from surplus. This transfer is likely to happen in whatever limited form in advanced economies as unemployment reaches explosive levels. But for capital, the second option is always preferable. The purpose of introducing new technology in capital relations is primarily to reduce per unit cost of production and increase profit and not be driven by any motive to augment knowledge for human civilisation in general. It is driven by competition within capitalists and acts as a spontaneous force which continuously increases the general levels of technology use in the production process. If the same purpose can be fulfilled by engaging low-waged labour and low-cost natural resources in the old forms of production, capitalists would not opt for technology upgradation and productive forces that demand a conducive environment of work relations that are essentially in tension to the foundations of capitalist work. Precarious labour, therefore, is a sign of decadence of capitalism – the more the plague spreads, the more it proclaims the failure of the system in accepting necessary changes fit for the future development of productive forces. Jobs are being outsourced to low-wage segments of the developing world and existing norms of employment are bypassed by subcontracting and outsourcing extending to homework. Wages paid to workers are below the value of labour power, working conditions are inhuman and keeping the workforce extremely vulnerable defines power relations that constitute the regime of capitalist accumulation. Domestic as well as international

---

[27] For a detailed discussion on sociological changes due to new productive forces, see Block and Hirschhorn (1979).

migration of a huge labour force contributes to the accumulation process by offering supply of labour that is structurally vulnerable, often considered to be informal or undocumented and denied all kinds of rights that a resident worker may claim. It is essentially a dysfunctional labour regime that increases dependence on a labour process characterised by a vicious cycle of low wage and low productivity.

## Informality as Discourse of Power

Each regime of accumulation creates its own truth and the truth that implicitly criminalises 'informality' is the norm of 'free-waged-labour' that capitalism upholds as its defining ideal of labour process. In classical political economy, the engaging of the worker by a capitalist is an act of market exchange where commodities are exchanged on the basis of equivalence of value and, hence, exploitation is invisible. As a critique of political economy, Marx in *Capital* showed that the apparent exchange of wage against labour power is the visible surface, beneath which exists a fundamental asymmetry flowing from property rights of capitalists that forces the property-less workers to produce more than the value of labour power. The critical assumption or the premise of the theory of surplus value that Marx embarks upon is the classical assumption of equivalence of value, precisely with the view to argue that the appearance of equivalence of exchange glosses over a power relation that keeps the worker unfree as a class and, therefore, even if the exchange takes place on the basis of equal value, the labour receives less returns than what it produces. But the value of labour power is not determined by some external yardstick measuring the physical and mental requirements of workers, but historically contingent upon the class struggle defined in terms of concrete space and time. In fact, the institutions and the particular state–labour–capital relationship which is often invoked to define the 'formal' refers to a very short period of inter-War years in the long history of capitalism and largely confined to a part of the Anglo-Saxon world. In fact, forcing labour to sell labour power below its value was the dominant feature of capital–labour relations throughout the history of capitalism in the larger part of the world under the capitalist order. The informal or the precarious forms of labour and the semi-proletariats were exploited through the ages to generate surplus and hardly any right for workers came as a voluntary gift flowing from capitalist morality or respect for rule of law.

The juridico-political structures that rest upon formal frameworks of 'rule' and 'right' tend to hide the real techniques of power that work through disciplining the subject in everyday life. The rule and rights are applicable to all subjects, but a defined coding of the 'normal' corresponds to a regime of subjectivity and the distribution of justice refers to this particular norm working through regulations, denials and restrictions. The disciplining mechanism is more close to real and also more effective. It is about internalising an untold order of the dominant power; it is 'instrumentalisation of reason' by way of creating micro techniques of treating the 'abnormal'.[28] Michel Foucault in *Discipline and Punish* discusses how power works through creating universal subjects on the one hand and disciplines on the other. 'Moreover, whereas the juridical systems define juridical subjects according to universal norms, the disciplines characterise, classify, specialise; they distribute along a scale, around a norm, hierarchise individuals in relation to one another and, if necessary, disqualify and invalidate'.[29] The denial of rights for the 'abnormal' does not work through regulations and restrictions but by way of exclusion as they are disqualified for the claim of rights applicable to the 'normal'. Capitalism had never survived with wage-contracted labour alone, neither did it create universal norms of labour contract applicable across the world, it had existed and negotiated with slavery, serfdom, bonded labour, undocumented labour, self-employment and various other forms of labour in the course of its history, but it could create a conceptual space centred around the wage-labour as the subject recognised in its juridico-political space.

Informality is essentially a discourse of power. The predominant labour processes are kept beyond the juridico-political structure that defines the loci of rules and rights. This huge labour force is denied rights as they are invisible within the juridical scope of modern capitalism, but at the same time they are the repositories of absolute surplus value upon which capitalist accumulation largely relies upon beyond the boundaries of factories. In case of India, Chirashree Das Gupta[30] offers a detailed account of the contestations between the capitalists and the labour unions on account of the evolution of the Industrial Disputes Act 1956 version. In course of the debate on defining the worker and the work place in the proposed act, it was the capitalist class of India which vehemently pushed for narrowing down the definition of worker so that labour rights and dispute adjudication process remain confined to the registered 'factory' sector only. The labour unions, on the contrary, were in favour of including all workers and workplaces within the ambit of law. Hence, informality was not something that

---

[28] Bidet argues that in the modern social order, the dominant class presents two poles in the rational mode of coordination at the social level: market and the organisation, one invokes the power of property and the other knowledge-power and this dual mode of coordination culminates not in the market, but in the supreme organisation, the modern state (Bidet 2015: 67–68).

[29] Foucault (1977).

[30] Das Gupta (2016: 135–37).

emerged out of some new elements in the labour process, but simply by way of defining the formal and delegitimising the rest as informal.

Capitalism has entered into a critical phase where the process of capitalist accumulation requires less and less living labour, both direct and indirect. Hence, the accumulation is increasingly delinked from the need of employing people joining the labour force. In other words, the reproduction of the entire labour force no longer seems to be a compelling need for capitalist accumulation. Such a process makes a huge number of workers simply redundant, but the system cannot shed off this entire mass of working people as it becomes politically exploding. It does not, however, imply that that world of labour is divided between unemployed and protected jobs, or a divide between 'accumulation' and 'need' as Sanyal-Chatterjee's schema would suggest, but precarious forms of employment creep into all work relations, as it offers capital additional opportunity to devalue labour. The larger share of this workforce, residing mainly in the developing world, are brought under capitalist relations through outsourcing and subcontracting. It dehumanises labour with the tag of 'informal' and tries to contain and control this labour force by disciplining beyond the realm of rights. Juridical power works within the realm of rights and obligations based on legitimising relations of power in terms of sovereignty. In a neoliberal regime where the state withdraws to proactively create a market society, employment of labour hardly invokes contracts according to the rule of law. This absence or silence of legality is the instrument of power that capitalism uses through the discourse of 'informal labour' and pushes the majority of the workforce at the margin of legitimacy. The informal exists not because there is a lack of regulation appropriate for this workforce, but because capitalism cannot afford the 'norms' which it had to concede to in its 'Golden Age.' It can rather survive only taking recourse to unprotected and undocumented workers, while at the same time exclusion continues using the normative imagery of the 'formal'.

# 7

# Self-Employment as Disguised Dispossession

One of the most startling features of capitalist development in India is that more than half the working population is engaged in non-wage employment. However, one can account this to the high share of employment in agricultural activities that had largely remained a site bearing marks of 'pre-capitalist' production relations. Nevertheless, self-employment and other precarious forms of non-wage employment assume a large share even in non-agriculture. This is quite peculiar since capitalism is largely characterised by an economic space in which not only produce is turned into commodities, but labour-power itself assumes the commodity form as wage labour. The worker works under the capitalist to whom the labour power belongs and the product of labour is appropriated by the capitalist net of wages. The problem is further complicated because wage employment, in the Marxian sense, is the only source of surplus-value that the labourer creates in the process of earning his/her living, precisely creating value beyond necessary labour time. The persistence of high share of non-wage employment in India and in other developing countries as well as a non-declining floor, if not a rising trend even in developed capitalism, is worrying at the conceptual level as well. Sometimes, the fact is attributed to cyclical fluctuations. That is, self-employment mushrooms in periods of economic downturn when employability of the economy declines and non-wage segment swells as a micro-level, counter-cyclical response. But this explanation is only partial because studies focus on a historical trend of declining influence of unemployment on self-employment.

How do we appreciate this apparent unity of producer with the means of production in the context of capitalism which is primarily defined as a system reproducing the alienation of the direct producer from the means of production? At a conceptual level one needs to comprehend the fact of rise in non-capital space within capitalism. It manifests articulation of various modes of production while capital relation assumes dominant position within the totality of social organisation. Neoliberalism is the paradigmatic mode of articulation in which capital relations intend to entangle and hegemonise every other mode of production by creating a market society. In fact, the withdrawal of the state in neoliberalism is never meant to be a state remaining passive. Indeed, the state reduces its intervention in the realm of economy, but is very active in destroying barriers of regulation that limit the space for private capital. Hence, the withdrawal of the state in neoliberalism is the active process of creating space for private capital articulated through a market society. Expanding space of self-employment, particularly in non-agriculture, needs to be diagnosed vis-à-vis accumulation of capital and, therefore, the relation between self-employed, wage-employed and unemployed becomes crucial in understanding capitalist development in India.

Many studies appreciate rising self-employment as a technology-driven flexibilisation of production. In other words, it is an outcome of a complex process involving increased modularisation of production, servicification as well as a response to a changing demand pattern that shifted more towards customised goods replacing standardised products, making large-scale production increasingly inefficient. It is also supplemented by the notion of 'cooperative efficiency' suggesting that instead of stand-alone enterprises, a dense network of producers, suppliers and service providers embedded in a conducive cultural milieu of mutual trust and related institutions can create a virtuous circle of cumulative growth. This narrative is part of the broader strand of literature of 'flexible specialisation' of the post-Fordist regime which, of course, captures certain aspects of self-employment, but one needs to see whether such a technology-centric explanation really explains the swelling of self-employment in developing countries such as India.

## Non-wage Employment in India

The stylised fact of high non-wage employment in India demands a closer look into empirical evidence. Non-wage work takes two different forms, namely self-employment and unpaid family work. A self-employed person might be defined as one who earns income by her/his own labour, but does not sell labour power to some other in return for wages. A self-employed person is neither a wage-earner who sells labour to others nor a rentier who could earn income without expending any labour. A self-employed person can employ hired labour in his/her enterprise in return for wages or salaries or might run an own account enterprise (OAE) without hiring any labour. Unpaid family labour is recognised in official accounting only when that labour helps in producing commodities. Otherwise, the household labour that contributes to the production and reproduction of labour power is excluded from value calculations. Household labour is needed to transform wage goods into subsistence basket, but since it creates only use values and is not meant for exchange, such labour is not even recognised and banished from the 'paid-unpaid' determinations of labour process.

Table 7.1 shows the share of self-employed in India within the labour force by region and gender. It covers a period which includes episodes of high growth as

**Table 7.1** Percentage distribution of self-employed by usual status of employment by gender and sector

| | Rural | | | Urban | | | Rural + urban | | |
|---|---|---|---|---|---|---|---|---|---|
| | Male | Female | Persons | Male | Female | Persons | Male | Female | Persons |
| 1993–94 | 57.7 | 58.6 | 58.0 | 41.7 | 44.8 | 42.3 | 53.7 | 56.8 | 54.7 |
| 1999–2000 | 55.0 | 57.3 | 55.8 | 41.5 | 45.3 | 42.2 | 51.5 | 55.8 | 52.8 |
| 2004–05 | 58.1 | 63.7 | 60.2 | 44.8 | 47.7 | 45.4 | 54.7 | 61.4 | 56.9 |
| 2007–08 | 55.4 | 58.3 | 56.3 | 42.7 | 42.3 | 42.6 | 52.0 | 56.0 | 53.2 |
| 2011–12 | 54.5 | 59.3 | 55.9 | 41.7 | 42.8 | 41.9 | 50.7 | 56.1 | 52.2 |

*Source*: NSS report on Employment and Unemployment Situation in India, various years.

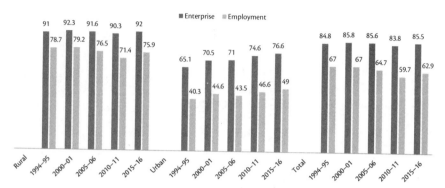

**Figure 7.1** Share of own account enterprises in total enterprises and employment in unorganised manufacturing sector

*Source*: NCEUS (2009); NSSO (2012, 2017).

well as a longer term trend of robust GDP growth. But the notable fact is that the share of self-employed within the labour force has remained consistently above the 50-per cent mark in the entire reference period. In other words, in spite of high growth, what is significant is that more than 50 per cent of the workforce in India was not employed in capitalist production relations involving a separation of direct producer from the means of production or capital–wage–labour relationship. The share of self-employed has been higher in rural areas compared to that in the urban labour force. More importantly, the share has been higher for the female labour force compared to that within employed men. Figure 7.1 shows the share of OAEs in total enterprises and employment within unorganised manufacturing. On an average in rural India, 91.4 per cent of enterprises in unorganised manufacturing have been OAEs that do not hire any labour and account for 76.3 per cent share of employment of unorganised manufacturing during this period. The corresponding shares for the urban, unorganised manufacturing has been 71.6 and 44.8. Overall for India, the average share of OAEs during the period 1994–95 to 2015–16 out of the total enterprises in unorganised manufacturing has been 85.1 per cent and share of employment turns out to be 64.3 per cent. The share of OAEs has increased both in terms of enterprise share and employment share in 2015–16 compared to 2010–11.

Table 7.2 shows the share of OAEs within unincorporated, non-agricultural enterprises that include broad activity categories such as manufacturing, electricity, trade and other services. The figures show that in rural areas, more than 84 per cent of enterprises involving these non-agricultural activities in unincorporated space are OAEs and their share in total employment in this segment has been more than 62 per cent in both the reference years.

**Table 7.2** Share of own account enterprises in total unincorporated non-agricultural enterprises and employment

|  | 2010–11 | | 2015–16 | |
|---|---|---|---|---|
|  | Enterprises | Employment | Enterprises | Employment |
| Rural | 91.44 | 78.41 | 91.40 | 76.45 |
| Urban | 76.78 | 51.21 | 76.57 | 50.42 |
| All | 84.63 | 64.61 | 84.17 | 62.09 |

*Source*: NSSO (2012, 2017).

Therefore, in unincorporated, non-agricultural activities excluding construction, self-employment accounts for 91.4 per cent of rural enterprises and 76.6 per cent of urban enterprises in 2015–16, accounting for 76.4 per cent and 50.4 per cent of employment respectively.

Studies related to the informal sector often argue that the dynamics of self-employment is related to the cyclical fluctuations in the economy, meaning self-employment increases during downturn and its share declines in periods of high growth.[1] The stability in the share of self-employment in India, however, does not provide sufficient empirical evidence for such hypothesis. This is primarily because of the following reasons. First, the above proposition assumes a positive relationship between growth and employment. That is, in periods of upswing, more labour is pulled into wage employment from the 'reserve army' in the waiting. But such assumption hardly captures the dominant trend of high growth accompanied by rising unemployment. Second, the argument ignores the fact that because of a downturn, some might lose their job and consequently, shifted from wage employment to self-employment. The other possibility could be that many of the existing self-employing enterprises are likely to be shut down due to lack of demand. And higher the share of self-employment in the labour force *ex ante,* higher would be the probability of the first trend being outweighed by the second in balance. Third, there could also be a process of self-exploitative fragmentation under way that might result in higher self-employment which we take up in the last section of this chapter.

One way of looking into changing technologies and resultant production organisation underscores the fact that the more the knowledge component increases in the production, the more the autonomy of the person who possesses that knowledge assumes importance.[2] The rise in the relative scarcity of tacit

---

[1] Mead (1994); Mead and Liedholm (1998).
[2] Drucker (1993).

knowledge and the increasing need of transforming knowledge output into commercial products increases the importance of autonomy in the work process. Autonomy of the worker in the capitalist-labour process is directly related to the importance of tacit knowledge and inversely related to standardisation and codification of such knowledge. The more the knowledge is codified, the more it can be separated from its possessor and hence, the labourer becomes increasingly replaceable. Knowledge workers can be defined as those workers whose knowledge has been tacit in nature and cannot be easily replaced. In the case of knowledge-intensive industries, that is, where the component of non-standard, intangible knowledge inputs are high, new start-ups emerge as a result of an employee quitting his/her job to realise higher gains from acquired knowledge and specialisation by catering to niche markets. While in the case of traditional sectors, where knowledge and skills are easily replaceable, self-employment cannot be explained by the fact of increasing need of autonomy for specialised production. In fact, despite having a sense of ownership, the self-employed person is generally more vulnerable to cyclical fluctuations compared to the wage worker since for the latter, the wage contract is independent of the act of sale of produced goods or services at least in the short run, while the self-employed person can realise the return of labour only after being able to sell the produce.

## Capital and Non-capital

The conceptual discomfort regarding persistent high share of non-wage employment together with high growth emanates from a notion of 'pure' capitalism which as an advanced mode of production is supposed to replace non-capital. In this context, the high share of non-wage employment appears to be a sign of unfulfilled capitalist development. As capitalism matures, concentration and centralisation will eventually destroy self-employed, petty production and give rise to a bipolar production relation consisting of wage workers and capitalists as contesting poles. It invokes a linear progression of history driven by the dialectic of productive force and production relations. In Marxian literature, although the concept of 'productive force' assumes causal primacy in social change, it is not unambiguously defined. In some texts, it has a technical connotation while in others, it encompasses broader aspects of class consciousness. In fact, such conceptual divergences led to differences in the interpretation of social change that finally crept into the seminal 'mode of production debate'.[3]

---

[3] Holton (1981).

There seems to be three broad perspectives within Marxist scholarship analysing capital–non-capital relationship. The first one being derived from teleological interpretation of history assuming 'petty production' as a transitory phase pre-destined to be destroyed by the capitalist process of centralisation and concentration. In this view, capital replaces non-capital as capitalism develops. The second strand of literature assumes a permanent relationship between capital and non-capital in which the existence of non-capital is seen as a contingent requirement for maintaining stability of capitalism at the core. Hence, coexistence of capital and non-capital is intrinsic to the capitalist mode of production. The third perspective assumes capitalism as a complex articulation of various modes of production and there is no unique or optimal combination of elements or subsystems and institutions within capitalism that would necessarily triumph over other combinations.

Maurice Dobb[4] argued that the rise in capitalist relations did not happen simultaneously with the decline in feudalism, but there was a phase of 'petty-commodity production'. Commoditisation of production took the initial form of simple commodity production where the producer sells his produce in order to procure other commodities for use. However, commercialisation of production, that is, transforming goods into commodities could not in itself lead to capitalist production because capitalism does not signify only production of commodities, but labour power has to be commodified as well. And this requires a forced separation of the mass of producers from their own means of production that Marx characterised as the 'primitive accumulation of capital'.[5]

Hence, 'petty-commodity production' was conceived as a transitory phase in Marxian literature that could never withstand in the face of capitalist development.[6] The destruction of non-capitalist relations may manifest either in forms of dramatic social change or it can happen gradually by way of erosion of the economic viability of the earlier system. The most important reason for capitalist sway over 'pre-capitalist' relations was the intrinsic trend of concentration and centralisation of production. Capitalism favours concentration to reap the benefits of increasing returns to scale and hence, smaller structures could hardly survive in the face of capitalist competition. Therefore, petty commodity-production was conceived as a transient category that is supposed to wither away as capitalism matures.

Rosa Luxemburg[7] (1951) was among the first to theorise the need for non-capitalist markets and argued that in the case of expanded reproduction, a 'closed'

---

[4] Dobb (1946).
[5] Marx (1958: Part VIII).
[6] Moser (1978).
[7] Luxemburg (1951).

capitalist system can never resolve the realisation crisis without a non-capitalist 'external market' that is used to absorb part of the surplus. While acknowledging the requirement of external stimuli, Michal Kalecki's[8] critique, also echoed by Paul Sweezy,[9] suggests that in a balanced trade between capitalist and non-capitalist segment, that is if net exports are zero, then the non-capitalist segment plays no role in absorbing the unrealised surplus. Prabhat Patnaik[10] refuted the need for export surplus in stimulating investment in the capitalist sector. This is precisely because expansion of exports and contraction of import-competing activities have asymmetrical effects upon domestic investment and the positive effects of the former would be larger than the negative effects of the latter. Second, balanced trade between two economies might imply export surpluses from the capitalist to pre-capitalist sector if imports from under-developed economies are used to replace domestic pre-capitalist producers within the developed capitalist economy. Though Patnaik's theorising of engagement with the pre-capitalist sector bears resemblance to Luxemburg's argument of the theoretical impossibility of capitalism existing in isolation, it is different in that the necessity of engagement does not arise to realise the entire unconsumed surplus of the core as argued by the former. Rather, it provides a 'reserve market' that stimulates investment. The central argument runs as follows: Being a demand-constrained system, capitalism has a tendency to move away further from the central position and there is obviously no spontaneous mechanism that ensures the functioning of the system within the upper bounds of 'inflationary barrier' and lower bounds of activity related to the minimum acceptable rate of profit to the capitalists. The coherence and viability of capitalism can only be maintained when the capitalist sector is ensconced with a pre-capitalist setting, when the distant reserve army consisting of a vast pauperising mass created within the pre-capitalist sector and geographically separated from the reserve army at the core plays the role not only of containing real wages, but also stabilising the wage-unit. Hence, the value of money.[11]

The basic difference between Kalecki's analysis and that of Patnaik's lies in the fact that Kalecki implicitly assumes that a capitalist economy is viable at any rate of profit, while in Patnaik's scheme, there is a minimum rate of profit and hence, a level of activity slipping below which would make the system unviable. However, what is common to all of the above analyses is the necessity of creating

---

[8] Kalecki (1971)
[9] Sweezy (1942).
[10] P. Patnaik (1997).
[11] P. Patnaik (2008b).

hegemony over the existing non-capitalist segment because only then the capitalists would be induced to the required level of investment.

As against linear evolutionist perspectives, the concept of mode of production in L. Althussar and E. Balibar[12] is a 'complexly articulated' social totality conceived entirely in the formal abstract level. In Althussar, the concept of mode of production signifies an extended meaning. It is not only a specific combination of the forces of production and relations of production, but the determinate and specific relations of the former with economic moments as well as with other social mediations, namely political and ideological. The articulation of various elements in the mode of production is captured by the notion of 'overdetermination', a concept originally used by Sigmund Freud analysing representation of dream thoughts in images constituted by mechanisms of condensation and displacement.[13] In this scheme of analysis, none of the elements in the complex totality enjoys causal primacy over others. Rather, they overdetermine each other and get overdetermined in the same process. The elements of the mode of production exist in history in a 'floating state' and prior to their combination, each being the product of its own history and none being the teleological product of the others or their history. Althussar views the capitalist mode of production as the unintended and overdetermined effect of the 'aleatory' and contingent 'encounter' of the various historical processes. The emergence of capitalism is explained here not as an outcome of historical necessity, but as a point of 'radical indeterminacy' that brings together constituent elements floating in history, giving rise to a new social system. Hence, what follows also is that existence of non-capitalist production-relations might not necessarily have to have a causal determination. That is, they are not necessarily linked with capitalism for some purpose originating from the capitalist space. Rather, they may exist as independent processes, having interactions with capitalism in various moments, both overdetermining and being overdetermined by the same process. Therefore, there is absolutely no ontological reason to think of 'pure' system. Neither is there any reason to believe that coexistence of multiple systems indicates failure in evolving to some 'pure' capitalism.

The engagement of capital and non-capital entails a hierarchy of relationship where non-capital can valorise itself only through an asymmetric exchange not necessarily on the basis of equivalence of value as happens within capitalist relations. Labour in capitalism assumes a dual character: concrete that signifies the particular dimension and specifics of labour that produces commodities as use values and the other abstract, that is universal, social and general, producing

---

[12] Althussar and Balibar (1970).
[13] See Resnick and Wolff (1987).

exchange values of commodities. Differences in terms of use of various concrete labour or qualities of labour is abstracted into homogeneous labour articulated through quantities of labour time. A system of structural coherence is achieved through the act of exchange, giving rise to value relations where commodities are embodiments of various quantities of socially necessary labour time. To the non-capitalist segment, this articulation might not be binding in itself. However, the act of interaction between capital and non-capitalist production process takes place in the realm of value articulated through the market. The non-capital has to express itself in terms of exchange relations in order to get entry into the capitalist space, while it is also difficult for capital to intrude into all sorts of non-capitalist production processes.[14]

The non-capitalist site of production is not as something auxiliary to the capitalist labour process, clinging as an appendage to the latter. Rather, it constitutes the capitalist production of values although not recognised. The household labour is a classic example of such suppression. The conceptual act of assuming 'subsistence basket' as synonymous to wage goods is the silent process of ignoring the household labour that transforms wage goods into the subsistence basket.[15] The general rate of profit in the capitalist sector is constituted by the tendential equalisation of the rate of profit actualised through competition among capitals within and between sectors. In the sphere of self-employment, there is no reason to believe that this uniform rate of profit would be realised in the act of exchange between capitalist and non-capitalist segments. The terms of trade between the capitalist sector and the self-employed producer is completely arbitrary and accidental as it is impossible to establish a relation of equivalence in value theoretic terms. The capital advanced in self-employment is not 'capital' in the general sense, as these are hardly transferable to alternative sites of investments. It has to be applied in a way to valorise the family labour and markets for capital and labour are not separate and independent. They are both segmented markets, as the family labour cannot always take recourse to alternative occupations. However, return to labour in self-employment, once entering into exchange with the capitalist segment, should be at least not more than the average wage in the capitalist sector within a particular skill range. Otherwise, one would prefer to become self-employed rather than working as wage labour. This is ensured by the asymmetric relation between capital and non-capital together with the existence of a 'reserve army of labour' or sufficient number of people looking for subsistence income. Hence, return to self-employment and wages in the capitalist sector are mutually constitutive, one conditioning the other, not on

[14] Chakrabarti, Dhar and Cullenberg (2012).
[15] Quick (2004).

the same footing, but on the basis of asymmetry. Ajit Chaudhury et al.[16] termed this relationship as a 'mimicry of overdetermination'.

## Autonomy or Fragmentation

Self-employment has often been seen as a sign of proliferation of entrepreneurship facilitated by change in demand in the advent of new technology. There has been a shift towards customised goods instead of standardised products, product life cycles have shrunk and non-price qualitative dimensions such as exacting timeliness, punctuality in delivery and minimum inventory assume importance in new competition. Information and communication technology has reduced marginal transmission costs of information and physical capital to the minimum, facilitating further modularisation of production in the form of subcontracting and outsourcing. At the same time, with the rise in customised demand, the demand for tacit knowledge has increased, once again underlining the importance of space as a choice variable. In other words, the Fordist model of large-scale production with detailed command structure turned out to be outdated and has to be replaced by decentred production organisation, allowing more discretion and greater autonomy. The network of autonomous units, however, invoke space as a socio-cultural milieu defined by mutual trusts and related institutions. Neoclassical theory assumes space as synthetic and uniform. Distinctions of space become irrelevant as efficient allocation of labour and capital through perfect factor mobility eventually ensure convergence of factor productivities across space. But space is neither linear nor can it be seen as passive uniform containers. Space is relational and, therefore, investment in new technology and learning affects capabilities of other firms within proximity.[17] Since neoclassical theory assumes perfect mobility of factors, it is insensitive to spatial relations and can consider benefits of proximity only in terms of externalities. But such externalities may cause underinvestment because the producer cannot internalise those benefits received by others into prices. Hubert Schmitz[18] goes beyond the conventional perception of external economies and argues that in case of horisontal networks, economic agents are both recipients and producers of external economics. Hence, underinvestment ceases to be the dominant outcome. Various strands of post-Fordist literature, therefore, suggest that appropriate production organisation is a decentred structure of economic agents which do not require large-scale of operation in minimising costs. Rather, it uses

---

[16] Choudhury, Das and Chakrabarti (2000).
[17] For a detailed discussion, see Roy (2012, 2013: 14–29).
[18] Schmitz (1999).

multipurpose technologies and cooperative institutions sharing indivisible inputs. In such a milieu of 'cooperative competition', self-employment may flourish on the basis of flexible specialisation, enabling producers to respond to customised demand.

In the case of India, the above analysis seems plausible only for sectors where knowledge input is highly intangible and tacit in nature. For instance, in sectors such as information technology, the contribution of a programmer or an inventor is the highest in the production of output. In that case, if the gap on expected return from the potential innovation between the inventor and the corporate decision-maker is sufficiently large and the cost of starting a new firm is sufficiently low, then the employee might decide to establish a new enterprise.[19] Proliferation of new high-tech start-ups could be explained by such mismatch in expected returns, but one cannot appreciate the spawning of tiny units in traditional sectors on similar lines. The rise of small and tiny enterprises in traditional clusters of India is largely a result of an asymmetric relationship between trader and the small producer defined as contested exchange.[20] The trader has the power over the small producer to impose sanctions affecting the future stream of revenue while the latter lacks the capacity with respect to the trader. To the small producer, the objective function is not to maximise profits as they can hardly access the market independently. Rather, it is of maximising sales and increasing revenue. In that case, higher sale is subject to paying a greater premium of profit to the trader, be it directly or indirectly. Higher the degree of dependence on traders, the less will be the margin of profit for smaller units as the pressure for reducing costs cannot be transferred to the workers whose wage level has already touched the reservation wage. In that case, the only space left for an owner of a small unit is to restrict the upward mobility of labour by refusing to recognise skill accumulation and related claims for increased wage. And if the wage increment after a certain period is not remunerative to the skill and productivity that the worker attains, the skilled worker would be inclined to establish a new unit if the initial capital required is relatively low and thereby enjoy the 'freedom' of self-exploitation.[21] The small producer, in that case, might earn more than what s/he earned earlier as a wage worker, having the option of working for longer hours. However, she/he may end up producing goods that require less skill, but ensure higher income by way of selling more by lowering the offer price. Thus, the choice of self-employment in

[19] Audretsch and Aldridge (2009).
[20] Bowles and Gintis (1990).
[21] For a technical model of the above analyses, see Roy (2006).

most of the traditional sectors is the result of 'forced autonomy' driven by the dynamics of self-exploitative fragmentation.

Such fragmentation is not for the purpose of attaining higher flexibility required as a response to changing demand. Most self-employed manufacturers operate in the low end of the market and supply intermediate goods in the value chain at a lower cost. Customisation of production in place of standardised demand was the major challenge that new industrial organisations of the 'second industrial divide' seem to have addressed in the context of Europe.[22] In India, it is the absence of a standardised market that explains fragmentation in production structure. High inequality and existence of multiple layers of goods and services with quality standard grossly being compromised, defines the market for low-end products. These mass consumption goods like garments, leather goods, toys, sports goods, processed food and so on could have easily been produced at much lower unit cost and with uniform standard in a Fordist large-scale structure. In fact, India might have a higher edge compared to Bangladesh in terms of variety in garments, but products with similar quality and even with much higher value-added are being produced in large-scale units in China and also some in Bangladesh.[23] The underlying fact precisely is Indian firms, on an average, do not operate at a quality range and degree of customisation that is incompatible to the Fordist structure of production organisation. Hence, self-employment in India can hardly be explained as a result of rise in customised demand or driven by the need for functional flexibility.

Self-exploitative fragmentation rather than flexibilisation explains the Indian case of high non-wage employment. Capitalist accumulation entails an interaction between the capitalist and non-capitalist segment by continuously creating and destroying the 'other' through a contradictory process. On the one hand, we see increased concentration and centralisation of capital articulated through merger and acquisitions at the global scale, smaller entities being outcompeted and devastated. On the other hand, the same process of accumulation lower down the value chain instils fragmentation of existing units into tiny self-employing operations. The mode of accumulation in the neoliberal regime manifests a major departure from the expanded reproduction of the post-War Keynesian era. The realisation of excess capital was facilitated that time by mass consumption and large expenditures of the welfare state on account of public utilities and infrastructure. Under the neoliberal regime, accumulation relies heavily on dispossession taking various forms of loss of entitlements for the workers. Capital creates its own constitutive outside the non-capital, here in the form of self-employed, and sheds wage workers having defined entitlements. The self-employed, in this

---

[22] Piore and Sabel (1984).
[23] Roy (2009).

case, is a caricature of 'free owner' who can engage with capitalism not on the basis of equivalence, but by accepting unequal exchange symbolising devalued identity of the owner on the one hand and that of a vulnerable worker on the other. Self-employment in this case is nothing but disguised dispossession.

# 8

# Land Acquisition in India

## Revisiting Primitive Accumulation

The splurge of land grab across the world in the backdrop of financial crisis, rising food and energy prices and in India, particularly since 2005, several issues related to acquisition of farm land and consequent dispossession caused a huge furore and public debate. The primary concern expressed in the World Bank reports of 2008 and 2010[1] was that poverty alleviation needs to be linked to reducing 'yield gap' in agriculture and the necessary transformation of generating productive employment at least for the rural population has to be mediated by large land holdings engaging in commercial agriculture. Investment on land also became important due to a rise in food and energy prices and large capital investment moved on to acquire land to ensure food and energy security for the future. Apart from these stated goals of 'rational planning' in using resources of the planet, the discourses in favour of acquiring farm land for more productive use largely revolves on the modernist logic of transforming agricultural land either from small-holding, subsistence agriculture to agribusiness linked to the new commodity regime or to provide spaces for industry that would evict unproductive rural labour and employ them in more productive activities. Essentially, both these rationales invoke a teleology or an imagery of linear progress which is more or less decided by the past of advanced capitalist countries.

The Lewis–Kuznets[2] process of moving people out of agriculture, the classical trajectory of modernity where people of labour-surplus countries need to be pushed out from traditional low-productivity segments to high-productivity industry and service activities is the underlying teleology broadly invoked in these discourses. Because of surplus labour, real wage remains more or less the same, despite labour being drawn in more productive activities and the rising gap between wage and productivity becomes the source of capital accumulation in modern sectors. The process of accumulation in the modern sector will pull more labour from low-productive agricultural activity and absorb them in high-productive segments, eventually leading to an exhaustion of surplus labour which

---

[1] World Bank (2008, 2010).
[2] See Lewis (1954) and Kuznets and Murphy (1966).

will cause rise in wages. This path of 'modernity' from 'backward' agriculture was conceived in a classical setting when demand was not thought of as a problem and technological growth was supposed to engage more people through its direct and indirect effects rather than causing a scenario of net redundancy of labour.[3] This conceptual frame of marching forward towards industrial development with collateral damage of temporary dispossession as a pain for a larger gain is completely out of grid. Enclosure of small holdings and peasant agriculture for the sake of industrial development and commercial agriculture faces immense resistance across the world. This also, once again, brings to the fore the 'agrarian question' in the context of developing economies – how far the assumed and prescribed depeasantisation leads to proletarianisation of the work force. In other words, the relevant questions in concrete terms could be the following: How much of the land acquired for industrial development has been actually used for the stated purpose? Does this presumed trajectory absorb the dispossessed in productive activities and is it so that commercial agriculture be necessarily more productive than small-peasant farming? These are pertinent questions on the presumed trajectory of capitalist industrialisation.

Attraction towards land is also driven by financial interests independent of its productive capacity. Given the financial crisis and the resultant distrust towards existing financial instruments, large institutional investors are after land because it provides a tangible asset with much more stable expected returns in the future. Securitisation of any sort requires an underlying asset with expected flow of future returns. Land easily qualifies and is also inflation-hedging. Therefore, land as an asset enters into the aggregation of returns that various kinds of financial instruments offer in securitised form. Speculative prices of real estate and the growth of financial activities around a wide network of real estate and its ancillaries, particularly in metro cities and small towns in India, made land the core area of lucrative returns. Purchase and sale of land has also become a source of revenue for many state governments and the role of the state, therefore, aligns quite often with builders, corporates, contractors and tends to trivialise the legal protections that exist to defend the rights of those being dispossessed in the process of land acquisition.

In this chapter, we revisit Marx's notion of 'so-called primitive accumulation of capital' and its later versions proposed by Marxist scholars primarily to reflect upon bourgeoisie cannibalism and predatory capitalism prevalent in a neoliberal regime. Beginning from Rosa Luxemburg, Marxist analyses of capital accumulation was linked to the discussion on the relationship between capital at

---

[3] In the context of India this debate is addressed in Ghose (2016) and Roy (2008).

the core and the pre-capitalist periphery. There are debates on how such a relationship contributes to the process of capital accumulation at the core and also whether the creation and existence of 'pre-capitalist' periphery necessarily bears a temporal connotation. This is also related to various phases of the 'mode of production debate', referring to the articulation of coexisting production relations. But most of these arguments seem to agree that non-capital existed with capitalism and contributed to the process of capitalist accumulation.

Other views in the post-colonial context suggest that existence and creation of non-capital is not necessarily linked with the process of capitalist accumulation. Rather, it is a reunion of the direct producer with the means of production often facilitated by a transfer of surplus accumulated at the core. Non-capital, in this sense, is neither pre-capital, which is assumed to be transient, nor does it exist and persist as a reserve army of labour. This vast segment outside capital relations seems to be condemned forever. We also need to revisit Marx's later writings that help us throw light on the notion of primitive accumulation. The land acquisition debate in India has to be located in the larger context of agrarian change and social transformation. In that respect, the current spree of land grab resembles primitive accumulation of capital, a forcible engagement with non-capital which the development discourse acknowledges as a not-so-preferred, but unavoidable, path of industrialisation. Revisiting Marx would instigate a careful observer not only to question the pathway, but the end in itself.

## Triple Crisis and Development Discourse

Largescale land grab was very much a part of early accumulation such as the Irish and English enclosures from the seventeenth to nineteenth centuries, dispossession of native peoples of North America and Australasia and three distinct episodes of land rushes in Africa from 1855 to 1955. In the Global South, land grab in the pre-colonial period was a part of territorial conflict and during colonial rule, land was acquired and subjugated for the imperial division of labour.[4] In the current context, the renewed interest on land is primarily a response to the emerging crisis of capital accumulation owing to rising cost of production and reproduction. The narrative of rising prices of food, feed and fuel together with the meltdown of the financial bubble in 2007–08 once again brings land onto the centre stage. It is now linked to a food security discourse of feeding the future world and saving the planet. These concerns immediately mandate enhancing efficiency and mending the yield gap of small-farm peasant

---

[4] Wily (2012).

agriculture. The neoliberal regime, hence, facilitates commoditising land which was itself supposed to be producing commodities. It also enables a process of financialisation, aggregating large parcels of land and necessary securitisation to shift resources towards a new extractive food-fuel-biomass regime. This invokes the trope of modernity and 'food security' and aims to enclose the world's remaining land and water.

In developing countries, 227 million hectares, an area equal to the entire size of Western Europe, has been sold or leased since 2001.[5] It also entails a process of reversal of land reforms undertaken by late-colonial or post-colonial progressive regimes in many countries of the South. The World Bank, which advocated the breaking up of large plantations in favour of small holdings and relatively homogeneous 'family farms' in the second half of the twentieth century, has done a volte-face and began advocating corporate-led, large, farm-based agriculture. The World Bank Report of 2008, *Agriculture for Development*, put forth the imagery of a dualistic agriculture that would be centred around large farm mostly involved in export-oriented agricultural production and the small holder farms either gradually disappear or are hooked into the value chain through contract farming arrangements. The same process, therefore, entails proletarianising the existing peasantry attached to farmlands who would offer cheap labour to corporate agriculture. The ideology of enclosure in the name of food security and ecological sustainability mediates through the World Bank's notion of 'yield gap', the gap between actual and potential production which can be resolved by high-input, value chain agriculture. Therefore, largescale land grab was advocated to achieve higher productivity that takes care of the future demand for food. But this was not limited to food alone as the narrative goes with rising per capita income in India and China and growing 'meatification' due to changing diets lead to increase in demand for animal feed such as soya, corn and so on. The large, secret deals in Latin America were meant for expansion of soy plantation covering an area of 50 million hectares spanning southern Brazil, northern Argentina, Paraguay and eastern Bolivia, and the 'Republic of Soy' was created by evicting hundred thousands of small holders.[6] There was a rise in the demand for biofuels with the intent to substitute fossil fuels, given the rising oil prices and to reduce reliance on Middle East oil resources. Alliances between multi-national corporations emerge, involving countries both of the North and of the South in building feed-fuel alliances of soy-rapeseed or palm oil or ethanol alliances involving US, South Africa, Malaysia, Brazil, India, China and Mozambique. It also redefines the notion of crop diversification where the emphasis is to produce

---

[5] Oxfam (2011).
[6] Holt-Giménez (2007).

'flex crops' which have multiple use such as selling as sugar when ethanol price is low or selling as biodiesel in the form of palm oil when biofuel prices rise. Apart from the immediate concerns of food-feed-fuel security and self-reliance, land acquisition is also taking place as the 'great green land grab'[7] in the name of environmental concerns. Products and services relating to natural parks, wildlife, sanctuaries or plantations of pine and eucalyptus are commoditised as a resource for carbon credits to be traded with polluters elsewhere.

Utsa Patnaik[8] offers a critique of this food-fuel security narrative, foregrounding the inequality caused by the neoliberal regime which results in declining food availability for the poor, on the one hand, and overconsumption of the rich, on the other. As income increases, indirect demand for cereals in the form of animal products increases while the share of direct cereals in the consumption basket declines. This is true for an individual household, but as income increases, the total demand for cereal should increase if the distribution remains the same. But if inequality rises as it did in the current neoliberal regime, the demand for animal products and, hence, that of feed increases while the per capita availability of food declines as the vast section of the poor are unable to increase their intake of direct cereals. In India, the rise in food prices has to be attributed to transfer of huge tracts of land from foodgrain cultivation to producing exotic crops meant for export markets. Decline in public investment in agriculture and rising input prices have made peasant farming unviable. Growth of foodgrain production declines in most developing countries including India and China, including episodes of absolute fall in foodgrain production. The dominant argument in favour of export-oriented agribusiness is that there is no need to worry about self-reliance in food production in a globalised world. Producing exportables as part of global agri-business chains would earn enough to meet domestic demands for food. But this has not been the case as competition between developing countries brings down the reservation price and unit price declines even if exports increase in physical quantities over time.

In the case of India, the land grab was primarily linked to the discourse of development which includes infrastructure, industry, urbanisation, real estate and extracting mineral resources. It is largely driven by domestic corporate investors, notwithstanding the fact that multinational corporations and international agencies are also keen in developing infrastructure corridors, building links to extractive and agribusiness frontiers. Acquiring farmland for public sector projects such as dams and irrigation projects, steel towns, infrastructure and public sector mining was part of the Nehruvian vision of national development. Though such

---

[7] Fairhead, Leach and Scoones (2012).
[8] U. Patnaik (2009).

public purposes attained wide legitimacy, such acquisitions during the period 1951–90 caused dispossession to the tune of 21.3 million people.[9] India's Land Acquisition Act did allow acquisition of land for private ownership, but this was hardly the practice in the pre-liberalisation period. Private companies were allotted plots of land in industrial areas owned by the government on the basis of rent payments. This is not to argue that dispossession was justified and the benefits of development were evenly distributed among the 'public'. Rather, the capitalists, landlord classes and public sector elites disproportionately gained out of these projects. The post-liberalisation period was radically different in terms of defining and justifying land acquisition for 'pubic purpose'. In fact, post-colonial developmentalism was substituted by what Michael Levien calls a broker state[10]. Post-1991, we see a decline in the share of public investment and with liberalisation, private demand for land infrastructure and real estate increased. Since liberalisation, India experienced high growth episodes with huge private investment in construction, minerals and services particularly IT-BPO services. High growth in India and China generally increased the demand for space and infrastructure, particularly that of commercial spaces for service-related activities, triggering the construction boom as well as rise in mineral prices. Against this backdrop, liberalised India's accumulation of capital confronted a supply barrier of land which exists largely in the form of small holdings that were practically and legally very difficult to aggregate and acquire. The state comes to the aid of capital in this regard, applies force to dispossess people from their existing livelihood and this application of force is a crucial feature, according to Levien, in understanding 'accumulation by dispossession' executed by the broker state. Therefore, the problem of dealing with small land holdings and underdeveloped land markets in rural India was taken care of by state governments who were in competition with each other in wooing capital. Many studies, however, suggest that the developmental claim which tried to legitimise private ownership as public purpose is hardly tenable. A study on Mahindra Special Economic Zone (SEZ)[11] in Rajasthan, covering 3,000 acres of acquired land shows that the SEZ Act only requires 50 per cent of the land acquired by the developer to be used for productive purposes. Mahindra would be using more than thousand acres of acquired land to build luxury apartments, making huge profits by selling residential space. Only 14 per cent of the dispossessed households received some employment while it fragmented and individualised the peasantry in the process, created chains of brokers, speculators and underemployed labour in this new regime of dispossession.

---

[9] Fernandes and Paranjpye (1997).
[10] Levien (2017).
[11] Levien (2011).

## Financialisation and Real Estate

Global investors did not consider farmland and agricultural assets in general as a lucrative financial asset until 2007 as rate of returns from land were comparatively less than that of financial instruments. The agro industrialisation of the North, propelled by the corporate food regime, came to an end as food prices started climbing along with declining sustainability and rising energy costs. Industrial agriculture seemed to have approached a crisis of declining bio-physical productivity, soil depletion and reduction in efficiency of nitrogen use.[12] This was accompanied by rising input, irrigation and energy costs as well as enhanced risks due to climate change. A shift in focus was triggered also by the global financial meltdown in 2008 with declining trusts on financial assets. In this conjuncture, global investors were in search of cheap resources of land, water and labour located in the South, augmented by finance, which was looking for more stable and tangible real assets in the backdrop of the financial crisis. Land of the South assumed importance as a preferred asset for offshoring investment to operationalise agro value chains as well as a potential candidate for speculative returns from investments in food and biofuel. It is generally held that farmland values show high correlation with inflation and a low correlation with other investments.[13] Therefore, sovereign wealth funds and institutional investors show interest in land as an inflation hedge as well as a means to reduce portfolio risks through diversification.

Financialisation entails an exercise in building up assets that yield a clear, defined future income stream. Securitisation is the aggregation of future income streams from a pool of underlying assets bundled into a new financial asset in which investors buy shares. It makes illiquid assets liquid and, hence, mobilisation of funds through securitisation became possible even if land is fixed in space and emerges as an exchangeable asset by buying and selling titles of land. The global macro scenario, characterised by low interest spread and low inflation, gives rise to flat yield curves together with abundant liquidity in most economies. This is precisely the reason why global investors were keen in creating new asset classes that can generate an exciting future stream of returns. The phase of securitisation, predominant in the 1980s and 1990s, was followed by more recent focus on hedge funds which involve more creative forms of asset and offsets risks of securitisation through diversified portfolio of financial instruments. In other words, the assets created through securitisation were often backed by expected future income streams of large corporates or government while the current new

---

[12] McMichael (2012).
[13] Fairbairn (2014).

class of assets are more closely defined and linked to expected returns from roads, airports, water supply, solid waste management, telecommunication and power generation.[14] Land in the South enters into the new class of assets that can generate a future income stream and, therefore, small holders and settlers need to be uprooted from their livelihood, creating new enclosures of corporate agribusiness, producing export-oriented exotic crops or food and biofuel. Parcels of land are commoditised and securitised by fund management companies and institutional investors such as pension funds, hedge funds, university endowments, life insurance companies, sovereign wealth funds as well as 'high net worth individuals' like George Soros and Warren Buffet who can park their wealth, buying shares of reshaped assets and hedge inflation. In fact, Warren Buffet popularises the notion of 'value investing' that is linked to intrinsic value and long-term fundamentals attached to land, allowing returns to be insulated from the vagaries of investor sentiment.[15] The intrinsic productive capacity, regardless of whether the land is used for actual production or not, makes it a transparent asset in the midst of distrust of financial markets. Though actual investment committed by institutional investors in farmland assets has been less than one per cent of their total investment, the total investment globally amounts to US$30–40 billion, according to an estimate.[16]

Acquisition of land, however, does not immediately lead to creation of financial asset. Transforming physical objects into fungible assets that can be traded in domestic and international markets requires a social process of abstracting the object from its singular history, modifying and standardising with codifications describing a particular object delinked from its human attachments. It is also about establishing property rights, a forcible intervention on the part of the state in the case of land that defines private property and ownership essential to create markets for commodities. The neoliberal state apparently withdraws from economic activity, but actively intervenes in the realm of society to create an environment conducive for markets to come into play. Donald MacKenzie calls these creations of social relations as infrastructures of markets.[17] It includes a system of property rights, credit provisions, ideologies about market behaviour, technologies for grading, standardising, transportation and communication. Llerena Guiu Searle defines this socio-cultural infrastructure as 'routes of accumulation'.[18] Transforming small, peasant land

[14] Leyshon and Thrift (2007)
[15] Fairbairn (2014).
[16] Wheaton and Kiernan (2012).
[17] MacKenzie (2003).
[18] Searle (2016).

holdings into a large agribusiness unit of industrial agriculture or real estate is the key process in securitising land, making it attractive to domestic and foreign investors. Land is unique in the sense that it has productive capacity and can also yield financial returns. Land assumes 'moneyness' as a store of value, but beyond that, value is augmented by appreciation. Studies suggest that the greater share of internal rate of return (IRR) from land primarily originates as financial income. This makes land a 'pure financial asset', assuming properties of what Marx termed as 'fictitious capital' where the return on land as an asset holding is remotely linked to its productive capacity. Like loanable funds, 'idle lands' are identified and allocated for higher profitability. The World Bank's discourse on yield gap in the context of agricultural production is the cardinal concept to define 'idle land'. The land which is cheap and unused, according to the buyer, is the source of livelihood for a farmer involving human attachment of sense of prestige and security. The non-capital space is forcefully invaded, farmland is commoditised and then its value is determined by market principles with some notion of fair price. In fact, the violence tends to subvert the fact that the entire transaction has been forcefully imposed, a caricature of market is played out where the buyer might be willing to buy the land while the seller is not. Another dimension to this process of financialisation of land has been viewed by some scholars, paraphrasing Arrighi's systemic cycles of accumulation, as returning back of investment to productive assets in the terminal phase of a *longue duree* accumulation cycle.[19] This is, of course, too early to empirically substantiate the point that investment flocking around real physical assets such as land is significant enough in signalling a terminal crisis of the current phase of capitalist accumulation.

The dominant *avatar* of land as a financial asset in India is the real estate. Since 1998, real estate has been included in the 'priority sector' list in Indian banks and lending to private developers was made easy by relaxing existing norms. While anticipating a housing bubble in the making, Reserve Bank of India prohibited banks to lend to developers to purchase land. Subsequently, banks increased the interest rate of lending to developers in 2006, but the booming middle class market, primarily driven by IT-BPO services, created a huge demand for real estate. Beginning from 2002, foreign investors were allowed to invest in real estate in India and the existing restrictions were further relaxed in 2005. Decline in asset prices in advanced economies, together with huge capital overhang, led international investors to search for high returns, but at the same time for risky ventures. In India during the 2000s, the average IRR

---

[19] Arrighi (2009).

in real estate was at least 20 per cent plus, which was higher than that accruing
in any other industry in India and also, higher than returns from American real
estate projects. For instance, DLF reported 35–40 per cent return in mid-market
residential projects and for luxury apartments, it goes up to 75 per cent. The
average cost of construction is roughly 20–40 per cent of the total project cost
and the labour cost is 10 per cent of the total construction cost. Protracted
agrarian distress and consequent shift of employment from agriculture to non-
agriculture, creating a huge number of vulnerable, cheap, migrant labour looking
for jobs in urban India was the source of low-cost labour supply in the construction
sector.[20]

However, this is only one part of the story. Foreign investors such as American
International Group, Carlyle Group, J P Morgan and Lehman Brothers are some
of the international players who invested in India's real estate. Apart from
building residential apartments and shopping malls, one of the major sources of
profit for investors derived from the first stage of real estate operation itself was
gains from changing the title and use of existing land. It involves speculative
knowledge, imagination, influence and intense assessment of future returns that
drive investors to enter into such ventures. An early bird in India's real estate
market, Trikona Trinity Capital PLC listed in the London Stock Exchange
Alternate Investment Market in 2006, reported a return in the range of 27–179
per cent in 11 of its 12 investment projects for the fiscal year 2007–08. But this
is how the broker state comes in aid to both domestic and foreign capital in the
process of land acquisition and in transforming land use to get a share of
speculative gains as revenue, together with illicit kickbacks for various layers of
bureaucracy and politicians. Michael Levien's study on Mahindra SEZ in
Rajasthan offers a telling story of expropriation which is not particular to
Rajasthan, but a general template of state–private nexus in the regime of
dispossession.[21] Levien defines the ratio of the land's sale price and the sum
of costs involved in acquisition and development of that land as the 'ratio of
dispossession'. As mentioned, according to law, only 50 per cent of the total land
acquired for SEZ needs to be used for industrial purposes, and in Mahindra
SEZ, the 'ratio of dispossession' for land put to use for industrial development
amounts to 253 per cent and that part which would be developed and sold as
luxury apartments amounts to 625 per cent. These figures simply reflect the fact
of huge gains made by private developers by taking advantage of land arbitrage
and, in this process, the broker state has a key role to play in using force to
dispossess people and vacate land identified for sale as well as in defining the

---

[20] Searle (2016).
[21] Levien (2011).

acquisition cost. It also suggests that the rate of return is much higher in real estate than in industrial activities which precisely explains the fact that only 34 per cent of land acquired as SEZs in India is used for industrial development.

Real estate business involves a detailed value chain involving government officials, bankers, contractors, developers, architects, lawyers, brokers and international property consultants. The new-age apartments are not only places to live, but it attaches prestige to the owner, defines a particular lifestyle and also works as investments for future returns. The task of the builder is not only to construct apartments, but to create a representation adequate to capture value at various levels. Critical anthropologists suggest that producers not only supply according to demand expressed in the market, but also reshape and construct new demands in capitalism, according to the global image of a particular lifestyle. It also syncs well with the triumphant 'India story' as a country of high growth emerging to be a 'super power', a perceived growth and a delusional representation of economic projections and forecasts through cumulative fetishisation is what defines 'value' in real estate.

Elizabeth Ferry[22] defines value as the politics of making and ranking differences and deciding what kind of differences are important. It is remaking of the social world that not only defines prices of objects, but assigns values that create demand for new markets. The bottom line of all these representations and communications is to define a prescribed path towards achieving global, middle class lifestyle and the inevitable convergence to such a reified future is what keeps the ball rolling. Hence, 'catch up' is the buzz word and the *mantra* is to sell an intense belief that India can and needs to achieve the level of per capita hotel rooms or shopping malls in the near future that had been possible in the US or the West. This defines the 'yield gap' once again in a different way and, therefore, tends to legitimise the accumulation by dispossession in the name of development. Therefore, a conflict arises between the concerns of the 'noisy' poor who are evicted and dispossessed from their livelihood and cannot understand what actually 'public purpose' means with the neo rich, professionals and growing middle class, aspiring for lifestyles that resemble that of global citizens.

## Development Discourse and Primitive Accumulation

Dispossession of people from land and livelihood is sometimes viewed as an unavoidable collateral damage necessary for the sake of common societal goal of industrialisation. The assumption behind such a linear progression is a teleology

---

[22] Ferry (2013).

that capitalist industrial growth and the necessary process of capital accumulation should drive this pre-decided path of progress and, therefore, agricultural transformation should fall in line accordingly. Instead of transforming rural spaces of developing countries by resolving the 'agrarian question', the problematic is often misconceived and telescoped as a process of de-peasantisation, a shift of population from agriculture to non-agriculture without being proletarianised as imagined in the charted path of capitalist development. The assumed trajectory is premised on the Eurocentric view that the Industrial Revolution in the West was preceded by an 'agricultural revolution' in eighteenth- and nineteenth-century Britain that supported the demands of wage goods and raw materials needed for industrialisation. It is posed as a smooth process of transition wherein agriculture-produced raw materials and food for workers shifted to industry and increased productivity attained endogenously could create surplus that contributed to capital accumulation for industrialisation. Utsa Patnaik[23] demolished this narrative of transition that consciously misinterprets history making invisible the realities of forcible transfer in the form of primitive accumulation that actually contributed to Britain's capital formation. The demands for industrial transition of the West were actually met by heavily taxed peasantry and plantation agriculture set up in subjugated colonies for supply of raw materials and wage goods. The agrarian regimes that developing countries were historically engaged with were largely fitted according to the needs of accumulation of the uneven and combined development of global capitalism. Philip McMichael identifies three different phases of agricultural regimes that catered to the needs of industrialisation.[24] The pre-World War I phase of free trade primarily linked peasant production of Americas, South Africa, Asia and Australia to the needs of European industrialisation through unequal exchange. The second phase during the post-Second World War was largely state-driven, agricultural regime in decolonised and newly independent countries. This is the period when state investment in infrastructure and technology as well as provisioning of credit and control in prices led to a growth which was aimed to generate surplus in agriculture for the purpose of industrialisation as the national goal. The trajectory of such a regime was, however, not entirely independent as might appear, but was conditioned by particular histories of countries as well as their position in the global division of labour.

The current phase emerges as the regime of petty commodity production, once again, subjected to primary accumulation of global capital mediated through global food chains. It is understandable how these different phases of agrarian

---

[23] U. Patnaik (2011, 2006).
[24] McMichael (2009).

regimes and the related class combinations led to an 'incomplete transition' towards capital relations in the country-side of developing countries. The crux of the 'agrarian question' is related to the progress of capital accumulation that is supposed to guarantee material prosperity of all rural classes. It should generate surplus through stratification of rural class and consequent exploitation of wage labour and transfer the accumulated surplus as a source of capital for industrial progress. But this assumed trajectory of agrarian transition has not been realised in India. In a neoliberal regime, the interlinkage between agriculture and industry has been further weakened. Importance of agriculture as domestic suppliers of raw materials for industry and food for workers declines in a globalised regime as cheap imports might substitute domestic supply. Also, accessibility of foreign capital reduces the need of surplus being generated and transferred from domestic agriculture. But neither did such inflow of capital lead to successful transformation of agriculture nor did it increase the material well-being of rural people. Moreover, services that seem to drive the growth of the economy in the current phase generally show a weak backward linkage with agriculture relative to a manufacturing-led growth path. With declining share in GDP and dwindling growth, India's agriculture is being characterised by persistent subsistence economy without having any endogenous dynamic of capital accumulation.[25] The rural poor primarily moved within the regime of dispossession from rural subsistent agriculture to precarious labour in the urban or rural non-farm informal activities. The dependence on remittance has increased for average rural households as people move out from their village, losing kinship ties and joining the non-farm labour force as 'semi-proletariat' or as migrant workers.

The feudal relations of production in rural India have been weakened not by some radical transformation, but largely because of technological intervention of the green revolution in the 1960s, price incentives, irrigation management and credit provisioning as well as demography and fragmentation of holdings over the years.[26] The productivity gains of the green revolution were exhausted by the end of the 1980s and cost of agricultural production increased because of increased use of chemicals and fertilisers and also due to retreating water tables particularly in areas dependent on ground water irrigation. On top of that, as a fallout of reforms, public investment in agriculture declined, incentive pricing has been rationalised and credit flows to agriculture fell substantially. All these made peasant agriculture unviable. The distribution of operational holdings and ownership is highly skewed and inequality in land ownership has increased with

---

[25] D'Costa and Chakraborty (2017).
[26] Harris (2013).

rising landlessness. Vikas Rawal,[27] using data from the 59th round of the National Sample Survey for 2003–04, estimated that 31 per cent of rural households across the country as a whole own no land at all, and another 30 per cent own less than 0.4 hectare (or about one acre), only a little over 5 per cent of households own more than three hectares and just 0.52 per cent own more than ten hectares of land. Findings of the Foundation for Agrarian Studies from village surveys in Andhra Pradesh, Uttar Pradesh and Maharashtra suggest it is difficult for households holding less than two hectares of land to earn enough income for their survival. In a more recent study, Arindam Banerjee[28] has shown that 86 per cent of agricultural households in India have negative or very little investment and their farm and non-farm incomes taken together mostly fall short of consumption expenses. Land as a factor of agricultural production has become increasingly unattractive, pushing the agenda of redistribution of land to the backseat, while returns by changing the use of land have become an important source of speculative gains. The rural rich is more dependent on businesses allied to agriculture such as fertiliser, seeds and other non-farm income related to construction and so on rather than relying on agricultural activities. Hence, surpluses being generated are also shifting to non-agricultural activities. Therefore, capital relations penetrate and dominate rural production relations in India, but could not resolve the agrarian question. On the other hand, as discussed earlier, state-sponsored land acquisition has not led to an increase in industrial activity. Rather, the gains of developers primarily accrue from real estate business instead of renting out for industrial sites. This brings us to the more important question of whether capitalism possesses the assumed historical features and capacities to transform economies towards surplus-generating activities and involves people released forcefully or gradually from agriculture toward productive employment. In this context, we would once again revisit the Marxian notion of primitive accumulation. A process by which means of production and livelihood are forcefully transferred into capital by way of separating direct producers from their land, absorbing released labour from agriculture as workers in factories and, hence, also making them dependent on the market for consumption needs. This Marxian notion of rise of original capital is often misread as an inevitable violence, 'necessary' for the sake of capitalist progress. Major debates on India's industrialisation, land acquisition and consequent dispossession often invoke this element of inevitability some way or the other.

Capital relation in Marx is entirely different from the classical notion of 'accumulation of stocks' seen as vector of things used for productive activity. In

---

[27] Rawal (2008); Ramachandran and Rawal (2010).
[28] Banerjee (2017).

Marx, capital signifies a social relation of separation of direct producers from the means of production. This process of separation can take various forms, can be actualised through violence or can also be mediated through the legal, political and ideological structures as an accepted, regularised discipline. In *Capital I*, the chapters narrating the 'so-called primitive accumulation of capital' foregrounds a process of separation that involves non-economic interventions by the state, 'the enclosure', the creation of pastures expropriating producers from common property land. Marx was resolving the infinite regress, identifying the creation of original capital from where accumulation begins, a moment of original wealth coming in contact with people who have nothing to offer but their labour power. Adam Smith's explanation of this 'original sin' invokes differences in moral and human behaviour, distinguishing between people who are diligent, intelligent and eager to save and those who are lazy and spend what they earn. The first group of people, because of their thrift and hard work, eventually emerged as capital owners. Marx was critical about this behavioural prognosis saying, 'The legend of theological original sin tells us certainly how man came to be condemned to eat his bread by the sweat of his brow; but the history of economic original sin reveals to us that there are people to whom this is by no means essential. Never mind! Thus, it came to pass that the former sort accumulated wealth, and the latter sort finally had nothing to sell except their own skins.'[29] It seems that the inauguration of capital relations in classical theory, the 'previous accumulation' in Adam Smith is a 'blind spot'. It is an invisible moment, but a moment that can only be appreciated as something positive, giving rise to capitalism and, hence, the emergence had to be sought from some good human qualities or moral values.

In Marx, primitive accumulation is an act of violence, a destruction of existing property relations, a moment of redefining a new ensemble of relations that normalise the act of violence. It is the process of creating capital by expropriation of resources from direct producers, a forcible process of creating labour, where the subjective being, the human subjectivity, is objectified as a parcel of labour power. It is actualised by the predominance of a particular social mediation, namely, market, production of commodities and exchange values as the defining mode of societal interaction. But this creation of capital relation and the reproduction of capital and labour might not be a one-shot game. Neither can it be seen as a designed sequence of events, happening one after another or simultaneously happening as necessities coming together, giving rise to a new order. The separation once created forcibly has to be normalised and made invisible. People expropriated from land, according to Marx, were not immediately

---

[29] Marx (1958: 713).

transformed into workers for capitalist factories.[30] It had to be executed by 'bloody legislations',[31] a legal structure of enforcement, defining discipline of the new order and gradually, politically and ideologically, passed into the silent rules of exploitation. The separation is reproduced in an expanded scale in the regular functioning of capitalism, the act of violence is internalised within the objective laws of the system and, hence, become invisible. Therefore in Marx, primitive accumulation of capital is not a moment of pre-history, but a continuous process of redefining norms by capital to overcome its own limits. It is about continuously creating new enclosures when augmentation of capital within the existing norms faces challenges from its own boundaries. The ensemble of various processes which have their own independent history creates the moment of 'encounter', a condensation and mutual constitutivity that defines the new norm.[32] As a result, what is encroachment, expropriation, loot or plunder according to the existing rules, appears to be a norm accepted by consent in the new regime and the violence gets buried into the newly created objectivity.

The problem which is of immediate relevance in the current context of land acquisition in India, is that here we come across a conjuncture where primitive accumulation occurs through separation of land from the direct producers. The land is being capitalised, but the process of capitalist profit-making does not absorb the dispossessed peasants as workers. In other words, the current phase of primitive accumulation results in de-peasantisation together with incomplete proletarianisation. Whether it is done by force, as in most of the cases of land acquisition in India may suggest,[33] or without explicit application of force by silently changing the rules of the game and enfeebling peasant cultivation as a protracted process of primitive accumulation, the dispossessed people are not immediately turned into wage labour. In fact, the inauguration of capital relations that transforms collective properties and peasant cultivation into self-augmenting capital and erstwhile peasants into wage-labourers might be two completely separate processes divided in space and time. It need not be the case and had not been so earlier as well that people disposed were immediately absorbed as wage

---

[30] 'First of all, in Western Europe, the death of communal property [and the emergence] and the birth of capitalist production are separated by a [centuries-long] huge interval which covers a whole series of successive economic revolutions and evolutions, [The death of communal property did not give birth to capitalist production,] of which capitalist production is but [the last] the most recent.' 'The "Second" Draft', Marx-Zasulich Correspondence February/March 1881, available at https://www.marxists.org/archive/marx/works/1881/zasulich/draft-2.htm (accessed 11 March 2019).

[31] Marx (1958: ch. 28, p. 734).

[32] Read (2002).

[33] Levien (2015).

labour in capitalist factories. The becoming of capitalism is a protracted process acquiring systemic features where every relation is the presupposition of the other and this episode of emergence and reproduction of capital relations would not be the same in all countries.

Marx was careful in acknowledging the heterogeneity that existed across societies and restricted his generalisation of 'enclosure' and expropriation as final form in reference to England alone.[34] In his later writings and correspondences with Russian scholars, he was conscious about various collective forms of property existing in Russia, was aware of the realities of peasant and Cossack communes that covered three-fifths of arable land in European Russia.[35] In his later writings, particularly his correspondence with Vera Zasulich, Marx's position was close to the populists of Russia and Marx did not argue that common properties are archaic in form and need to be displaced for the sake of capitalist development as it happened in Western Europe. Marx was of the view that in case of Russia, it is not a transformation from one private property to another, but a common property existing and surviving, and denounced the argument of 'historical inevitability' of the annihilation of the commune as propounded by Russian Marxists. Therefore, Marx never saw primitive accumulation of capital as a brutal necessity for the progress of human civilisation as it is often narrated in evolutionary linear interpretations of history.[36]

Primitive accumulation, as conceived by Marx, and its later incarnations that emerged in the context of contemporary capitalism by Marxist scholarship of our time, addresses the critical engagement of capital and non-capital in concrete contexts which help capital accumulation in overcoming its existing barriers. Starting from Rosa Luxemburg's critique of Marx's expanded reproduction[37] and her proposition of the perpetual necessity of the periphery to realise the surplus produced at the core to contemporary versions of 'accumulation by dispossession' by David Harvey, 'accumulation by displacement' by Farshad Araghi and Prabhat Patnaik's 'accumulation through encroachment', through

---

[34] 'In discussing the genesis of capitalist production, I said [that the secret is that there is at bottom 'a complete separation of ... the producer from the means of production' (p. 315, column 1, French edition of *Capital*) and that '*the expropriation of the agricultural producer* is the basis of the whole process. Only in England has it been so far accomplished in a radical manner.... *But all the other countries of Western Europe* are following the same course'. Cited in 'The "First" Draft', Marx-Zasulich Correspondence February/March 1881 available at https://www.marxists.org/archive/marx/works/1881/zasulich/draft-1.htm (accessed 11 March 2019).

[35] Shanin (1983).

[36] See Chakrabarti, Cullenberg and Dhar (2017).

[37] Luxemberg (1951).

different routes of analyses, underline the importance of altering existing property rights and engulfing the non-capital space as a necessary requirement for capitalist accumulation to continue. In David Harvey, the notion of 'accumulation by dispossession' seems to encompass all dimensions of change in property rights and norms facilitated by financialisation and neoliberalism. Therefore, it includes a non-exhaustive list of activities related to predatory, speculative ventures, stock promotions, Ponzi schemes, asset destruction through inflation, asset-stripping through merger and acquisitions, debt peonage and corporate fraud, credit and stock manipulations, privatisation of pension funds, emphasis on intellectual property rights, patenting and licensing of generic material, seed plasma, biopiracy and depletion of global commons, privatisation of water and public utilities, commodification of cultural forms, histories and intellectual creativity.[38] This wide range of *modus operandi*, as discussed by Harvey, makes the notion of 'accumulation by dispossession' somehow diffused into everything under the sky in neoliberalism, but the crux of the argument seems to be the following. Overaccumulated capital needs fresh release of assets including labour power at very low or zero cost which could displace the crisis of overaccumulation by reducing input costs. Therefore, the broad idea is a new wave of enclosing the commons: 'Assets held by the state or in common were released into the market where over accumulating capital could invest in them, upgrade them and speculate in them'.[39] The 'other' in this case is not pre-fixed as the 'outside' of the closed system of capitalism and gradually get internalised, as Luxemburg argued, but the other is also created by the same process that usurps non-capital. Patnaik's 'accumulation through encroachment' integrates the subversion of 'non-capital' as well as other capital blocs in the hierarchy of uneven development as a process of containing the supply price of inputs required for capitalist accumulation at the core.[40] It is income deflation articulated through squeezing out agriculture, reducing government expenditure, de-industrialisation, net-unemployment generating structural change and secular shift in terms of trade against petty producers of primary commodities that characterise encroachment. Farshad Araghi's notion of 'accumulation by displacement' expands the scope of capital–non-capital relation by defining it as a process of accumulation, dependent on under-reproduction of labour and ecology where labour and its 'inorganic body' nature is being appropriated as surplus labour and surplus nature. It is once again an encroachment and curtailment of the necessary

---

[38] Harvey (2003).
[39] Ibid., 158.
[40] P. Patnaik (2008a).

and, hence, redefining the boundaries of 'necessary' and 'surplus', both in terms of labour and nature.[41]

Primitive accumulation in all the aforementioned analyses, despite their differences in conceptualisation, refers to a process of redefining the rules of 'silent exploitation' through expropriation and violence. It is a continuous process of encroaching commons when the existing forms of capital accumulation through expanded reproduction faces its own limits. Given the peculiarity of capitalist accumulation in the neoliberal regime where appropriation of surplus is largely mediated through finance, with rising competition between capitals and introduction of new technology increasingly replacing labour, absorption of dispossessed people as workers shows up as a remote possibility. But this does not, however, mean that increasing number of people who have nothing to sell, but their labour power or the expansion of relative overpopulation, is completely delinked from the process of capitalist accumulation as Kalyan Sanyal had suggested in his characterisation of the 'need economy'. The process of dispossession facilitates a huge supply of de-proletarianised, vulnerable, migrant labour which is the major absorber of income deflation or 'forced underconsumption' that facilitates capitalist accumulation. Sanyal grossly generalised the huge segment of unprotected labour and petty producers as delinked from the accumulation process, as part of the undifferentiated 'need economy' that clings to 'accumulation economy' as an appendage sustained through transfers of surplus. The sustenance of such a huge segment of non-capital in the post-colonial context is explained by the need for maintaining political stability of the system which is unavoidable for capital because of the exclusionary nature of capitalist accumulation.

In fact, the degree of absorption of labour in the core of capitalism depends on the conjectural nature of capitalist accumulation. By the end of the eighteenth century, the destruction of petty production and introduction of new machines created a huge mass of unemployment in Britain and these dispossessed people were not absorbed as workers in the domestic capitalist sectors of the metropolitan countries. Amiya Kumar Bagchi[42] had shown long back that immediately after the Napoleonic Wars, there was a simultaneous flow of mainly British capital and labour to other European countries and to new, White settlements as a process of diffusion of capitalism. During the nineteenth and twentieth centuries, there was huge migration from Europe to North America, Australia, New Zealand, Argentina and Brazil. In fact, this was part of the process of capitalist growth in White colonies that absorbed labour from Europe and, at the same time, was

---

[41] Araghi (2009).
[42] Bagchi (1972) and also see U. Patnaik (2012).

funded by transfer of surplus from non-White colonies. In the current context, given the backdrop of heightened capital intensity, on the one hand, and financialisation on the other, such an option of displacing the unemployment problem to distant new-found lands is no longer there. Therefore, perceiving land acquisition and related dispossession as the harbinger of capitalist development with people being absorbed as workers in factories is a chimera. Capitalism survives on the forced underconsumption and pauperisation of the huge mass of working people and Marx did not ever see the advent of capitalism as a moment of progress to be celebrated, as teleological interpretations would like to suggest. On the contrary, in his discussion on primitive accumulation, the narrative is the brutality that associates with the rise of capital relations. As he says, 'capital comes dripping from head to foot, from every pore, with blood and dirt'.[43]

---

[43] Marx (1958: 760).

# 9

# Decoding Resistance and Class Formation in the Neoliberal Regime

Appropriation of 'fictitious commodity' labour is the terrain of contestation between labour and capital throughout the history of capitalism. Labour is not produced for sale and, hence, marketisation of labour power entails a 'double movement' of reclaiming the social substance in the Polanyian sense. The conflict between labour and capital is mediated through complex processes and multiple identities, the degrees of resistance and its articulation take various forms depending on particular contexts and histories. Nevertheless, capital is not the sole author of history, as it appears to be, as if the labour passively responds to capital's domination for the sake of survival. Instead, history has also shown that cycles of crisis, either of profitability or that of legitimacy, prompted structural changes in capitalism which are primarily responses to the way labour impacted capital. Moments of crisis in capitalism are, therefore, always preceded by high tides of labour resistance, and if it does not lead to a radical rupture, it would necessarily be followed by the introduction of new dimensions of technology or labour arrangements that ultimately empower capital. In the current phase of globalisation, there is hardly any doubt that as global capital gets access to global labour reserve, the bargaining power of labour declines drastically. Neoliberal regime and the resulting withdrawal of the state from the economy is essentially supplemented by a conscious effort to intervene and create market society. It is an intervention on the part of the state to dislodge the social compact once capital had to live with during the Golden Age of capitalism, accepting institutions that de-commodify labour to some extent. The retreat of labour in the twenty-first century is effected through contradictory tendencies in the sphere of production. On the one hand, concentration in ownership was effected through mergers and acquisitions within the North and, on the other, global assembly line involves low-wage workers of the South in a de-centred network of outsourcing and subcontracting. The emergent structural divide between the stable working class and the overwhelming majority of precarious labour demands a relook at the idioms of resistance.

The diffusion of production and increased fragmentation of labour defines the new regime of capitalist accumulation which not only involves changes in the production process, but also in the reproduction of labour power. Boundaries between spaces of production and consumption and that between working time and disposable lifetime are increasingly fading out. Labour time approximates lifetime and individual capacities are largely subsumed to social labour. The decomposition of capital–labour relations, once embedded in the Fordist–Keynesian regime of accumulation, gives rise to an amorphous mass of working people with respect to which organised labour and its political representations hardly seem to be a force to reckon with. Class becomes apparently invisible and the politics of resistance seems to be increasingly muted to sporadic resentments. Labour is heterogeneous and, particularly in developing countries, the vast majority of working people including peasantry are involved in multiple occupations with varying interests which do not necessarily get subsumed into a single class identity. The vast majority of workforce today manifest precarious forms of unwaged labour which does not work under a defined employer and mass resentments voice issues of civic rights and other entitlements targeted at the state instead of being confined to wage-related issues. Sometimes, voices heard resemble a plebeian uproar rather than working class resistance and the 'worker' seems to be increasingly diffused into the nebulous space of citizen or a consumer.

Paradoxically, growing inequality in the current process of globalisation is far better captured by the notion of class than that of other social constructs. The distance between segments of people within a country has increased farther than between nations, but the articulation of discontent was hardly manifested in conventional class lines. In fact, the multiplicity of political contestations and the construction of the 'people' is increasingly emerging to be a dynamic and volatile process which can be used to mute resistance into some form of negotiable resentment. In this chapter, we dwell on the labour–capital conflict in the context of value capture articulated by capital at different levels. The onslaught on labour is linked to the specificity of the accumulation regime that tends to individuate labour, denounces collective identity, diffuses antagonism and creates an amorphous mass, such that resistance can be manipulated in the guise of 'populism'. Irreducible differences in identities are celebrated, nurtured and calibrated and, sometimes, stitched into a discursive space where primacy of individual freedom weakens the collective challenge to capital.

## Capital–Labour Relations in Globalisation

Eric Hobsbawm's Marx memorial lecture in 1978 was titled 'The Forward March of Labour Halted?'[44] The title ended with a question mark, not a final

---

[44] Hobsbawm (1978).

statement of conclusion but an apprehension based on observing the rise and decline of the working-class century. It is in the twentieth century, the century of the working class, when for the first time in history working people who were not owners of properties became a major political force. Scrolling through the century in the context of Britain, Hobsbawm's essay delineates the rise and fall of working-class politics. It was primarily about the sheer rise in the numerical strength of manual workers who constituted the larger section of the population. A high proportion of these workers, however, did not mean a homogeneous workforce but manifested a common culture and style of life – the rise of football as a mass proletarian sport and the ubiquitous fish-and-chip shops were some of the signifiers representing working-class life. Workers became heroes and models in cultural imageries and every political philosophy spanning from liberalism to fascism, in some way or the other, had to articulate political programmes addressing working class issues. The changes that Hobsbawm identified at the latter part of the century in the context of British labour are familiar features in the present context of developing countries. There has been a rise in the proportion of proletariats in the strict sense of the term, meaning the number of people who survive simply by selling skilled or unskilled labour, using different degrees of brains and brawns. However, the proportion of manual workers in the increased proletarian workforce has declined. The link between growth of output and employment has weakened, together with a rise in tertiary employment and the gap between different strata of working class increased. This may not be explained by their relative position in the technical ladder, but depends on many other factors which are beyond the realm of trade union control. Furthermore, there has been a continuous process of shifting skills from human beings to machines, increased substitution of skilled labour by relatively unskilled ones, resulting in a decline in the autonomy of the worker. The decline and disillusionment of working-class dominance in polity, however, could not erase the long-lasting effect of democracy that emerged in modern times as the universal model of organising politics and society. While commenting on the halt, Hobsbawm did not see this decline as inevitable, instead reiterating Marx that men make their history within the limits of circumstances that they face but it is human agency that makes history and it is never predestined. Even in the midst of the great capitalist boom during the 1960s, the working class could pose a serious challenge to capital with resumed growth of trade unions, sharp rise in labour votes and radicalisation of students.

The retreat which Hobsbawm perceived way back in the 1970s seems to be the hallmark of capital's ascendancy with the onset of globalisation. The 1970s mark the high point of the labour movement, union organisation and militancy in the global stage that was perhaps the precursor of the long retreat. Globalisation signifies capital's assault on labour often camouflaged in the garb of the neutral term 'competition'. This is the third phase of globalisation which is far more interpenetrative than the earlier phases. Production structures involve arms-length outsourcing and subcontracting in the low-wage South.[45] Roughly 60 per cent of gross exports accounts for intermediate goods and we increasingly perceive a global assembly line channelled through FDI or direct subcontracting. Free movement of capital, together with restrictions in the global movement of labour, allows differential labour regimes to exist within national boundaries which, in turn, allows substitution of similarly skilled workers by way of shifting production from high-wage to low-wage segments. In other words, labour arbitrage becomes possible as global capital gets access to global disposable labour. However, as developed countries de-industrialise with the declining share of manual workers, Marx's Little Dialectic of workers gaining strength with capitalist development and emerging as a challenger did not seem to materialise.

In the South, increased participation of labour in global production structures is coupled with massive outsourcing and subcontracting that allows bypassing of existing institutions of protecting labour rights. The bargaining power of workers, as defined by Eric Olin Wright, can be of two broad types: associational and structural.[46] Associational power consists of various forms of collective power such as trade unions or political parties and structural power relates to particularities of the labour market or strategic position of workers within the production structure. A tight labour market, acquiring some specific skills or alternative sources of non-wage income, increases the market bargaining power of workers. Strategic position of workers in a larger production process might increase the strength of the workers since a localised stoppage would jeopardise the entire production structure. Globalisation has affected all these dimensions of the bargaining power of workers. Access to global disposable labour sharply reduced the marketplace bargaining power of workers. In addition to that, increased privatisation and marketisation of agriculture and manufacturing shrunk access to community sources of income. Strategic position of workers in an integrated production structure leads to workplace bargaining power. This has been weakened by capital's technological fix, characterised by 'post-Fordist' production processes. Malleable technologies and multitasking allow low average costs at a smaller scale of operation and production increasingly becomes a network of temporary and cursory relationships that subvert the strategic position of the worker. Some, however, have argued that the decline of labour is not much about the structural transformations in the production process but rather because of a

---

[45] J. Smith (2016).
[46] Wright (2000).

discursive shift that punctured the century-old belief of working-class power.[47] The relation between labour and capital is essentially political. This political contestation is often reified by the 'phantom of objectivity' as if the spontaneity of competition gives rise to technological change that has nothing to do with power relations.[48] In fact, a political reading of Marx's *Capital* allows us to see how production structure from handicrafts to factory and machinofacture changed as a means to curb the bargaining power of workers. Marx read this change as a response of capital to workers' resistance to exploitation at the point of production. But as the production process changes, workers' power, although temporarily undermined, bounces back with new forms having larger disruptive power in terms of scale and scope. In a similar vein, capital's response to crisis, either of profitability or that of legitimacy, has been a reorganisation of production.[49]

The reorganisation of the production process as a response to the crisis of profitability changed the world of work in the twenty-first century. Proletarian mass constitutes two broad categories and the distinction is evident in both the developed and the developing world. The relatively small portion of the workforce comprises workers who have acquired certain professional skills and a secure job, fetching wages and emoluments capable of meeting reasonably decent living standards. They are endowed with certain rights that allow associational bargaining power or trade union participation and also some social security benefits. A small portion of this workforce can overcome the restrictions of global mobility of labour through their professional qualities and are endowed with bargaining power even at the individual level because of their marketable skills.

The vast majority of the workforce that comprises roughly 40 per cent of the popular classes in the developed countries and 80 per cent of that in the developing world are mostly low-skilled, low-waged or non-waged workers. These workers have very weak bargaining power, hardly any institutional protection of wages or social security, extremely vulnerable in terms of employment conditions and often without any political voice. Samir Amin qualified these two categories as 'stable' and 'precarious' forms of labour, signifying the great divide of the twenty-first-century working class.[50] The majority of the workforce, this precarious labour, is not at all redundant in the process of capitalist accumulation, but often politically marginalised. Increase in outsourcing at the global and local level, various forms of subcontracting, increased recourse to casualisation and home-based work constitutes this

---

[47] Piven and Cloward (2000).
[48] For a detailed discussion, see Lucaks (1975).
[49] Silver (2003).
[50] Amin (2008).

precarious segment, a significant part being wageless labour. The change is caused by capital's assault on labour, redefining the composition of workforce, fragmenting and segmenting them through creating new hierarchies. This has been the usual strategy of capital when it faces a crisis. When Marx talked about 'abstract' labour, he did not mean this abstraction as a thought process, a conceptual category required to explain a theoretical construct. Rather, this abstraction takes place in the concrete form of exchange. Capitalism requires to homogenise the particular concrete forms of labour and their use values into exchange values and, finally, into the general form of value. The chain of equivalence, on the other hand, is problematic for capitalism because it gives rise to a discursive space where different categories of working people exchange and negotiate their interests through a shared experience against capital. Capital, being a social relation, reproduces class domination and that is not only manifested in terms of wage compression within the factory, but also includes other dimensions of exploitation, oppressions and subordinations that feed into the social configuration of capital as a totality.[51]

The neoliberal age signifies a different phase of capitalist accumulation. Michael Aglietta defined a new phase of capitalist regulation when the accumulation of capital finds its content no longer simply in a transformation of the reproduction of the labour process, but above all, in a transformation of the reproduction of the labour power.[52] It is not only about changing the organisation of production, but also reconstructing the structure of reproduction of labour power. The precarious form of labour which is predominant in today's world of work essentially explodes the notion of 'working day' which was a result of protracted class war. The concrete division of labour time between 'necessary', 'surplus' and 'free lifetime' is jeopardised. In other words, the idea of 'labour power' being sold for a defined portion of the day, distinct from disposable time, which is termed as 'leisure' or 'unproductive' according to capital, no longer exists for the vast majority of the workforce. The assembly line, in fact, is stretched out to the household and not limited to the premise of factory. It is more of a decentred network of production where capitalist relations emerge as something like a universal imperative. The other way is to confine labour into factory campuses where life time of the labour is appropriated as work time. It is the rise of the 'social factory' where the realm of production and that of reproduction comes close to each other.[53] The production process, in that way, is increasingly socialised. Labour becomes social labour and the general appropriation of

---

[51] For a detailed discussion, see Roy (2019b).
[52] Aglietta (2000).
[53] For a detailed discussion, see Negri (1991, 1988).

productive power becomes more important compared to the skill of individual labour. Antonio Negri argues that the diffusion of the 'normal' working day unsettles the value calculus based on individual labour power:

> The time of social labour power is a working day so extended as not only to comprise within itself the relation between production time and reproduction time, as a single whole, but also and above all to extend the consideration of time over the entire life-space of the labour market.[54]

The diffusion of factory, stretching the global assembly line to the poor households of the South, blurs the distinction between the sphere of production and reproduction. The boundaries of working day become meaningless to the vast section of precarious labour and, with the rise of social labour, the image of the unionised worker with institutional protections of job and related stability begins to resemble a new labour aristocracy. Neoliberalism and dismantling of institutions that protected labour rights is a process of mainstreaming the so-called informal labour. And the discourse on 'formal' upon which the notion of informality is predicated allows the state to politically marginalise the majority workforce and deprive them of the rights which are posed as 'privileges' attributable to the formal workforce. The empirical category of factory and the factoryst definition of worker, however, overwhelmed the notion of proletariat, making it synonymous with the imagery of a factory worker. But the rise of factory and the image of a typical worker, defined by certain rights and entitlements, is essentially a social historical construct. The post-War changes in capitalist production structure, which was dependent on large factories, reduced the autonomy of the individual worker to a great extent. Assembly lines homogenised workers and created stable hierarchies within them.

Furthermore, the Fordist structure of production, together with mass consumption, was supported by Keynesian policies that sought to resolve issues of conflict through the entire span of production and circulation. The Keynesian theory of involuntary unemployment was premised on the acknowledgement of downward rigidity of wages and, hence, accepting working class as a counter pole, that the dynamics of capitalist accumulation has to live with. The resolve was sought as an economy-wide intervention instead of viewing it as a capital–labour power conflict confined to a particular enterprise. It was essentially a class response which was forced upon the capitalist class to recompose the command structure, effective both in the sphere of production and in the larger societal space. The social democratic normalisation of the factory worker was useful for

---

[54] Negri (1988: 110).

capitalism to contain the spectre of informality. In fact, the precarious forms of work which have become so endemic today existed throughout the entire history of capitalist development, but it was invisible and unheard of in the narrative of 'capitalism' idealised in the context of the metropolitan North. In that way, the factory worker, the masculine protagonist of a collective voice, captured the image of the working class of the last century. Collective bargaining for wages and other benefits through trade unions and other institutions used to be the axis of working-class resistance. In today's world of work, capital's response to the emergent social labour is altogether different. It is an annihilation of the 'social' labour through a continuous process of individualising and atomising the labour force. The working class is ripped off its institutional voice, trade unions no longer represent the majority of the labouring class and the political centrality of organised labour has indubitably diminished.

## Resistance and Class Formation

In the backdrop of a visible decline of working-class politics, both in terms of trade unions and of political representations, we envisage two important trends in the realm of resistance. The universal project of emancipation led by the proletariat of the twentieth century appears to be replaced by a politics of aspiration and articulation of resentment by the middle class. Middle class, as many scholars see it, is a sociological category, a construct that goes beyond economic parameters. It is about an assertive imagery of an individual who is an aspirational consumer and, at the same time, a responsible citizen who is energetic enough to vent his or her resentment against unfulfilled aspirations. Therborn (2012) aptly captures the aspiration of the emerging middle class:

> The core of this utopia is a dream of boundless consumption, of a middle class taking possession of the earth, buying cars, houses and limitless variety of electronic goods and sustaining a global tourist industry. But at the same time.... Middle class consumption also has the great advantage of accommodating the privileges of the rich while supplying a quiescent horizon of aspiration to the popular classes.[55]

Their position vis-à-vis state policies and democracy has always been highly situational and opportunistic. Any of the sensational upsurges in India and abroad that have shaken the middle class in recent times, however, did not intend to pose any fundamental challenge to the neoliberal regime.

---

[55] Therborn (2012: 17).

The second, and perhaps a deeper challenge to working-class politics, is the emergence of 'neo-populism' as a popular articulation of the plebeian voice. Populism in its classical form emerged in the 1930s in Latin America when the agro-export-led economy was turning towards policies of import-substitution. The traditional forms of oligarchy were gradually getting displaced by a multi-class alliance in the early phase of industrialisation. In the 1980s, debt crisis and economic austerity followed by structural reforms increasingly contracted the space of fiscal populism. But there again, since the mid-1990s, a new version of populism emerged in Peru, Brazil and Equador which coincided with the neoliberal regime. Despite differences in contexts, populism, as it is broadly defined, bears a common thread cutting across its old and new versions.[56] It is a 'top-down' process of political mobilisation where a charismatic leader establishes a direct, unmediated relationship with the unorganised mass of people. It is embedded in a reciprocal relationship where immediate benefits given to the people create effective claims for political support. It thrives on the backdrop of weakening of political institutions and party system of loyalty and representation together with fragmentation of the civil society. Selective targeting of sections of the popular mass works in both ways. Universal rights and expansion of entitlements are constrained by the neoliberal mandate of fiscal responsibility. But using the available fiscal space to cater to the needs of shifting sections of popular masses are much more visible and, hence, produce huge political returns. A paternalistic structure that never challenges the neoliberal regime, often using the 'politics of apolitics' or the image of 'leader from within', grows with increased social atomisation. The functional need of political organisation declines and is often consciously curtailed with a view that a party structure tends to reduce the leader's autonomy. Televised interactions and opinion surveys as modes of direct communication and responses overtake organisational structures, as the politics of neo-populism hardly promises any challenge to the entrenched power structures. Neoliberalism and populism reinforce each other in de-institutionalising labour rights, and contribute in fragmenting, segmenting and individuating the working poor. Increase in direct bargaining power vis-à-vis the state as perceived by the subaltern comes under siege with rising authoritarianism and denial of democratic rights, and the art of manoeuvring popular electoral support gradually domesticates the working mass and derails the art of insurrection. Politics of neo-populism in its various shades largely depends on mobilising support from the subaltern, the amorphous mass of working poor who spill over boundaries of class. Rina Agarwala discusses how, in the Indian context, informal labour negotiates with the state in realising welfare demands and how the worker identity

---

[56] Roberts (1995).

is increasingly replaced by the politics of welfare, largely relying on the basis of citizenship.[57]

The factoryst notion of proletariat had been predominant among the political left which often leads to abandoning the rest of the working people as *lumpenproletariat*, denouncing them as the 'social scum', 'rotten lower strata', 'the mob', 'the dangerous class', and so on, as it appeared in *The Communist Manifesto* and other Marxist literature. In fact, before Marx, proletariat was also synonymous with the poor, ragpickers and nomads.[58] Marx wanted to make a distinction between the agents of social change between proletariat and the lumpenproletariat who are the 'refuse of all classes' and immune to historical transformation. In the *Eighteenth Brumaire*, Marx was keen to identify this social group that went with the coup of Louis Bonapart.

> Alongside decayed *roues* with dubious means of subsistence and of dubious origin, alongside ruined and adventurous offshoots of the bourgeoisie, were vagabonds, discharged soldiers, discharged jailbirds, escaped galley slaves, swindlers, mountebanks, *lazzaroni*, pickpockets, tricksters, gamblers, *maquereaus*, brothel keepers, porters, literati, organgrinders, ragpickers, knife grinders, tinkers, beggars – in short, the whole indefinite, disintegrated mass, thrown hither and thither, which the French term *la boheme*.[59]

This is a group of people largely 'parasitic' and cannot be defined by particular relational position in terms of historical or production relations. One can easily make out that today's working class, which includes heterogeneous forms of waged and non-waged workers, are very much integrated with the production process and hardly resemble the lumpens that Marx was referring to. The other intention of Marx to distinguish and construct the category of proletariat as a collective agency was to reverse the bourgeoisie logic of calling the working class as a parasitic rotten mass, instead proving the whole society being parasitic on their labour. In this context, the proletariat was distinct from the 'refuse of all classes'. The distinction was also made to contest Bakunin's position who held that the outlaw, criminal and the bandits are the real revolutionary forces. The characterisation of lumpenproletariat in Marx, therefore, was largely pathological and contingent upon particular historical context. At the same time, it was viewed as amorphous and volatile, difficult to be defined by a concrete historical process. It is an unnamed class which is amenable to political articulation. The 'political' is the field within which the social groups are shaped by institutions,

---

[57] Agarwala (2013).
[58] See Stallybrass (1990).
[59] Marx (1937 [1852]: 38).

norms, culture and ideology. And this was aptly captured in Fanon's *The Wretched of the Earth*. 'The lumpen proletariat once it is constituted brings all its forces to endanger the security of the town and it is the sign of the irrevocable decay, the gangrene ever-present at the heart of colonial domination.'[60]

Fanon discusses how this 'horde of rats' were used by the colonial oppressors in Algeria, Angola and Congo, how colonialism finds in the lumpenproletariat a considerable space of manoeuvring. And, therefore, instead of abandoning this class as prone to reactionaries, Fanon suggests that progressive movements should pay fullest attention to this amorphous mass. The political has to assert instead of assuming a predisposition of this heterogeneous mass to reactionary forces. And the making of a class is never predetermined. Rather, it is a conscious political process that eschews reactionary tendencies, and gives rise to a collective hegemonic project which emerges to be the beacon of all excluded and exploited.

> So the pimps, the hooligans, the unemployed, and the petty criminals when approached, give the liberation struggle all they have got, devoting themselves to the cause like valiant workers.... These jobless, these species of subhumans, redeem themselves in their own eyes and before history. The prostitutes too, the domestics at two thousand francs a month, the hopeless cases, all those men and women who fluctuate between madness and suicide, are restored to sanity, return to action and take their vital place in the great march of a nation on the move.[61]

'People' is a political construct and the construction of populism by right-wing combinations invokes a mobilisation against the bureaucratic state, suggesting a separation of political system from society, functioning of the economy through experts and without any public debate, emphasises democracy as a celebration of difference and liberty, rather than a homogenising process of generating collective will. Radical resistance to capital, on the contrary, is a construction of people of diverse occupations attached to different vintages of capital relations. The working class has been heterogeneous and E. P. Thompson's *Making of the English Working Class* provides a graphic analyses how dispersed groups of working people with their radical populism and Jacobin agitations of the eighteenth century emerged to be a class-conscious group in nineteenth-century Britain.[62] The radical insurgencies of working people in the 1790s in Britain were largely motivated by the French Revolution which was ruthlessly

---

[60] Fanon (2004: 81).
[61] Ibid., 81–82.
[62] Thompson (1963).

crushed by the ruling class and, later on, was diverted to religious lines by Methodism and also into middle class-led constitutional radicalism. The radical and democratic sense, however, spread deep roots on working people and, with the advent of the industrial revolution, the shared experience of dehumanisation of production, moral and social degradation and immiseration with rising conflicts brought together diverse groups of working people making them see as a class in opposition to the capitalists. Resistance had been multidimensional; sometimes artisans had been radically against capitalism – they had a social base while the industrial proletariat, although relatively small in number, confronted capital within the ambit of new industrial relations. What is important is a discursive space, a social premise that legitimises the idea of equality and dignity of human beings and then a political process that makes multiple conflicts share a common cause.

Globalisation has created enormous opportunity for capital to create, access and reproduce heterogeneity in the labour market. There are workers who have stable jobs; others are employed in precarious modes for whom 'working day' has no particular meaning, work time and life time overlap and the space for disposable time shrinks to a minimum. This segment also includes the unemployed, the spectacular redundant 'waste labour' of post-colonial capitalism that could not be shifted to new-found lands or could be absorbed by a protracted process of labour-intensive industrialisation as it happened in the case of Europe. They are worse off in capitalism for not being exploited! But this heterogeneity, which capital tends to create within the working class either by legal structures, social norms, culture, and so on, to confront the homogenising tendency of its own dynamics is what is realised in the 'social'. It is also the space of creative politics where exclusion, exploitation and oppression mingle with concrete determinations. Within the factory, the worker fights to increase emoluments, a struggle to increase the value of labour power, the 'necessary' labour time, equivalent to the value of goods and services considered to be necessary in maintaining a continuous supply of labour. However, the notion of 'necessary' in capitalism does not invoke any moral or ethical point of view. Maintaining of labour, instead, is only necessary because labour produces surplus value. Apart from those being employed, there exists a huge mass of labour which is not employed by a capitalist employer, namely unpaid family labour, self-employed and unemployed, and their maintenance never comes under the calculus of 'necessary'. This huge segment of working poor mostly depends on the state to fulfil their bare needs of food, shelter, water supply, sanitation and health and other services. Chakrabarti et al. distinguish the politics of 'need', the developmental struggle, as separate from class struggle arguing that the notion of need has to be problematised from the idea of justice and the contestation here is about redistribution of social surplus rather than production surplus.[63] In fact, Marx did distinguish between 'necessary' from 'need'. Capital recognises labour as 'necessary' only when it contributes to the accumulation of surplus, otherwise the 'need' of those who are excluded from the capitalist accumulation process are not at all 'necessary' in the eyes of capital. This is what Marx conveyed in the beginning of *Grundrisse*: 'It is already contained in the concept of the free labourer, that he is a pauper: a virtual pauper ... if the capitalist has no use for his surplus labour then the worker may not perform his necessary labour.'[64] In other words, the selling of labour power is incidental to the worker and the recognition of necessary as the organic needs for the worker's reproduction is subject to producing surplus.

The expanding mass of proletariat who were rightly equated to factory workers in the twentieth century, given the predominant form of production then, now largely exists beyond the factory. Production is far more socialised today in the form of using information, networks and knowledge and individual productivity as a measure of worker's contribution hardly makes sense. Wages or other forms of returns to labour, therefore, are largely determined by political conflicts rather than relying on economic calculus of individual productivity and efficiency. The focus of the struggle of the working people, therefore, has to be targeted towards expanding the allocation of social labour for 'necessity and need'. It is, of course, destined towards breaking the boundaries between the two and the expansion of 'necessary' in this case, means a struggle at the point of production, a struggle for wage increase, while the struggle for need spans the whole society and both can be integrated in the process of class formation.

The larger aspect of the struggle, however, relates to what is being and not being recognised as necessary by capital, an ontological expansion of the notion of need, greater allocation of social labour in the form of 'social wage', which is essentially a struggle of de-commodification of labour. In this struggle, one part relates to protecting the rights once achieved. These, according to Silver, are Polanyian battles of restoring the social substance over market by re-creating institutions.[65] But the other component is a struggle for transformation that new production organisations and labour compositions often give rise to. Labour movements at the current juncture, therefore, should take into account the changes in production process, should include the waged and the unwaged, the dispossessed and the excluded in their struggle towards emancipation. The whole of society becomes the scope of struggle in the age of social labour. And it cannot

---

[63] Chakrabarti, Dhar and Dasgupta (2015).
[64] Marx (1993 [1973]: 604).
[65] See Silver (2003).

be limited only to juridical modes of indignation, but involves a creative process of class formation going beyond the imagery of the 'factory worker'. The mediation of class interests within various ranks of the proletariat would include a process of cooperation and self-valorisation that is not only based on the power of refusal but has to be supplemented by a power of constitution, bridging interests through creating alternative spaces where solidarity and sharing of interests are driven by a different kind of rationality.

# 10

# Conclusion

Capitalism proved itself to be a peculiar organism that survived cycles of expansion and crisis, mutating with new challenges and giving rise to innovative sparks that kindled the new wave of expansion. Spheres of production and finance attracted capital in successive phases and at predictable sequence in search of profit, giving rise to a dynamism often supplemented by the rise of a new technological paradigm. It seems we arrived at a phase of capitalist growth that manifests contradictory tendencies in its various aspects – ignoring those might indulge pragmatic pretence but actually do not contribute to resolving persistent problems. We need industrial growth, but industrialisation cannot be a goal in itself. Delinking of industrial production from employment is not a problem of industry *per se,* but of a mode of industrialisation that invokes an exclusionary trajectory. It is indeed true that the communication and information revolution reduces transaction costs to almost zero and, therefore, human interaction is bound to be globalised. Developing countries participate in global trade and production, ideas flow across borders, workers migrate, capital's movement becomes seamless, but all these transactions are embedded in a structure of asymmetry in which human contributions are valued in different ways, exploitation and expropriation continue with a recreated institutional structure. Capitalism, in its highly financialised phase, can earn profits without producing and it appears that financial transactions and profits emerging out of it do not require labour exploitation as it used to be in twentieth-century factories. The apparent invisibility of labour and exploitation in the maze of financial transactions is because it is seen as separated from the 'dirty' world of production, a real non-hazardous, technical, neutral face of capitalism. It is also notable that the information revolution has permeated every bit of productive activity and is increasingly corrosive to the institution of private property and appropriation of private gains. Information is abundant and, hence, price mechanisms which are only capable of sensing scarcity are gradually losing acceptability in many social transactions. Knowledge commodities, being 'non-rival' in nature, can only be owned through a continuously growing monopoly structure which prevents use of knowledge, excluding its potential users. Neoliberal capitalism falls apart as newer technologies demand less hierarchical collaborative production structures that rising monopolies fail to offer. We need to face and recognise these conflicts, the structures that impinge upon proximate economic, political and social outcomes.

De-industrialisation sets in most of the developing countries and high-growth economies such as India and China will not be able to compensate the slowdown of advanced economies which are sunk into a protracted crisis. The difference from earlier cycles this time seems to be the missing spurt of productivity-enhancing technologies, that used to emerge in the backdrop of rising working-class resistance. Resistance shrunk options for increasing labour exploitation, then cheap capital amassed in the realm of finance looks forward for green offshoots of innovation and with rising synergies and interdependence, evolved a new technological paradigm as the harbinger of new cycles of production. In the case of new-phase capitalism empowered by the ICT revolution, the productivity gains are not so spectacular compared to previous new waves.[1] But labour being fragmented and weakened at the global scale allows dragging the growth process for longer periods. The disconnect between growth and employment poses a larger challenge. With new machines, the need for human physical labour, in any case, is going to decline. Capitalism, so far, only recognised factor incomes, and wages have been the remuneration against work. The income earned by the vast majority of people has been against some work done for others. Therefore, a disconnect between growth and employment is essentially leading to a tension between income and work. The various proposals of *universal basic income* in advanced economies are primarily acknowledgement of the fact that capitalism as a system is no longer capable of employing the available labour force. On the other hand, the hollowing out of work, particularly in the manufacturing sector, has been responded to by neoliberalism by commodification of all kinds of services which were earlier not meant for sale. This wholesale privatisation of services, health, education, care work, entertainment, and so on, emerges as the new area of work which offers income against paid work. Suppression of wages and expropriation of entitlements contributed to the edifice of capital's new empire. Work on demand, creating the huge gig-economy or platform-based work, is the height of 'labour in the abstract': a huge labour force, with no face or identity, as the worker confronts capital, a distant corporate entity often beyond reach, and switches from one work to another or from one employer to another employer. Under-reproduction of labour and nature has been the hallmark of neoliberal capitalism. Outsourcing and subcontracting, creating layers of self-employed or petty production and integrating the chain of exploitation and expropriation through a network of production and finance defines the growth

---

[1] David (1990: 355–61).

process of neoliberal capitalism. Challenges of global warming as well as various ecological imbalances threaten the existence of living beings in various parts of the globe. It is increasingly evident that 'market for pollution' or other market-based solutions such as carbon credits will not resolve distortions created in the relation between nature and human beings.

Developing countries in the post-colonial phase primarily engaged in the process of nation-building. The mandate had to be compulsively inclusive, as it was a process of realising the imaginations of masses who contributed to anti-colonial struggles. In course of time, particularly in the post-Cold War scenario, the ruling elite of most of these countries became subservient to the imperatives of global capital. The growth process became increasingly dependent on profit income and that also influenced the priorities of the development trajectory. In the case of India, the manufacturing sector stagnated and import intensity of exports as well as capital intensity in general increased over time. Due to a sharp decline in the share of wages in value added and consequent increase in inequality, the demand for manufacturing could not reach the levels of 'massification' of consumption demand as experienced by most of the advanced countries in their early periods of industrialisation. The expansion of services need not be seen as a separated process from productive activities. In fact, in many cases, services are embedded in manufactured goods and the production process responds to feedback shared through service loops. The creation of values and surplus depends on creating commodities which may not have to have some physical existence as goods, but it should necessarily involve exploitation of labour power whose value is independent of the nature of commodities it produces. Hence, we come across a huge array of precarious labour in the services sector, particularly in developing countries such as India where demand for such services emerges because labour is cheap and, second, because of commodification of services which were earlier provided through public provisioning.

Growth of manufacturing in India is dependent on radical redistribution of income which would reduce inequality and expand the middle class. Such a change would release the potential for massification, increase the demand for standardised goods and services which could be produced in modern, small enterprises that internalise the capacities of customisation often difficult in large, rigid structures. This process also requires calibration of technology use and prioritising preferences. In other words, phases of industrialisation should be in sync with society and the economy, particularly specialising in standardised mass production, instead of high-valued luxuries as it used to be the case in the Asian tributary mode of production. An economy driven by demand for high-valued luxuries would disfavour technologies suitable for mass production, would rely more on technology rents than profits based on competition. On the other hand, empowerment of labour in capitalism has historically been linked with full employment scenario and since neoliberalism sustains itself on wage repression, it has continuously displaced the agenda of full employment. Profit making in a neoliberal regime increasingly depends on offering assurance for future consumption or returns for the rich, rather than current consumption of the masses.

Rising inequality and persistent deficient demand was at least temporarily managed by increasing financialisation of the economy. The huge accumulation of surplus in the hands of a few rich demands commodification of future risks in the form of securitised assets claiming to assure future returns. Financialisation, on the other hand, is a fetishised reification of objectivities of social reproduction of capital. It is the game of earning profits without productive investment and, therefore, the disconnect between growth and employment is also manifested as a disconnect between growth of profits and that of physical investment. The primacy of shareholder returns undermines the need to enhance productive capacity and manifests itself as a trade-off between profit and growth. Fictitious capital and profit, through alienation, assume autonomy from the realm of production and tend to subvert profit realised through productive activities. This, however, does not imply that capital in finance and that in production are independent and separate subjects. Rather, they manifest different phases of the metamorphosis of capital in totality which are part of the same circuit of accumulation. The unifying feature of capital accumulation is ultimately realised through repression of labour, either in the form of labour arbitrage, or of dismantling existing structures of social wage. It also becomes imperative to deregulate the labour market with financialisation because, with rising debt and interest payments, the only way to maintain profitability is to suppress the claims of workers. The suppression of workers' entitlements and consequent contraction of demand is partially compensated by rise in credit or wealth-based consumption, which, in turn, conditions at least the working class of advanced countries to internalise the fluctuations of financial markets and the imperatives of social reproduction of capital. In developing countries, the permeation of financial transactions, although increasing, has been relatively less compared to developed countries. Hence, wealth-based consumption is restricted within a thin, middle-class base.

Industrialisation as a strategic agenda has been aborted by the unfounded belief that integration with global production networks and specialising in tasks assigned by value chains is the process by which the long-run trajectory of creating industrial base can be short-circuited. Post the financial crisis, the enthusiasm towards outward-looking policies has slightly altered due to de-globalisation or rebalancing, resulting in shrinking of global value chains in the recent past. But the point is not of degree only, it is about prioritising industrial growth as a strategy rather than being conceived as a passive outcome of liberalised markets. The history of industrialisation, either of the North or of late industrialisers of South East Asia, does not, in any case, subscribe to the view that the market did it all. Neither is it true that industrialisation necessarily has to be conflicting or competing with resources deployed in agriculture. In fact, success stories of the South narrate a case of partial proletarianisation and that of labour using technologies with calibrated transfer of population from rural to urban areas. But all these are policy induced rather than market driven. The process of integration, either in the form of involving with the global production networks or through financial flows, actually reduces the policy options available to the state to act upon. Developing countries are inserted into a global structure which is asymmetric and hierarchical and the role of that particular country is defined by the global division of labour. It is also important that participation in these structures does not necessarily increase the share of gains for developing countries because the distribution of gains is not determined by the contribution of these countries in a particular stage of production. Rather, it is governed by the distribution of profits according to hierarchies of capital involved in the global division of labour. Therefore, the imperatives of global capital are being internalised by capitalists of developing countries, which is entirely in conflict with strategies for independent industrial policy.

On the other hand, the financial structure influences the activity levels and allocation of resources that are suitable for higher profitability mediated through standardisation and commodification of risks. The institutional structures are completely in sync with such global imperatives, which, in turn, are very much linked with defining and protecting contributions and returns that favour the North by creating propertied knowledge while labour, which is in abundance in the South, is made easily accessible to global capital. The undervaluation of the contribution of developing countries cannot be captured by movements of price, as such figures only rationalise the outcomes that emerge through contestation between capitals as well as between labour and capital as a whole. This is precisely the reason why a persistent gap between advanced and developing countries exists and the developing countries accrue increasingly lesser share of gains the more they participate in this asymmetric global structure. The participatory nature of the current phase of globalisation often manifested through decentred network of production is essentially a myth. Concentration and centralisation of capital has been actualised through waves of mergers and acquisitions at the global level and the same process involves the contradictory tendency of fragmentation of production down the line. With the rise of the knowledge component in the production process and since it is even more difficult to restrict flow of accumulated knowledge, establishing global monopolies becomes increasingly necessary in capturing knowledge rents by global corporates.

Labour lost immensely in the process of neoliberal globalisation. Issues of labour rights and entitlements are increasingly being seen as impediments to industrial growth and development. Capitalism considers labour as input, but often fails to recognise that people who sell their labour power and receive payments as wages or salary are also the purchasers of the goods and services produced in the production process. And it is only when goods and services are sold that capitalists can realise produced surplus value as profits. Therefore, for an individual capitalist, the rationale to reduce wages or input costs appears meaningful, but for the capitalist class as a whole, similar tendencies would push down the share of working people in output and hence create constraints in realising profits. The history of capitalism, however, faced crises most of the time because such periods are preceded by ascendancy of labour which puts constraints on capital in pushing down wages and increase profitability. And such conflicts not only triggered new onslaught on labour but also facilitated fresh drives for technological innovation or recomposition of production organisation. Rise in productivity through these technological changes created new areas of production and boosted demand due to income effect caused by rise in real income through cheapening of products. Hence, technological development was accompanied by a process of absorbing labour, triggered by rise in demand. But capitalism seems to have passed through this classical phase and at the current phase capitalist accumulation no longer requires the huge available labour force.

This does not, however, imply that the capitalist does not need to cheapen labour. Surplus value emerges out of squeezing labour and cheapening of labour always gives additional profit to capitalists besides advantages of costs on other inputs. But the vast labour force is no longer required for capitalism to continue accumulation. They are not all part of the reserved army of labour either, to be called whenever required. Rather, a majority of them is actually condemned forever, and would never get the opportunity to be exploited. The political manoeuvring of this oppressed class often takes the form of shifting contours of patronage where the discourse on rights is increasingly surpassed by quid-pro-quo arrangements between the rulers and the ruled in which economic benefits are exchanged against political support. What seems notable is the expansion of the non-capital space within capitalism in the form of self-employed and petty producers who are not wage labourers but can survive only through engaging with capital relations in an asymmetric mode of exchange. In the margin, exchanges, however, do not take place on the basis of equivalence of value as it is supposed to be in capital relations, but through a subversion of such relations. In other words, whether in the global scale or in the context of the domestic economy, exploitation alone does not explain capitalist accumulation. It also requires expropriation of value in different layers in the form of primitive accumulation which in so many ways is nothing but a process of undervaluing nature and labour. It often entails a forcible subjugation of non-capital by capital, but the coercion involved in this process can be momentary or protracted in nature and can also assume explicit or implicit forms.

Capital relations tend to occupy all spaces by way of commodifying existing relations. In this process, it creates detailed hierarchies of capital spanning the global to the local; such extensions of capital relation spill over the location of production and intrude into the process of reproduction. The life processes of workers get subsumed into the work process where every moment and every aspect of life seem to be governed by the needs of hegemonic capital. The dominance of global capital and wage repression is articulated through the reified objectivity of financial fluctuations. It imparts a governance structure mediated through the state and other institutions, ensuring profitability for capital in its purest form. Increasing displacement of capital–labour relations from its conventional employer–employee relationship destabilises the existing regulatory structures of institutional protection. Individual capitalists are increasingly relieved by the state in making payments that are necessary for maintaining the future stream of labour and, in this process, labour rights are replaced by entitlements provisioned for citizens in the form of social security. The shift in discourse from worker to citizen becomes enormously problematic for the rising proportions of migrant workers. Huge number of migrant workers moving from one place to another or across borders provide the most vulnerable workforce at the disposal of capital. They are often forced to accept sub-human conditions of work, extended working hours, low wage and denied any support from the employer, state or the local community. They can easily be left out from social security benefits and other rights and entitlements that a citizen is supposed to get from the state. They are the illegitimate children of capitalism who contribute in the process of capital accumulation while hardly being recognised for the same.

Capitalism is going through the fourth decade of stagnation. The persistence of stagnation for prolonged duration without significant rise in productivity growth has something to do with the possibility and realities of wage repression. Upswings from depression in earlier capitalist cycles have been generated by technological innovations where capital amassed as finance in the matured phase of the cycle moved out to invest in emerging areas of technical innovation. Although new technologies such as network and digital technologies and mobile communications as well as the sudden burst in the application of artificial intelligence, robots and the Internet of Things impacted particular sectors heavily, they could not trigger a long-term growth in productivity. One of the reasons which might explain this lack of dynamism in capitalist recovery has been identified as the weakening of market relations that had been the major conveyors of dynamic growth in earlier phases of recovery. It is primarily because of the nature of technology, which contains an immense amount of shared knowledge that cannot be priced by the usual market mechanisms. This is because knowledge is essentially 'non-rival' in nature and the value of such knowledge to its possessor does not decline by sharing it with others. Rather, it increases through infinite feedback loops. Once it is produced, sharing of knowledge products involve zero marginal costs. It is also important to note that a large chunk of knowledge created by society is available through the internet free of cost and the very process of consumption of knowledge or information itself can produce new information through an unending chain.[2] The rules of the game based on scarcity seem to be becoming ineffective in this process and market modes of exchange are heavily corroded by the burgeoning free space of knowledge and information. In this context, appropriating private gains from emerging knowledge goods demand much larger monopolies and control which is evident from the fact that few companies seem to fight against each other to have control over the current as well as future flow of information.

It also has wider impact as use of direct labour and human efforts decline with the use of new technology. The metrics of individual contribution based on productivity measures essentially become a formal exercise. For instance, huge replacement of shop floor workers by robots that are monitored by the human supervisor increase the productivity of the supervisor manifold, but that does not manifest the increase of capability of the human being who happens to be the supervisor. Instead, it is a product of social knowledge which cannot be attributed to any particular individual. The decline of the use of direct labour, for the capitalists, has increased the need for having control over knowledge by way of creating propertied knowledge which not only restricts the access to knowledge goods and services but also threatens the production of knowledge upon which the current phase of capitalist recovery largely depends. In fact, Marx indicated such tendencies long back in *Grundrisse*:

> Labour no longer appears so much to be included within the production process; rather, the human being comes to relate more as watchman and regulator to the production process itself.... No longer does the worker insert a modified natural thing as middle link between the object and himself; rather, he inserts the process of nature, transformed into an industrial process, as a means between himself and

---

[2] For detailed discussion, see Riffkin (2013) and Mason (2015).

inorganic nature, mastering it. He steps to the side of the production process instead of being its chief actor. In this transformation, it is neither the direct human labour he himself performs, nor the time during which he works, but rather the appropriation of his own general productive power, his understanding of nature and it is, in a word, the development of the social individual which appears as the great foundation-stone of production and of wealth. The theft of alien labour time, on which the present wealth is based, appears a miserable foundation in face of this new one, created by large scale industry itself.[3]

Recent studies suggest that the use of new technology is disruptive in nature as it is going to create huge unemployment in the middle segment of repetitive jobs. Indications of such technology-driven unemployment is evident in developed as well as developing countries. An ILO report quotes a study of Bank of America Merrill Lynch in 2015 that 35 per cent of workers in the UK and 47 per cent of those in the USA are at risk of being displaced in the next 20 years. Such estimates on developing countries done by the World Bank suggest that 69 per cent in India, 72 per cent in Thailand, 77 per cent in China and 85 per cent in Ethiopia would be facing technology-led displacement.[4] It is argued that the 'hollowing out' of the middle-level workers is likely to increase inequality in societies further. Moreover, as wages increase in developing countries over time and cost of robots decline, jobs that can easily be replaced by robots need not be relocated to developing countries anymore in search of cheap labour reserves. In other words, capitalism with its new technology is no longer in a position to absorb the huge labour force that exists. Ironically, capitalism can only recognise remunerations as waged labour or labour power sold as commodity in different forms and, hence, faces the problem of irreconcilable tension between wage and income. It is forced to talk about *universal basic income* which recognises the separation between wage and income and blurs the distinction between work and free time.

Technological development is a product of human knowledge in progress and in so many ways it reduces work time required as necessary for human survival. On the contrary, when we see that a vast section of population would become redundant, that they are not required, it does not mean that disposable free time in society increases. Rather, they become a burden for capitalism and need to be managed politically. On the other hand, labour time has not reduced for the majority of workers; instead, 'working day' has no boundaries for the vast majority of precarious labour. All these contradictory tendencies suggest that saving work

---

[3] Marx (1993 [1973]: 705).
[4] Ernst, Merola and Samaan (2018: 3).

time through the introduction of new technology, instead of increasing free time, poses a challenge to the reproduction of the existing production process. Increased use of knowledge in production demands a collaborative production structure where existing technology and its progress would be recognised as fruits of social labour, where people collaborate not only in producing goods and services but actively take part in improvising them through sharing knowledge and production models. New technology reduces the use of direct labour time, but knowledge being appropriated and restricted to private ownership does not lead to increase in free time for society and, hence, grossly limits the learning and sharing space and progress of technology in general.

# References

Acemoglu, Daron and Pascual Restrepo. 2017. 'Robots and Jobs: Evidence from US Labor Markets'. NBER Working Paper Series No. 23285.

ADB. 2010. 'The Rise of Asia's Middle Class'. In *Key Indicators for Asia and the Pacific, 2020*. Manila: Asian Development Bank.

Agarwala, Rina. 2013. *Informal Labour, Formal Politics, and Dignified Discontent in India*. Cambridge: Cambridge University Press.

Aglietta, Michael. 2000. *A Theory of Capitalist Regulation: The US Experience*. London: New Left Books.

Akamatsu, Kaname. 1962. 'A Historical Pattern of Economic Growth in Developing Countries'. *The Developing Economies* 1(s1): 3–25.

Ali-Yrkkö, Jyrki Petri Rouvinen, Timo Seppälä and Pekka Ylä-Anttila. 2011. 'Who Captures Value in Global Supply Chains? Case Nokia N 95 Smartphone'. *Journal of Industry, Competition and Trade* 11(3): 263–78.

Althussar, L. and E. Balibar. 1970. *Reading Capital*. London: New Left Books.

Amin, Samir. 2008. 'Foreword: Rebuilding the Unity of the "Labour Front"'. In *Labour and the Challenges of Globalisation: What Prospects for Transnational Solidarity?* ed. Andreas Bieler, Ingemar Lindberg and Devan Pillay, xiv–xxii. London: Pluto Press.

———. 2010. *The Law of Worldwide Value*. New York: Monthly Review Press.

Anthony P. D'Costa and Achin Chakraborty. 2017. 'The Land Question in India: State, Dispossession and Capitalist Transition'. In *The Land Question in India: State, Dispossession and Capitalist Transition*, ed. Anthony P. D'Costa and Achin Chakraborty, 16–45. New Delhi: Oxford University Press, South Asia edition.

Araghi, Farshad. 2009. 'Accumulation by Displacement: Global Enclosures, Food Crisis, and the Ecological Contradictions of Capitalism'. Review (Fernand Braudel Center), *Political Economic Perspectives on the World Food Crisis* 32(1): 113–46.

Arestis, P. and M. Sawyer. 2004. *Re-examining Monetary and Fiscal Policy for the 21st Century*. Aldershot: Edward Elgar.

Arndt, S. and H. Kierzkowski, eds. 2001. *Fragmentation: New Production Patterns in the World Economy*. Oxford: Oxford University Press.

Arrighi, Giovani. 1994. *The Long Twentieth Century*. London: Verso.

———. 2009. 'The Winding Paths of Capital: Interview by David Harvey'. *New Left Review* 56 (March–April): 61–94.

Arrow, K. J., H. B. Chenery, B. S. Minhas and R. M. Solow. 1961. 'Capital–Labor Substitution and Economic Efficiency'. *The Review of Economics and Statistics* 43(3): 225–50.

Audretsch, B. David and T. Taylor Aldridge. 2009. 'Knowledge Spillovers, Entrepreneurship and Regional Development'. In *Handbook of Regional Growth and Development Theories*, ed. Roberta Capello and Peter Nijkamp, 201–10. Cheltenham, UK, and Northampton, USA: Edward Elgar.

Bagchi, Amiya Kumar. 1972. 'Some International Foundations of Capitalist Growth and Underdevelopment'. *Economic and Political Weekly* 8(31–33): 1559–70.

Bairoch, Paul. 1982. 'International Industrialisation Levels from 1750 to 1980'. *Journal of European Economic History* 11(2): 269–333.

Balassa, Bela. 1977. '"Revealed" Comparative Advantage Revisited: An Analysis of Relative Export Shares of the Industrial Countries, 1953–1971'. *The Manchester School* 45(4): 327–44.

Baldwin, Richard. 2012. 'Global Supply Chains: Why They Emerged, Why They Matter, and Where They Are Going'. Fung Global Institute Working Paper No. 2012-1. Asian Perspectives Global Issues series, Fung Global Institute, Hong Kong.

Banerjee, Arindam. 2017. 'Agrarian Crisis and Accumulation in Rural India: Locating the Land Question within the Agrarian Question'. In *The Land Question in India: State, Dispossession and Capitalist Transition*, ed. Anthony P. D'Costa and Achin Chakraborty, pp. 101–25. New Delhi: Oxford University Press, South Asia edition.

Baumol, W. J. 1967. 'Macroeconomics of Unbalanced Growth: The Anatomy of Urban Crisis'. *American Economic Review* 57(3): 415–26.

Bhaduri, Amit. 2014. 'What Remains of the Theory of Demand Management in a Globalizing World?' Public Policy Brief No. 130, Levy Economics Institute of Bard College, Annandale-On-Hudson, USA.

Bhagwati, J. 1984. 'Splintering and Disembodiment of Services and Developing Nations', *The World Economy* 7(2): 133–44

Bidet, Jacques. 2015. *Foucault with Marx*. London: Zed Books.

Bienefeld, Manfred. 1979. 'Urban Employment: A Historical Perspective'. In *Casual Work and Poverty in Third World Cities*, ed. Ray Bromley and Chris Gerry, 27–44. New York: John Wiley.

Blair, Jennifer. 2005. 'Global Capitalism and Commodity Chains: Looking Back, Going Forward'. *Competition and Change* 9(2): 153–80.

Block, Fred and Larry Hirschhorn. 1979. 'New Productive Forces and the Contradictions of Contemporary Capitalism: A Post-Industrial Perspective'. *Theory and Society* 7(3): 363–95.

Bose, Ahana and Parthapratim Pal. 2018. 'External Commercial Borrowings: Is It a Boon or a Bane?' *Economic and Political Weekly* 53(30): 19–22.

Bowles, Samuel and Herbert Gintis. 1990. 'Contested Exchange: New Micro Foundations for the Political Economy of Capitalism'. *Politics and Society* 8(2): 165–222.

Boyer, Robert. 2011. 'Is a Finance-led Growth Regime a Viable Alternative to Fordism? A Preliminary Analysis'. *Economy and Society* 29(1): 111–45.

Braudel, Fernand. 1980. *On History*. Chicago: University of Chicago Press.

Bromley, Ray. 1978. 'Introduction – The Urban Informal Sector: Why Is it Worth Discussing?' *World Development* 6(9/10): 1033–39.

. Carrera, Iñigo Juan. 1998. 'A Model to Measure the Profitability of Specific Industrial Capitals by Computing Their Turnover Circuits'. CICP Working Paper, Centro para la Investigación como Crítica Práctica la Investigación como Crítica Práctica, Buenos Aires.

Castells, M. and A. Portes. 1989. 'World Underneath: The Origins, Dynamics, and Effects of the Informal Economy'. In *The Informal Economy*, ed. Alejandro Portes, Manuel Castells and Lauren A. Benton, 11–37. Baltimore: John Hopkins University Press.

Centre for Sustainable Employment. 2018. *State of Working India 2018*. Bengaluru: Azim Premji University.

Chakrabarti, Anjan, Stephen Cullenberg, and Anup Dhar. 2017. 'Primitive Accumulation and Historical Inevitability: A Postcolonial Critique'. In *Knowledge, Class, and Economics: Marxism without Guarantees*, ed. Theodore A. Burczak, Robert F. Garnett, Jr, and Richard McIntyre, 288–306. London and New York: Routledge.

Chakrabarti, Anjan and Atanu Thakur. 2010. 'The Making and Unmaking of the (In)formal Sector'. *Critical Sociology* 36(3): 415–35.

Chakrabarti, Anjan, Anup Dhar and Byasdeb Dasgupta. 2015. *The Indian Economy in Transition: Globalisation, Capitalism and Development*. New Delhi: Cambridge University Press.

Chakrabarti, Anjan, Anup Dhar and Stephen Cullenberg. 2012. *World of the Third and Global Capitalism*. Delhi: Worldview Publications.

Chancel, Lucas and Thomas Piketty. 2017. 'Indian Income Inequality, 1922–2015: From British Raj to Billionaire Raj?' WID.world Working Paper No. 2017/11.

Chandrasekhar, C. P. 2015. 'Promise Belied: India's Post-Independence Industrialization Experience.' In *Indian Industrialisation: ICSSR Research Surveys and Explorations*, ed. C. P. Chandrasekhar, Vol. 1, pp. 1–48. New Delhi: Oxford University Press.

Chandrasekhar, C. P. and Jayati Ghosh. 2015. 'The Ever Expanding Debt Bubbles of China and India'. *Business Line*, 2 March.

Chang, Ha-Joon. 2010. *23 Things They Don't Tell You about Capitalism*. Allen lane: Penguin Group.

Chatterjee, Partha. 1988. 'On Gramsci's Fundamental Mistake'. *Economic and Political Weekly* 23(5): PE24–PE26.

———. 1993. *The Nation and Its Fragments: Colonial and Postcolonial Histories*. Princeton, New Jersey: Princeton University Press.

———. 2011. *Lineages of Political Society: Studies in Postcolonial Democracy*. New York: Colombia University Press.

Chaudhury, Ajit, Dipankar Das and Anjan Chakrabarti. 2000. *Margin of Margin: Profile of an Unrepentant Post-Colonial Collaborator.* Kolkata: Anustup.

Chenery, Hollis B. 1960. 'Patterns of Industrial Growth'. *American Economic Review* 50(4): 624–54.

Clark, Collin. 1940. *The Conditions of Economic Progress.* London: Macmillan.

Crotty, J. 2003. 'The Neoliberal Paradox: The Impact of Destructive Product Market Competition and "Modern" Financial Markets on Nonfinancial Corporation Performance in the Neoliberal Era'. *Review of Radical Political Economics* 35(3): 271–79.

CSO. Various years. *Annual Survey of Industries.* New Delhi: Central Statistics Office, Government of India.

Dallery, T. and T. van Treeck. 2008. 'Conflicting Claims and Equilibrium Adjustment Processes in a Stock-Flow Consistent Macro Model'. IMK Working Paper 9/2008.

Danies, Rob. 1979. 'Informal Sector or Subordinate Mode of Production? A Model'. In *Casual Work and Poverty in Third World Cities*, ed. Ray Bromley and Chris Gerry, 87–104. New York: John Wiley.

Das Gupta, Chirashree. 2016. *State and Capital in Independent India: Institutions and Accumulation.* Cambridge: Cambridge University Press.

Das, Santosh and P. S. Rawat. 2018. ICSSR sponsored project report on 'Asset Quality of Indian Scheduled Commercial Banks: Issues and Concerns'. New Delhi: Institute for Studies in Industrial Development.

David, P. A. 1990. 'The Dynamo and the Computer: A Historical Perspective on the Modern Productivity Paradox.' *American Economic Review Papers and Proceedings*, 355–61.

Dobb, M. 1946. *Studies in the Development of Capitalism.* London: Routledge and Kegan Paul.

Drucker, P. F. 1993. *Post-Capitalist Society.* New York: Harper Business.

Eichengreen, B. and P. Gupta. 2009. 'The Two Waves of Service Sector Growth'. NBER Working Paper No. 14968, Cambridge, MA.

———. 2010. 'The Service Sector as India's Road to Economic Growth.' ICRIER Working Paper Series, Number 249, Indian Council for Research on International Economic Relations, New Delhi.

Elsby, Michael W., Bart Hobijn and Ayşegül Şahin. 2013. 'The Decline of the U.S. Labor Share'. *Brookings Papers on Economic Activity* 2(Fall): 1–63.

Elsenhans, Hartmut. 2015. *Saving Capitalism from the Capitalists.* California: Sage.

Ernst, Ekkehard, Rossana Merola and Daniel Samaan. 2018. 'The Economics of Artificial Intelligence: Implications for the Future of Work'. ILO Future of Work Research Paper Series 5, ILO, Geneva.

Epstein, G. A. (ed.). 2005. *Financialization and the World Economy.* Cheltenham: Edward Elgar.

Ercel, Kenen. 2006. 'Orientalization of Exploitation: A Class-Analytical Critique of the Sweatshop Discourse'. *Rethinking Marxism* 18(2): 289–306.

Fairbairn, Madeleine. 2014. '"Like Gold with Yield": Evolving Intersections between Farmland and Finance'. *The Journal of Peasant Studies* 41(5): 777–95.

Fairhead, J., M. Leach and I. Scoones. 2012. 'Green Grabbing: A New Appropriation of Nature?' *The Journal of Peasant Studies* 39(2), special issue: 237–61.

Fama, E. F. 1965. 'Random Walks in Stock Market Prices'. *Financial Analysts Journal* 21(5): 55–59.

———. 1970. 'Efficient Capital Markets: A Review of Theory and Empirical Work'. *The Journal of Finance* 25(2): 383–417.

Fanon, Frantz. 2004. *The Wretched of the Earth*, with commentary by Jean-Paul Satre and Homi K. Bhaba. New York: Grove Press.

Fernandes, Walter and V. Paranjpye. 1997. *Rehabilitation Policy and Law in India: A Right to Livelihood*. New Delhi: Indian Social Institute.

Ferry, Elizabeth Emma. 2013. *Minerals, Collecting and Value across the US–Mexico Border*. Bloomington: University of Indiana Press.

Foucault, Michel. 1977. *Discipline and Punish*. London: Penguin Books.

Gereffi, Gary. 1994. 'The Organisation of Buyer-driven Global Commodity Chains: How US Retailers Shape Overseas Production Networks'. In *Commodity Chains and Global Capitalism,* ed. G. Gereffi and M. Korzeniewicz, 95–122. Westport, CT and London: Greenwood Press.

———. 1999. 'International Trade and Industrial Upgrading in the Apparel Commodity Chain'. *Journal of International Economics* 48(1): 37–70.

———. 2001. 'Beyond the Producer-Driven/Buyer-Driven Dichotomy: The Evolution of Global Value Chains in the Internet Era'. *IDS Bulletin* 32(3): 30–40.

———. 2018. 'Protectionism and Global Value Chains'. In *Global Value Chains and Development: Redefining the Contours of 21st Century Capitalism,* 429–52. Cambridge: Cambridge University Press.

Ghani, Eijaz, William R. Kerr and Alex Segura. 2015. 'Informal Tradables and the Employment Growth of Indian Manufacturing'. World Bank Group, Policy Research Working Paper No. 7206.

Ghose, Ajit K. 2016. *India Employment Report 2016: Challenges and the Imperative of Manufacturing-Led Growth*. New Delhi: Institute for Human Development and Oxford University Press.

Goyal, S. K. 2014. *India's Policy Milieu: Economic Development, Planning and Industry*. New Delhi: Academic Foundation.

Goyal, S. K. and K. S. Chalapati Rao. 2002. 'Savings and Capital Formation of the Indian Private Corporate Sector'. ISID Report submitted to the Department of Economic Affairs, ISID, New Delhi.

Greenwood, Jeremy and Bruce Smith. 1997. 'Financial Markets in Development, and the Development of Financial Markets.' *Journal of Economic Dynamics and Control* 21(1): 145–81.

Grossman, S. and J. Stiglitz. 1980. 'On the Impossibility of Informationally Efficient Markets'. *American Economic Review* 70(3): 393–408.

Hall, P. A. and D. Soskice (eds). 2001. *Varieties of Capitalism: The Institutional Foundations of Comparative Advantage*. Oxford: Oxford University Press.

Hallward-Driemeier, Mary and Gaurav Nayyar. 2018. *Trouble in the Making? The Future of Manufacturing Led Development*. Washington: The World Bank Group.

Harris, J. 2013. 'Does "Landlordism" Still Matter? Reflections on Agrarian Change in India'. *Journal of Agrarian Change* 13(3): 351–64.

Hart, K. 1973. 'Informal Income Opportunities and Urban Employment in Ghana'. *Journal of Modern African Studies* 11(1): 61–89.

Harvey, David. 2003. *The New Imperialism*. New York: Oxford University Press.

Hein, Eckhard. 2009. 'A (Post-)Keynesian Perspective on "Financialisation"'. Working Paper 1/2009 Macroeconomic Policy Institute (IMK) at Hans Boeckler Foundation, Duesseldorf.

Heintz, James. 2006. 'Low-wage Manufacturing and Global Commodity Chains: A Model in the Unequal Exchange Tradition'. *Cambridge Journal of Economics* 30 (4): 507–20.

Henderson, Jeffrey, Peter Dicken, Martin Hess, Neil Coe and Henry Wai-Chung Yeung. 2002. 'Global Production Networks and the Analysis of Economic Development'. *Review of International Political Economy* 9(3): 436–64.

Hilferding, R. 1981. *Finance Capital: A Study of the Latest Phase of Capitalist Development*. London: Routledge and Kegan Paul, 1st German edition 1910.

Hill, T. P. 1977. 'On Goods and Services'. *Review of Income and Wealth* 23(4): 315–38.

Hobsbawm, Eric. 1978. 'The Forward March of Labour Halted?' *Marxism Today*, September, 279–86.

Hodgson, G. 1980. 'The Theory of Exploitation without the Labour Theory of Value'. *Science and Society* 44(3): 257–73.

Holt-Giménez, E. 2007. 'Biofuels: Myths of the Agro-fuels Transition'. *Food First Backgrounder* 13(2). Available at http://www.foodfirst.org/node/1711 (accessed on 22 February 2019).

Holton J. Robert. 1981. 'Marxist Theories of Social Change and the Transition from Feudalism to Capitalism'. *Theory and Society* 10(6): 833–67.

Hopkins, T. and I. Wallerstein. 1986. 'Commodity Chains in the World Economy prior to 1800'. *Review* 10(1): 157–70.

ILO. 2015. *World Employment Social Outlook 2015: The Changing Nature of Jobs*. Geneva: International Labour Organization.

IMF. 2007. *World Economic Outlook, April. 2007: Spillovers and Cycles in the Global Economy*. Washington, DC: International Monetary Fund.

———. 2017a. *Financial System Stability Assessment Report: India*. IMF Country Report No. 17/390.

————. 2017b. *World Economic Outlook, April 2017: Gaining Momentum?* Washington, DC: International Monetary Fund.

————. 2018. *World Economic Outlook, April 2018: Cyclical Upswing, Structural Change.* Washington, DC: International Monetary Fund.

Itoh, Makoto and Costas Lapavitsas. 1999. *Political Economy of Money and Finance.* New York: Palgrave Macmillan.

Kaldor, N. 1966. *Causes of the Slow Rate of Economic Growth of the United Kingdom.* London: Cambridge University Press.

Kalecki, Michal. 1971. *Selected Essays on the Dynamics of the Capitalist Economy.* Cambridge: Cambridge University Press.

Kaplinsky, R. 1998. 'Globalisation, Industrialisation and Sustainable Growth: The Pursuit of the nth Rent'. Discussion Paper 365, Institute of Development Studies, University of Sussex.

————. 2000. 'Spreading the Gains from Globalisation: What Can Be Learned from Value Chain Analysis?' Working Paper 110, Institute of Development Studies, University of Sussex.

————. 2005. *Globalization, Poverty and Inequality: Between a Rock and a Hard Place.* Cambridge: Polity Press.

————. 2007. 'Capability Building in SSA: What Difference Do the Asian Drivers Make?' SLPTMD Working Paper Series, 10, Department of International Development, University of Oxford.

Kapoor, Radhicka and P. P. Krishnapriya. 2019. 'Explaining the Contractualisation of India's Workforce'. Indian Council for Research on International Economic Relations (ICRIER) Working Paper no. 369. ICRIER, New Delhi.

Kemeny, Thomas. 2009. 'Are International Technology Gaps Growing or Shrinking in the Age of Globalization? *Journal of Economic Geography* 11(2011): 1–35.

Kenny, Martin. 2013. 'Where Is the Value in the Value Networks?' In *Twenty-First Century Manufacturing*, ed. J. Zysman, M. Kenney, D. Breznitz and P. Wright, 13–36. Report to the United Nations Industrial Development Organisation, Vienna.

Keynes, J. M. 1930. *Economic Possibilities for Our Grandchildren.* In *Essays in Persuasion*, 358–73. New York: Harcourt Brace, 1932.

————. 1973 [1936]. *The General Theory of Employment Interest and Money.* Cambridge: Cambridge University Press.

Krippner, G. R. 2005. 'The Financialization of the American Economy'. *Socio-Economic Review* 3(2): 173–208

Kuznets, Simon. 1957. 'Quantitative Aspects of the Economic Growth of Nations: II. Industrial Distribution of National Product and Labor'. *Economic Development and Cultural Change* 5(4) Supplement: 1–111.

Kuznets, Simon and John Thomas Murphy. 1966. *Modern Economic Growth Rate, Structure, and Spread*, Vol. 2. New Haven: Yale University Press.

Lapavitsas, Costas. 2013. *Profiting without Producing: How Finance Exploits Us All*. London: Verso.

Leontief, W. 1952. 'Machines and Man'. *Scientific American* 187(3): 150–64.

LeRoy, S. F. 1989. 'Efficient Capital Markets and Martingales'. *Journal of Economic Literature* 27(4): 1583–621.

Levien, Michael. 2011. 'Special Economic Zones and Accumulation by Dispossession in India'. *Journal of Agrarian Change* 11(4): 454–83.

———. 2015. 'From Primitive Accumulation to Regimes of Dispossession: Six Theses on India's Land Question'. *Economic and Political Weekly* L(22), 30 May: 146–57.

———. 2017. 'From Primitive Accumulation to Regimes of Dispossession: Thesis on India's Land Question'. In *The Land Question in India: State Dispossession and Capitalist Transition*, ed. Anthony P. D'Costa and Achin Chakraborty, 49–75. New Delhi: Oxford University Press, South Asia edition.

Levine, Ross. 1997. 'Financial Development and Economic Growth: Views and Agenda'. *Journal of Economic Literature* 35(June): 688–726.

Lewis, Arthur. 1954. 'Economic Development with Unlimited Supplies of Labour'. *The Manchester School* 22(2): 139–91.

Leyshon, Andrew and Nigel Thrift .2007. 'The Capitalization of Almost Everything: The Future of Finance and Capitalism'. *Theory, Culture and Society* 24(7–8): 97–115.

Linden, Marcel Van Der. 2011. *Workers of the World: Essays toward a Global Labor History*. Leiden, Boston: Brill.

Linder, Peter and Sung Eun Jung. 2014. 'Corporate Vulnerabilities in India and Banks' Loan Performance'. IMF Working Paper 14/232.

Liu, Runjuan and Daniel Trefler. 2008. 'Much Ado about Nothing: American Jobs and the Rise of Service Offshoring to China and India'. NBER Working Paper 14061, 2008.

Lucaks, George. 1975. *History and Class Consciousness*. Cambridge: The MIT Press.

Lucas, R. E., Jr. 1987. *Models of Business Cycles*. New York: Basil Blackwell.

Luxemberg, Rosa. 1951. *The Accumulation of Capital*. London: Routledge & Kegan Paul (first published in German in 1913).

Lysandrou, Photis. 2011. 'Global Inequality, Wealth Concentration and the Subprime Crisis: A Marxian Commodity Theory Analysis'. *Development and Change* 42(1): 183–208.

MacKenzie, Donald. 2003. 'Long Term Capital Management and the Sociology of Arbitrage'. *Economy and Society* 32(3): 349–80.

Maizels, A., K. Berge, T. Crowe and T. B. Palaskas. 1998. 'Trends in the Manufacturing Terms of Trade of Developing Countries'. Mimeo, Oxford, Finance and Trade Policy Centre, Queen Elizabeth House.

Marx, Karl. 1937 [1852]. *The Eighteenth Brumaire of Louis Bonaparte*. Available at www. marxists.org/archive/marx/works/download/pdf/18th-Brumaire.pdf (accessed 11 September 2018).

————. 1958. *Capital I*. Moscow: Foreign Languages Publishing House.

————. 1957. *Capital II*. Moscow: Foreign languages Publishing House.

————. 1959. *Capital III*. Moscow: Foreign languages Publishing House.

————. 1963. *Theories of Surplus Value, Part I*. Moscow: Progress Publishers.

————. 1993 [1973]. *Grundrisse*. London: Penguin Books.

Mason, Paul. 2015. *Postcapitalism: A Guide to Our Future*. London: Penguin Books.

Mazumdar, Surajit. 2010. 'Indian Capitalism: A Case That Doesn't Fit?' Working Paper ISID 2010/10.

————. 2015. *The Indian Corporate Sector*. Corporate Governance. New Delhi: Taxmann and Indian Institute of Corporate Affairs.

McKinsey Global Institute. 2003. 'Offshoring: Is It a Win-Win Game?' Report. August.

McMichael, Philip. 2009. 'A Food Regime Genealogy.' *Journal of Peasant Studies* 36(1): 139–69.

————. 2012. 'The Land Grab and Corporate Food Regime Restructuring'. *Journal of Peasant Studies* 39(3–4): 681–701.

Mead, C. Donald. 1994. 'The Contribution of Small Enterprises to Employment Growth in Southern and Eastern Africa'. *World Development* 22(12): 1881–94.

Mead, C. Donald and Carl Liedholm. 1998. 'The Dynamics of Micro and Small Enterprises in Developing Countries'. *World Development* 26(1): 61–74.

Milberg, William. 2007. 'Shifting Sources and Uses of Profits: Sustaining U.S. Financialization with Global Value Chains'. Working Paper 2007–9, December, W Schwartz Center for Economic Policy Analysis, Department of Economics, The New School for Social Research, New York.

Milberg, William and Deborah Winler. 2010. 'Capturing the Gains: Economic and Social Upgrading in Global Production Networks: Problems of Theory and Measurement'. Capturing the Gains Working Paper 4, The New School for Social Research, New York.

Mill, J. S. 1852. *Principles of Political Economy*, Vol. 1. London: J. W. Parker & Son, 3rd edition.

Morawetz, David. 1974. 'Employment Implications of Industrialisation in Developing Countries: A Survey'. *Economic Journal* 84(335): 491–542.

Moser, C. 1978. 'Informal Sector or Petty Commodity Production: Dualism or Dependence on Urban Development'. *World Development* 6(9/10): 1041–64.

Murthy, M. R. and K. V. K. Ranganathan. 2013. 'Structural Characteristics of the Large Indian Private Corporate Sector in the Post-Liberalisation Period'. ISID Working Paper No, 2013/03, Institute for Studies in Industrial Development, New Delhi.

Nagaraj, R. 2017. 'Economic Reforms and Manufacturing Sector Growth: Need for Reconfiguring the Industrialisation Model'. *Economic and Political Weekly* 52(2): 61–68.

Nathan, Dev. 2018. 'GVCs and Development Policy: Vertically Specialized Industrialisation'. In *Development with Global Value Chains: Upgrading and Innovation in Asia,* ed. Dev Nathan, Meenu Tewari and Sandip Sarkar, 373–408. Cambridge: Cambridge University Press.

Nayyar, Deepak. 2013. *Catch Up: Developing Countries in the World Economy.* Oxford: Oxford University Press.

Nayyar, Gaurav. 2012. *The Service Sector in India's Development.* New York: Cambridge University Press.

Negri, Antonio. 1991. *Marx beyond Marx: Lessons on the Grundrisse.* London: Pluto Press.

———. 1988. 'Archaeology and Project: The Mass Worker and the Social Worker'. In *Revolution Retrieved: Selected Writings on Marx, Keynes, Capitalist Crisis and New Social Subjects,* 199–228. London: Red Notes.

NCEUS. 2009. *The Challenge of Employment in India: An Informal Economy Perspective,* Vol. I. New Delhi: National Commission for Enterprises in the Unorganised Sector.

Ngai, Pun and Jenny Chan. 2012. 'Global Capital, the State, and Chinese Workers: The Foxconn Experience'. *Modern China* 38(4): 383–410.

NSSO. 2012. 'Key Indicators of Unincorporated Non-agricultural Enterprise (Excluding Construction) of the 67th'. Round (2010-11) KI (67/234). National Sample Survey Organisation, New Delhi.

———. 2014. 'Informal Sector and Conditions of Employment in India NSS 68th'. Round Report No. 557(68/10/2). National Sample Survey Organisation, New Delhi.

———. 2017. 'Key Indicators of Unincorporated Non-agricultural Enterprise (Excluding Construction) of the 73rd'. Round (2015-16) KI (73/234). National Sample Survey Organisation, New Delhi.

———. Various years. *Report on Household Consumption of Various Goods and Services in India.* New Delhi: National Sample Survey Organisation. Available at www.mospi.nic.in.

———. Various years. *Employment and Unemployment Situation in India.* New Delhi: National Sample Survey Organisation. Available at www.mospi.nic.in.

Obstfeld, Maurice. 1994. 'Risk-taking, Global Diversification, and Growth'. *American Economic Review* 84(5): 10–29.

OECD. 2012. 'Global Production Networks and Employment: A Developing Country Perspective'. OECD Conference Centre Working Paper No. TAD/TC/WP (2012)29, Organisation for Economic Co-operation and Development, Paris.

Organhazi, O. 2006. 'Financialisation and Capital Accumulation in the Non-financial Corporate Sector: A Theoretical and Empirical Investigation on the US Economy: 1973–2003'. In *21st Century Keynesian Economics,* ed. Philip Arestis and Malcolm Sawyer, 81–119. London: Palgrave-Macmillan.

Oxfam. 2011. 'Land and Power'. Oxfam Briefing Paper 151 (2), Oxfam GB, Oxford, UK, 22 September.

Palley, T. 1994. 'Debt, Aggregate Demand, and the Business Cycle: An Analysis in the Spirit of Kaldor and Minsky'. *Journal of Post Keynesian Economics* 16(3): 371–90.

———. 1996. *Post Keynesian Economics: Debt, Distribution and the Macro Economy.* Basingstoke: Macmillan.

Pasinetti, L. L. 1981. *Structural Change and Economic Growth: A Theoretical Essay on the Dynamics of the Wealth of Nations.* New York, NY: Cambridge University Press.

Patnaik, Prabhat. 1997. *Accumulation and Stability under Capitalism.* Oxford: Clarendon Press.

———. 2008a. 'The Accumulation Process in the Period of Globalization'. *Economic & Political Weekly* 43(26–27): 108–13.

———. 2008b. *The Value of Money.* New Delhi: Tulika Books.

Patnaik, Utsa. 2006. 'The Free Lunch: Transfers from the Tropical Colonies and Their Role in Capital Formation in Britain during the Industrial Revolution'. In *Globalization under Hegemony: The Changing World Economy,* ed. K. S. Jomo, 30–70. Delhi: Oxford University Press.

———. 2009. 'Origins of the Food Crisis in India and Developing Countries'. 1 July. Available at https://monthlyreview.org/2009/07/01/origins-of-the-food-crisis-in-india-and-developing-countries (accessed 19 March 2019).

———. 2011. 'The Agrarian Question in the Neoliberal Era'. In Utsa Patnaik and Sam Moyo with Issa G. Shivji, *The Agrarian Question in the Neoliberal Era: Primitive Accumulation and the Peasantry.* Oxford: Fahamu Books and Pambazuka Press.

———. 2012. 'Capitalism and the Production of Poverty'. *Social Scientist* 40(1–2): 3–20.

Piore, J. M. and C. F. Sabel. 1984. *The Second Industrial Divide: Possibilities for Prosperity.* New York: Basic Books.

Piven, Frances and Richard Cloward. 2000. 'Power Repertoires and Globalization'. *Politics and Society* 28(3): 413–30.

Pollin, Robert. 1996. 'Contemporary Economic Stagnation in World Historical Perspective'. *New Left Review* I/219(September–October): 109–18.

Porter, M. 1985. *Competitive Advantage: Creating and Sustaining Superior Performance.* London: Macmillan.

———. 1990. *The Competitive Advantage of Nations.* London: Macmillan.

Quick, Paddy. 2004. 'Subsistence Wages and Household Production: Clearing the Way for an Analysis of Class and Gender'. *Review of Radical Political Economics* 36(1): 20–36.

Ramachandran, V. K. and V. Rawal. 2010. 'The Impact of Liberalisation and Globalisation on India's Agrarian Economy'. *Global Labour Journal* 1(1): 56–91. Available at www.digitalcommons.mcmaster.ca.

Ravallion, M. 2009. 'The Developing Worlds' Bulging (but Vulnerable) "Middle Class"'. Policy Research Working Paper, No. 4816, World Bank, Washington, DC.

Rawal, Vikas. 2008. 'Ownership Holdings of Land in Rural India: Putting the Record Straight'. *Economic and Political Weekly* 43(10): 43–47.

Ray, Partha, Abhisek Sur and Amarendu Nandy. 2017. 'India's External Commercial Borrowing: Trends, Composition, and Determinants'. Working Paper Series 802, IIM Calcutta, Kolkata.

RBI. 2019. *Handbook of Statistics on the Indian Economy, 2018–19.* Mumbai: Reserve Bank of India. Available at https://www.rbi.org.in/scripts/AnnualPublications. aspx?head=Handbook%20of%20Statistics%20on%20Indian%20Economy (accessed 9 September 2019).

Read, Jason. 2002. 'Primitive Accumulation: The Aleatory Foundation of Capitalism'. *Rethinking Marxism* 14(2): 24–49.

Resnick, Stephen A. and Richard D. Wolff. 1987. *Knowledge and Class.* Chicago and London: Chicago University Press.

Rifkin, Jeremy. 2013. *The Zero Marginal Cost Society.* New York: Palgrave Macmillan.

Roberts, Bruce. 1987. 'Marx after Steedman: Separating Marxism from "Surplus Theory"'. *Capital & Class* 11(2): 84–103.

Roberts, Kenneth M. 1995. 'Neoliberalism and Transformation of Populism in Latin America: The Peruvian Case'. *World Politics* 48(1): 82–116.

Rodrik, Dani 2011. 'The Future of Economic Convergence'. Working Paper No. 17400, National Bureau of Economic Research (NBER), Cambridge, MA.

———. 2016. 'Premature Deindustrialization'. *Journal of Economic Growth* 21(1): 1–33.

Roy, Satyaki. 2006. 'Do Minimum Wages Reduce Employment in the Small Enterprise Clusters?' *Indian Journal of Labour Economics* 49(4): 709–19.

———. 2008. 'Structural Change in Employment in India since 1980s: How Lewisian Is It?' *Social Scientist* 36(11–12): 47–68.

———. 2009. 'Garments Industry in India: Lessons from Two Clusters'. Working Paper 01/2009, Institute for Studies in Industrial Development.

———. 2012. 'Spatial Organization of Production in India: Contesting Themes and Conflicting Evidence'. *Journal of Regional Development and Planning* 1(1): 1–16.

———. 2013. *Small and Medium Enterprises in India: Infirmities and Asymmetries in Industrial Clusters.* London: Routledge.

———. 2016. 'Faltering Manufacturing Growth and Employment: Is "Making" the Answer?' *Economic and Political Weekly* LI(13): 35–42.

———. 2017. 'Rent and Surplus in GPN Framework: Identifying "Value Capture" from the South'. *Agrarian South: Journal of Political Economy* 6(1): 32–52.

———. 2019a. 'Structural Asymmetry in Global Production Network: An Empirical Exploration'. Background Paper submitted for the ICSSR sponsored Programme on Pathways to India's Industrialisation Addressing Select Critical Issues and Concerns, ISID, New Delhi.

————. 2019b. 'Labour–Capital Conflict and Permeation of Class in Marxian Categories'. In *Perspectives on Neoliberalism, Labour and Globalization in India,* ed. K.R. Shyam Sundar, 61–78. Singapore: Palgrave Macmillan.

————. 2019c. *Financialisation in India: Nature and Implications with Special Focus on Corporate Sector.* Report submitted to the Indian Council of Social Science Research, ISID, New Delhi.

Sanyal, Kalyan. 2007. *Rethinking Capitalist Development: Primitive Accumulation, Governmentality and Post-Colonial Capitalism.* London, New York, Delhi: Routledge.

Schmitz, Hubert. 1982. 'Growth Constraints on Small-scale Manufacturing in Developing Countries: A Critical Review'. *World Development* 10(6): 429–50.

————. 1999. 'Collective Efficiency and Increasing Return'. *Cambridge Journal of Economics* 23(4): 465–83.

Searle, Llerena Guiu. 2016. *Landscapes of Accumulation.* Chicago: The University of Chicago Press.

Sen, Sunanda and Zico Dasgupta. 2015. 'Financialization and Corporate Investments: The Indian Case'. Working Paper No. 828, Levy Economics Institute of Bard College, Annandale-On-Hudson, USA.

Shanin, Teodor. 1983. 'Late Marx: Gods and Craftsmen'. In *Late Marx and the Russian Road: Marx and the Peripheries of Capitalism,* ed. Teodor Shanin, 3–39. New York: Monthly Review Press.

Sheikh, Anwar. 1982. 'Neo-Ricardian Economics: A Wealth of Algebra, a Poverty of Theory.' *Review of Radical Political Economics* 14(2): 67–83.

Silver, Beverly. 2003. *Forces of Labor: Workers' Movements and Globalization since 1870.* New York: Cambridge University Press.

Smith, Adam. 2003 [1904]. *The Wealth of Nations.* Edited by E. Cannan. New York: Bantam Dell, 5th edition.

Smith, John. 2012. 'The GDP Illusion: Value Added versus Value Capture'. *Monthly Review* 64(3): 86–102.

————. 2016. *Imperialism in the Twenty-First Century: Globalization, Super Exploitation and Capitalism's Final Crisis.* New York: Monthly Review Press.

Sotiropoulos, Dimitris P., John Milios and Spyros Lapatsioras. 2013. *A Political Economy of Contemporary Capitalism and Its Crisis: Demystifying Finance.* London and New York: Routledge.

Stallybrass, Peter. 1990. 'Marx and Heterogeneity: Thinking the Lumpenproletariat'. *Representations* 31 (Special Issue: 'The Margins of Identity in Nineteenth-Century England'): 69–95.

Standing, Guy. 2016. *The Precariat: The New Dangerous Class.* London, New York: Bloomsbury Academic.

Steedman, I. 1977. *Marx after Sraffa.* London: New Left Books.

Stiglitz, Joseph E. 1985. 'Credit Markets and the Control of Capital'. *Journal of Money, Credit, Banking* 17(2): 133–52.

Stockhammer, E. (2005–06). 'Shareholder Value Orientation and the Investment–Profit Puzzle. *Journal of Post Keynesian Economics* 28(2): 193–215.

Sturgeon, T. J. 2001. 'How Do We Define Value Chains and Production Networks?' *IDS Bulletin* 32(3): 9–18.

Sundaram, K. 2008. 'Employment, Wages and Poverty in the Organized and the Unorganized Segments of the Non-Agricultural Sector in India: All-India, 2000–2005'. Working Paper no. 165, Centre for Development Economics Department of Economics, Delhi School of Economics, New Delhi.

Sweezy, Paul M. 1942. *The Theory of Capitalist Development*. New York: Monthly Review Press.

The Economist. 2018. 'India Has a Hole Where Its Middle Class Should Be'. 13–19 January.

Therborn, Goran. 2012. 'Class in the 21st Century'. *New Left Review* 78(November–December): 5–29.

Thompson, E. P. 1963. *The Making of the English Working Class*. New York: Vintage Books.

Trotsky, Leon. 1973. *Our Revolution: Essays on Working Class and International Revolution 1904–17*. Westport, CT: Hyperion Press.

UNCTAD. 2013. 'Global Value Chains: Investment and Trade for Development'. World Investment Report, United Nations Conference on Trade and Development, Geneva.

UNIDO. 2017. *Demand for Manufacturing: Driving Inclusive and Sustainable Industrial Development*. Industrial Development Report 2018, United Nations Industrial Development Organization, Vienna.

Vernon, Raymond. 1966. 'International Investment and International Trade in the Product Cycle'. *Quarterly Journal of Economics* 80(2): 190–207.

Wheaton, B. and W. Kiernan. 2012. 'Farmland: An Untapped Asset Class?' *Food for Thought*, December 2012. Macquarie Agricultural Funds Management, Sydney, Australia. Available at http://www.macquarie.com/dafiles/Internet/mgl/com/agriculture/docs/food-for-thought/food-for-thought-dec2012-us.pdf (accessed on 1 March 2019).

Wily, Liz Alden. 2012. 'Looking Back to See Forward: The Legal Niceties of Land Theft in Land Rushes'. *Journal of Peasant Studies* 39(3–4): 751–75.

Wise, Raúl Delgado and David Martin. (2015). 'The Political Economy of Global Labour Arbitrage'. In *Handbook of the International Political Economy of Production*, ed. Kees van der Pijl, 59–75. Cheltenham, UK, and Northhampton, USA: Edward Elgar Publishing.

Wolff, Richard D., Bruce Roberts and Antonino Callari. 1984. 'Marx's (not Ricardo's) "Transformation Problem": A Radical Reconceptualization'. *History of Political Economy* 16(3): 564–82.

World Bank. 2008. *World Development Report 2008: Agriculture for Development.* Washington, DC: World Bank.

———. 2010. *Rising Global Interest in Farmland: Can It Yield Sustainable and Equitable.* Washington, DC: World Bank.

———. 2017. *Measuring and Analyzing the Impact of GVCs on Economic Development.* Global Value Chain Development Report. Washington, DC: World Bank.

———. 2018. *The Trouble in the Making? The Future of Manufacturing-led Development.* Washington, DC: World Bank.

Wright, Eric Olin. 2000. 'Working-class Power, Capitalist-Class Interests, and Class Compromise'. *American Journal of Sociology* 105(4): 957–1002.

Wuyts, Marc. 2001. 'Informal Economy, Wage Goods and Accumulation under Structural Adjustment: Theoretical Reflections Based on Tanzanian Experience'. *Cambridge Journal of Economics* 25(3): 417–38.

Xing, Yuqing and Neal Detert. 2011. 'How the iphone Widens the United States Trade Deficit with the People's Republic of China'. Working paper Series 257, Asian Development Bank Institute, Tokyo.

Ye, Ming, Bo Meng and Shang-jin Wei. 2015. 'Measuring Smile Curves in Global Value Chains'. IDE Discussion Paper No. 530, Institute of Developing Economies, Japan External Trade Organization (JETRO).

# Index

*Note*: 't' denotes table and 'f' denotes figure.